FULL CIRCLE

FULL CIRCLE

Shakespeare and Moral Development

By

Alan Hobson

BARNES & NOBLE, Inc.

NEW YORK

PUBLISHERS SINCE 1873

PUBLISHED BY
CHATTO & WINDUS LTD
40 WILLIAM IV STREET
LONDON W.C. 2

*

First published in the United States of America, 1972
by Barnes & Noble, Inc.

ISBN 389 04584 5

© ALAN HOBSON 1972

Printed in Great Britain

To
The Memory of
Harry Proudfoot of Stacksteads
The Most Inspiring of my Teachers
and to
'Auntie' Maud Seville of Loughrigg

Acknowledgements

Profoundest debts cannot be acknowledged. To say that without my brother Bob this book would not have been written is to desecrate by convention the intertwining of our lives and minds from which it has grown.

If I speak of the slogging hard work that my wife has done on the copy, none but other authors will really know what I want to say.

If I mention distinguished scholars to whom I am indebted, I do injustice to the larger number of unknown people, many quite unfamiliar with literature, to whom I have owed even more, not only in life, but also in the study of Shakespeare.

The opportunity to write came through the generosity of the Caernarvonshire Education Committee and the University College of North Wales. I am grateful for the advice and encouragement I received from Professor J. F. Danby, Professor A. R. Jones and the staff of the English Department at Bangor.

NOTE

References to the text of the following plays are to the revised Arden edition, published by Methuen:

King Lear, The Tempest, Macbeth, The Merchant of Venice, Richard II, Henry IV Parts I and II, Henry V, Titus Andronicus, Love's Labour's Lost, Julius Caesar, Measure for Measure, The Winter's Tale.

Otherwise, references are to the Alexander Text of the Complete Works of Shakespeare, published by William Collins, London.

Contents

Introduction

A FRAGMENT of the rim, a couple of spokes and a segment of the hub suggest a wheel. From a space-ship in orbit no two views of Earth with its moving shadow and its shifting cloud will be identical, and none will be complete, but the total unity is divined. Glimpses of several plays linked to *The Tempest* by common themes may intimate the complex unity of Shakespeare's dramatic work.

The Tempest makes us think about the proper exercise of power, the relation between love and power, between love and reason, between love and duty, between authority and freedom, between service and slavery. It is about wisdom and choice, about charity and equality, about deprivation and destructiveness and hate, about responsibility and answerability, about punishment, vengeance and forgiveness. It is also about aspirations, ideals and dreams – of which last it is an example as well as an exposition. Meditation upon dreams raises questions of perception and illusion and causes us to reflect upon imagination and judgement, education and insight, art and morals.

All these themes will occupy our attention in varying degrees as we study *The Tempest* and other plays in the ensuing pages.

But there is a central theme that links all these. *The Tempest* is the last of the long series of Shakespeare's plays about how to be happy, and it makes a final statement upon the conditions for happiness. Our main concern will be with the nature and the processes of that moral and spiritual transformation which is, in this and other plays, the pre-requisite of human happiness and the establishment of a harmonious order. Among other things, this will entail a study of conscience. The progress is from egoism to altruism, and to love, which includes both. It takes place in all healthy maturation, but it is seldom or never carried far enough in any individual, and certainly has never yet been carried far enough in a sufficient number of individuals to bring harmony and happiness to the human race. Shakespeare's recreation of the tragedy of our failure to achieve that progress we shall contemplate in our first chapter, on *King Lear*, but in *King Lear* itself there is a better hope, and one that Shakespeare, though he is no easy optimist, does not relinquish.

FULL CIRCLE

CHAPTER ONE

This Child-Changèd Father

O NCE upon a time all creation was harmony – of sound, of
motion, of feeling, thought and action.

> That undisturbèd song of pure concent,
> Aye sung before the sapphire colour'd throne
> To Him that sits thereon

was not in Heaven only: for 'we on earth with undiscording
voice' rightly answered 'that melodious noise'

> till disproportion'd sin
> Jarr'd against nature's chime and with harsh din
> Broke the fair music that all creatures made
> To their great Lord, whose love their motion sway'd
> In perfect Diapason, whilst they stood.
> In first obedience and their state of good.[1]

But, from the Beginning, there was also Chaos:

> . . . a dark
> Illimitable ocean without bound,
> Without dimension, where length, breadth, and highth,
> And time and place are lost; where eldest Night
> And Chaos, ancestors of Nature, hold
> Eternal anarchy, amidst the noise
> Of endless wars, and by confusion stand.[2]

The words are John Milton's. Shakespeare's universe is
substantially the same; there is the dimension of Order, of
Degree, of the Cosmic Dance, of harmony in music, of the
bonds between man and man, man and nature, nature, man
and God (usually called 'the gods' or 'heaven', etc.); and
there is – or rather there will be – Chaos; for chaos will come
again, and 'in those days shall be affliction, such as was not

---

[1] Milton: 'At a Solemn Music'.
[2] Ibid.: *Paradise Lost:* II. 891–7.

from the beginning of the creation which God created unto this time, neither shall be'.[3] When Duncan, symbol of earthly order and of the divine purpose in that order, is slain, Macduff cries (using the word later used by Milton):

> Confusion now hath made his masterpiece!
> Most sacrilegious murther hath broke ope
> The Lord's anointed temple, and stole thence
> The life o' th' building.

But, in Shakespeare, the masterpiece of chaos is the doom of Lear, when these words break from by-standers:

> KENT: Is this the promis'd end?
> EDGAR: Or image of that horror?
> ALBANY: Fall and cease! (V. iii. 263-4)

Horror – the Elizabethan reaction to broken bonds, disharmonies, each one

> a breach in nature
> For ruin's wasteful entrance.
> (*Macbeth:* II. iii. 113-14)

The contrasting image of the heavenly harmonies, as we have it in Lorenzo's words, has the same nostalgia as Milton's ode, but in a different mood. It has a Platonic rather than a Hebrew version of The Fall, and, instead of the saintly choir, the lovely myth of the music of the spheres:

> Sit Jessica. Look how the floor of heaven
> Is thick inlaid with patens of bright gold,
> There's not the smallest orb which thou behold'st
> But in his motion like an angel sings,
> Still quiring to the young-ey'd cherubins;
> Such harmony is in immortal souls,
> But whilst this muddy vesture of decay
> Doth grossly close it in, we cannot hear it:
> (*Merchant of Venice:* V. i. 58-65)

This image of the immortal soul in the dark prison of the body is sad and sweet compared to the jarring of Milton's 'disproportion'd sin'; and the tone of Milton's passage is more

[3] *Mark:* XIII, 19.

12

reminiscent of Shakespeare's explorations of discord and ruin. Shakespeare writes comedies and tragedies; that is, he is concerned with happy endings and unhappy endings; hence he explores proportion and disproportion, not only as elements in artistic form, but as features of human life. Not only his tragic heroes, but Falstaff and Toby and Bolingbroke and Achilles and Angelo and Malvolio and Shylock and Benedick and Beatrice are images of disproportion'd life, though not all monstrous in Milton's sense of 'disproportion'd sin'.

In the very depths of Chaos, God placed Hell; and there was Satan nursing

> th' unconquerable will
> And study of revenge, immortal hate
> And courage never to submit or yield.

preferring 'to reign in Hell, than serve in Heav'n',[1] bent on reducing the whole of creation once more to that chaos from which it had been reft by 'th'Omnific Word'. So Milton.

In Shakespeare the Adversary is not Satan, but egocentric man. Macbeth is drawn 'to his confusion' by the Witches, the powers of evil, but the source of their power is his own 'vaulting ambition'. At first alive in conscience he suffers torture of the mind and, in the vain hope of finding relief without having to repent, he calls on those Powers that first called on him: the voice is the voice of command, but the power is with those he conjures – the witches:

> I conjure you, by that which you profess,
> Howe'er you come to know it, answer me:
> Though you untie the winds, and let them fight
> Against the churches; though the yesty waves
> Confound and swallow navigation up;
> Though bladed corn be lodg'd, and trees blown down;
> Though castles topple on their warders' heads;
> Though palaces and pyramids, do slope
> Their heads to their foundations; though the treasure
> Of Nature's germens tumble all together,
> Even till destruction sicken, answer me
> To what I ask you.   (*Macbeth:* IV. i. 50–61)

[1] *Paradise Lost:* I. 107–9 and 263.

Such reckless self-will, such Satanic defiance of the proper order of things, not only in man's world of the churches and castles but in the natural order, the very sources of life, amounts to an invocation of Chaos. Like Satan, calling destruction on God's creation he brings it upon himself. Egoism is in the tone of the whole, in the violent repetitions, in the terrible climax, but pointed twice in 'answer me', each time powerfully placed at the end of the line, and the second time the grammatical pivot preserving the sense after the long crescendo of concessional clauses. This is the image of 'disproportion'd sin': he is be-monstered by this frantic affirmation of himself.

But Macbeth is not Satan: he is a good man who chooses Wrong, and whose wrong choices have their inevitable and inexorable consequences, not merely or even mainly in the world, but in himself. Not every man kills a king, literally, but Macbeth is Everyman in the *nature* of his choice and its consequences.

King Lear is even more distinctly a morality play with Lear as Everyman; for Lear is not Satanic. He is not a bogey-man or stage devil as Richard III often seems to be. Shakespeare's recipe for a convincing play about that chaotic period of the Wars of the Roses was this: make images of ruthless self-interested men and let them work; let love be named only by the feeble and cynical; confound the bonds of nature and of nations by letting loose the individual will. Richard Crookback is the agent:

> Then, since the heavens have shap'd my body so,
> Let hell make crook'd my mind to answer it.
> I have no brother, I am like no brother;
> And this word 'love', which greybeards call divine,
> Be resident in men like one another,
> And not in me! I am myself alone.
>
> (*Henry VI, Pt. III:* V. vi. 78–83)

This is Satanic, Shakespeare suspends disbelief, for the duration of the plays, but this figure does not readily convince as an image of a historical human being. It does, however, convince as an image of something in man, and it provokes rejection, yet also fascination and a terrified admiration. This is The Temp-

14

ter. The fate he tempts us to he himself suffers in the play, *Richard III*: the moral of his story is strongly, but unsubtly, pointed in his dreams and his doom. *Macbeth* is a deeper exploration of that moral; *King Lear*, deeper still.

A child is egocentric. We say this now without the connotations of selfishness or original sin. Maturation is thus growth in relationship, a progress to altruism. Maturity, in this sense, is never reached. The protective egoism of childhood retained in later life is called selfishness and is condemned.

King Lear, 'fourscore and upward', remains a great baby, but a ranting, towering, very dangerous baby. He is also a mighty king, majestic and terrible. The time has come to divest himself of the cares and responsibilities of kingship. 'The best and soundest of his time hath been but rash,' and, now, in the division of the kingdom, he is moved by violent impulse and childish vanity. The startling naïvety of his plan to divide the kingdom into three for his three daughters 'that future strife may be prevented now', but not into three equal parts (for he is not impartial: Cordelia is his joy and he thinks to set his rest 'on her kind nursery') – such naïvety is credible only in dotage, or in one whose course of royalty has run smooth and whom there has been none to gainsay. The same naïvety accompanies the childish vanity which, not content with the love of a true daughter, will have that love displayed in open court for all to see, and yet so disposes as to choke and curb true love and give the rein to flattery and falsehood:

> Which of you shall we say doth love us most
> That we our largest bounty may extend
> Where nature doth with merit challenge.
>
> (I. i. 51–3)

Upon such a public bribe only the daughters who hate him can profess natural affection. His natural (that is, properly dutiful and loving) daughter can only reject him, or seem to reject him, and this double injury, to his thwarted will and his inordinate vanity, wrenches his frame of nature from the fix'd place so that he does not even notice what is most mighty in her brief and somewhat obstinate replies:

> I love your Majesty
> According to my bond; no more, nor less.

This draws from him a mere threat that is the obverse of his original bribe:

> How, how, Cordelia! Mend your speech a little,
> Lest you may mar your fortunes.   (I. i. 92–5)

But Cordelia has professed to love him no less than according to her bond; that is, with the full affection of a true daughter. Shakespeare does not permit his audience to think this reference to the bonds of nature a mere form of words. Cordelia firmly reiterates:

> Good my lord,
> You have begot me, bred me, lov'd me: I
> Return those duties back as are right fit,
> Obey you, love you, and most honour you.
> Why have my sisters husbands, if they say
> They love you all?   (I. i. 96–9)

Lear does not hear; his favourite daughter will bandy words with him in public:

> LEAR: So young, and so untender?
> CORDELIA: So young, my Lord, and true.

Deafened and blinded by his thwarted affection, frustrated beneficence and injured vanity, and childishly petulant in all, Lear breaks out into the most terrible blasphemies against those bonds of nature – which are the sinews of the Divine Order. This is the way of one who

> – carries on the stream of his dispose,
> Without observance or respect of any
> In will peculiar and self admission.
> (*Troilus & Cressida:* II. iii. 159–61)

But in this instance the offender is a king, symbol of the bond between God and man, custodian of earthly order, image of the sun which is the giver of light and life and fosterer of 'nature's germens'. He is a father, too. His curse reverberates through every link of the great chain of being from the highest, in Heaven, to the lowest.in 'the green mantle of the standing pool'. The reverberations do not cease till Lear is dead. Every deed of good or ill has its inevitable consequences: there is no remission, even when there is redemption. That is the burden of this play.

The words on the page are as a score to be interpreted in voice and gesture and feature: majesty and magnificence and power, perversity and petulance and anguish, terrible finality and the cataclysmic anger of a frantic child are all in the sound pattern of this score; what has been noted above is in the imagery:

> Let it be so; thy truth then be thy dower:
> For, by the sacred radiance of the sun,
> The mysteries of Hecate and the night,
> By all the operation of the orbs
> From whom we do exist and cease to be,
> Here I disclaim all my paternal care,
> Propinquity and property of blood,
> And as a stranger to my heart and me
> Hold thee from this for ever. The barbarous Scythian,
> Or he that makes his generation messes
> To gorge his appetite, shall to my bosom
> Be as well neighbour'd, pitied and reliev'd,
> As thou my sometime daughter.   (I. i. 108–19)

It is a rejection of what Milton calls 'that first obedience' and that 'state of good', an image of the Fall; it is an invocation of Chaos more terrible than Macbeth's, being hurled against a living person, his child and his good angel, on whose kind nursery he had thought to set his rest: the little world of the family and the great order of the universe (which he invokes for a sacrilegious purpose) are desecrated at once. And Lear is choosing Satan, for there are three Satanic figures in this play, Goneril and Regan being two, and there are two angelic ones, the rejected Cordelia and the Earl of Kent, who is also rejected as he tries to check Lear's hideous rashness. Silencing Kent, Lear poses as the dragon:

17

Peace, Kent!
Come not between the Dragon and his wrath.

(I. i. 121–2)

But Lear is by no means 'th' old dragon underground'[1] – no Satan: he is not even, like Macbeth, a mature man making a deliberate choice: his choice is almost a reflex. Hence he can say at a later stage, 'I am a man more sinned against than sinning' and hence readers like Dr. Johnson have been offended by what they saw as the lack of poetic justice in the play: his punishment they have said is too harsh. This play follows the workings of a blind choice. Words from *Measure for Measure* describe Lear:

> But man, proud man,
> Dressed in a little brief authority,
> Most ignorant of what he's most assur'd,
> His glassy essence, like an angry ape,
> Plays such fantastic tricks before high heaven
> As makes the angels weep;   (II. ii. 116–21)

Every play, and every scene in a play, is an extended image made up of a complex of images; each character too is an image of some single grouping of human qualities; and, in a Shakespearean scene, there is the imagery in the language, which presents the scene, helps to delineate the characters, and establishes the thought and feeling patterns of the whole. Through the imagery in this last and more usual sense we experience Lear's predicament in the context of Heaven and Earth and Chaos and Hell. In the total image of the scene, we have this child-man at the centre, drunk with self, the world at his command but crying for the moon, howling with the pain of the conflict between his embryo-love and his injured vanity, tearing his guardian angel Cordelia and repulsing the clear-souled King of France, clasping to his bosom the self-interested Duke of Burgundy and the satanic daughters – and all with most horrible blasphemies against life and nature.

But this is not merely a symbolic play. The huge and mighty forms set moving in the mind are shadows of the images of flesh and blood in the foreground. Even Goneril and Regan are

[1] Milton: *On the Morning of Christ's Nativity*; The Hymn, XVIII.

encountered as human; Cordelia and Kent are very human indeed – sharing some of Lear's faults. If Lear is wilful, Cordelia and Kent are obstinate; if he is violent and unrestrained in speech, they are at least blunt and uncompromising. We are thus made to feel his deeper bonds with them and to sense the underlying goodness in him that has no part in the smooth, calculating, only too competent self-interest of those in whose power he places himself. Such is the interrelation of the character images, giving us an experience both of people and of a moral order. Shakespeare, looking at man, sees the particular instance, and the eternal situation.

But the play, typically, is about change. Shakespeare has long been praised for what has usually been called development of character: when Shakespeare looks at man, he sees him grow – grow and wither – and the changes Shakespeare observes and creates in image have their laws and patterns.

At the end of Scene I, Goneril and Regan, true children of Lear's hate, but inheriting none of his generous and often tender impulses, assess his folly and calculate his future in cold prose. He has chosen to lodge a month with each, attended by a hundred knights to be maintained by his sons-in-law. He will retain, he says, the name and ceremonial of a king. The daughters prepare the curbs to his will.

The first month is with Goneril. In less than a fortnight his train is disquantitied by half; orders are given to the servants to 'come slack of former services'; Goneril would 'have it come to question'. She knows him well – knows, that is, his weaknesses:

> Idle old man,
> That still would manage those authorities
> That he hath given away! Now, by my life,
> Old fools are babes again, and must be us'd
> With checks as flatteries,   (I. iii. 17–21)

He has given his daughters the rod, as his Fool says, and put down his own breeches. Soon he feels the checks, and then the strokes.

The first scene of his humiliation opens with his guardian

angel, Kent, disguised as the poor man, Caius, who seeks service
with the King:

LEAR: Dost thou know me, fellow?
KENT: No, Sir; but you have that in your countenance which I
would fain call master.
LEAR: What's that?
KENT: Authority. (I. iv. 28–32)

Lear has just entered, from hunting, with the words, 'Let me
not stay a jot for dinner: go get it ready.' But he is met with the
insolence of a servant and the contempt of his daughter. There
is grandeur in the fury of his anger, and there is pathos in his
suffering, for generosity and tenderness and remorse appear in
him, and, by that species of association of character-images
already mentioned, something of the innocence and devotion
of his Fool is imparted to him. His curses on Goneril, rending
over again the bonds of Nature and of family, are made the more
agonising by self-pity and the self-torment of impotent rage.
Wishing his own fate on Goneril, he expresses his suffering:

Turn all her mother's pains and benefits
To laughter and contempt, that she may feel
How sharper than a serpent's tooth it is
To have a thankless child! (I. iv. 295–8)

In helpless rage he curses his own weeping eyes:

Old fond eyes,
Beweep this cause again, I'll pluck ye out,
And cast you, with the waters that you loose,
To temper clay. (I. iv. 310–13)

Self pity, self-hate, shame and threats of vengeance – but other
words have burst from him earlier in the scene and the tenor of
his thought is made clear by the mysterious interplay of the
character images: the Fool is present and with witless wit
speaks what is in all minds but none dares say. Through him we
know Lear's mind. Impressions of inner conflict and remorse in
Lear's own words, the mixture of mild jest and agonising truth
in the words of the Fool, the uselessness of Lear's commands to
the Fool, who speaks not what he will but what is torn from

him – 'Prithee, nuncle, keep a schoolmaster that would teach thy fool to lie: I would fain learn to lie' – all these and like impressions convey the strongest possible sense of the disturbed mind long before Lear cries:

> O let me not be mad, not mad, sweet heaven
> Keep me in temper: I would not be mad!   (I. v. 47–8)

The terrible might of his resistless will is now impotent and the sense of inner stress that Shakespeare has created in this scene is indescribable.

Henceforth we witness the stages of the disintegration of Lear's mind. The chaos he has invoked enters into him. His curses fall upon himself. Indeed they always were upon himself; for it was he who rejected obedience and the bond of rule; it was he who was a thankless father and a biased and partial one; it was he who was the faithless and ungrateful master. But, although he regrets what he has done, he does not yet know himself. Realisation at first comes slowly. First comes regret, but not the acceptance of his own guilt:

> O most small fault,
> How ugly didst thou in Cordelia show!
> Which, like an engine, wrench'd my frame of nature
> From the fix'd place,   (I. iv. 275–8)

Her 'fault' is still the cause, and her thanklessness only less than Goneril's; he, himself, is the sufferer.

> Woe that too late repents;

His own pain is still to the fore. But remorse comes:

> I did her wrong,   (I. v. 24)

This last, the fuller recognition of his own fault, is what is almost beyond his power to endure, and it is here that he cries: 'O let me not be mad.' But it is also the most striking sign up to this point of what I shall call altruism. His tenderness to Cordelia and his fool, his warm recognition of the worth of his new servant Caius (Kent) – these have not been opposites of his egoism. They have shown his need of others but with a grand, or a petulant, or a pathetic possessiveness. His struggle for sanity from now on – when it is not merely a cry for attention and for pity – is a struggle to become aware of others./Though he, and we, are most aware of the disintegration, the shattering of what he now is, yet he is being made anew, and we are being prepared for a reversal, in which altruism will prevail over egoism. He will learn something of love.

Seeking Regan, Lear comes to Gloucester's castle, only to find that his faithful servant, sent on ahead, has been put in the stocks – a slight and an insult to the master. The old fury rages, especially when Regan and her husband, Cornwall, refuse to see him. Cornwall sends excuses, saying he is not well – 'Mere fetches', cries Lear, but in the full career of his rage something quite new happens: he stops and considers, falling out with his 'more headier will':

> My breath and blood! –
> Fiery! the fiery duke! Tell the hot duke that –
> No, but not yet; maybe he is not well:
>
> (II. iv. 103–5)

For a moment he considers the duke: he has been unjust before in his rage; he will not be so again. But he turns and sees his servant in the stocks; the torrent of rage bursts forth again until, at the point of exhaustion, he is aware that he has been out of control:

> O me, my rising heart! – but, down!

And again, when Goneril has arrived:

> I prithee, daughter, do not make me mad:
> I will not trouble thee my child; farewell:
> We'll no more meet, no more see one another;
> But yet thou art my flesh, my blood, my daughter;
> Or rather a disease that's in my flesh,
> Which I must needs call mine: thou art a boil,
> A plague-sore, an embossed carbuncle
> In my corrupted blood.

The torrent roars, but this time to be more quickly stanched:

But I'll not chide thee;
Let shame come when it will, I do not call it;
I do not bid the thunder-bearer shoot,
Nor tell tales of thee to high-judging Jove.

(II. iv. 220–30)

The irony of his prayers to the heavens, whose order he has blasphemed and rejected, is not at first noticed, but now the thunder breaks, not on the head of Goneril, but on his own. The sisters flay him with their tongues, stripping him cut by cut of his retinue, his dignities, his very manhood, till he flies weeping from the castle to the shelterless heath as the thunder rolls and a terrible storm breaks. His daughters, like Fate, shut their doors against him. There is no going back: the deeds are done that have led him to this. They are irrevocable and in their consequences inexorable.

At first, Lear,

Contending with the fretful elements;
Bids the wind blow the earth into the sea,
Or swell the curled waters 'bove the main,
That things might change or cease.

(III. i. 4–7)

And once again, using Macbeth's image, calls down destruction on the world that has rejected him:

And thou, all-shaking thunder,
Strike flat the thick rotundity o' th' world!
Crack nature's moulds, all germens spill at once
That make ingrateful man. (III. ii. 6–9)

And then he scorns the heavens

That will with two pernicious daughters join
Your high-engender'd battles 'gainst a head
So old and white as this. O! O! 'tis foul.

In this last line his ranting breaks down into self-pity, and exhaustion once again gives a respite in which his 'better judgement' speaks:

No, I will be the pattern of all patience;
I will say nothing.

23

But the self-pity grows:

> Let the great Gods,
> That keep this dreadful pudder o'er our heads
> Find out their enemies now.

Let the thunder strike the consciences of the real sinners, he cries:

> I am a man
> More sinn'd against than sinning.
>
> (III. ii. 59–60)

Self-pity is perhaps better than no pity. It is a softening of heart and perhaps a step towards sympathy. Certainly it serves this kind of purpose in Shakespeare's modulation of the feeling in this scene; for, after some gentle and considerate words of Kent, the great reversal begins. First come the ominous words,

> My wits begin to turn,

Then, suddenly, unexpectedly, comes Lear's realisation of someone else's suffering. He turns to the Fool:

> Come on, my boy. How dost, my boy? Art cold?
> I am cold myself.

That last remark is not self-pity, but a sharing and an encouragement. And it is followed by a moment of wise detachment:

> Where is this straw, my fellow?
> The art of our necessities is strange,
> That can make vile things precious. Come, your hovel.
>
> (III. ii. 69–71)

That this is no accidental arrangment or expediency of art in this particular scene is evidenced by the fact that it is repeated in the very next scene on the heath, outside the hovel now, their only place of shelter. The great rage is dying: there is only the pathetic impotence of one empty threat, checked as before:

> But I will punish home:
> No, I will weep no more.

THIS CHILD-CHANGÈD FATHER

In such a night as this? O Regan, Goneril!
Your old kind father, whose frank heart gave all, –
(III. iv. 19–20)

Hardly a just claim in view of the motives for his giving and the mode of his original division of the kingdom! However, he breaks off; but not to face the truth:

O! that way madness lies; let me shun that;
No more of that.

Again come the gentle words of Kent, and again both self-pity and the fear of madness are forgotten:

KENT: Good my lord, enter here.
LEAR: Prithee go in thyself; seek thine own ease;

and as he turns once more and sees the Fool, there comes the point of reversal itself:

In, boy; go first.

Lear was formerly the one to take precedence. Now he thinks of the Other – and not of one only. The next words are from the same line:

You houseless poverty, –
Nay, get thee in. I'll pray, and then I'll sleep. –

Pray! He has prayed before – the most hideous prayers for vengeance; and, later, pathetic cries for help and sanity and patience and protection. Self-centred prayers all. In this prayer the only references to himself are condemnations of his own most heinous faults, dignity, and property, and ignorance or, to smooth it a little, pomp and excess, and self-centredness. The prayer is a meditation on suffering humanity and the injustice of man to man; it is a reflection on politics and economics and government, the responsibilities of kingship that Lear thrust aside before he even knew them; but it is an outward movement of the heart and an enlightening of the mind: egoism has given way to altruism:

Poor naked wretches, whereso'er you are
That bide the pelting of this pitiless storm,
How shall your houseless heads and unfed sides,
Your loop'd and window'd raggedness, defend you
From seasons such as these? O! I have ta'en
Too little care of this! Take physic, Pomp;
Expose thyself to feel what wretches feel,
That thou mayst shake the superflux to them
And show the heavens more just.   (III. iv. 28–36)

The strain of realisation proves too great; a bedlam beggar, the
image of madness, comes screaming from the straw; and Lear's
mind is overturned. But in his last lucid moment he contemplates the bedlam:

> Is man no more than this? Consider him well. Thou ow'st the
> worm no silk, the beast no hide, the sheep no wool, the cat no
> perfume. Ha! here's three on's are sophisticated. Thou art
> the thing itself; unaccommodated man is no more but such a
> poor, bare, forked animal as thou art. Off, off, you lendings!
> come; unbutton here.

(III. iv. 105–12)

The moment of insight is the flash that accompanies the
explosion. His mind disintegrates. Realisation moves him to
action, but the action, like his rages ever since he gave away
his power, is pointless, irrelevant, impotent: that is, insane. And
now the prevailing sense of social, moral and spiritual horror is
made more hideous by the tumbling imagery of Tom o'
Bedlam; and the larger image of Lear's disintegrated mind is
compiled out of three characters in a burlesque of justice inter-
mingling grotesque humour and extreme pathos in the presentation of distorted items from Lear's experience.

Out of the mouths, not so much of babes and sucklings as of
fools and madmen, Shakespeare brings forth wisdom. Lear's
fool has already shown much insight, but now he disappears
from the play; for Lear is mad, and it is now for Lear to turn
the accepted notions upside down and inside out and expose
unpalatable truths, hidden from *common* sense. In a fit of
what Olivia would call 'merry madness'[1] he escapes from his

[1] *Twelfth Night:* III. iv. 15.

protectors and meets the blinded Duke of Gloucester, whose faults and sufferings have paralleled his own, and whose wisdom also has been increased and sympathies enlarged.

> LEAR: What! art mad? A man may see how this world goes with no eyes. Look with thine ears: see how yond justice rails upon yond simple thief. Hark, in thine ear: change places, and, handy-dandy, which is the justice, which is the thief?
>
> (IV. vi. 151–6)

Lear had called for justice when he was being most unjust. That this speech and what follows confirms the burlesque of justice, and constitutes a rejection of the distribution of punishments among men, is confirmed in the next line:

> None does offend, none – I say none; I'll able 'em:

Nor is this an isolated thought in Shakespeare's plays. From *The Merchant of Venice* to *The Tempest* mercy is a recurring theme; and forgiveness, in the last plays, is a major ingredient in Shakespeare's recipe for a happy ending. In *King Lear* the reversal of the common view will be confirmed when Lear is no longer mad. Here it is a hope, as well as a challenge; Lear needs to be forgiven: 'forgive us our trespasses as we forgive them that trespass'; but here the hope, the realisation and the challenge are quickly submerged in the 'impertinency' of madness. Here is the germ of altruism, but it becomes overlaid by shreds of the old vengefulness and self-pity.

To recapitulate. The individual, placing himself at the centre of things, asserting his private will, violates the WHOLE, disrupts the political and social order, chokes all pity with 'custom of fell deeds' and, striving to gain the whole world for himself, loses his own soul. But human nature has its contraries: there is a complementary impulse, the need to relate to others. Extreme suffering intensifies this need and *can* evoke the means to satisfy the need, can stimulate the latent altruism. That is the thread of this story so far. Lest anyone should miss the implications of it or be so misguided as to think Lear's story is merely the story of one man, Shakespeare shows us the same moral law working in the life of Gloucester. Gloucester's 'self-admission' has issued in adultery and a subsequent rejection of his truest and best-loved child. He is afflicted with moral blindness similar to Lear's, and only when his physical eyes have been put out and he himself is cast out into a shelterless world does he begin to see the truth about himself. He has been less indifferent to the sufferings of others than Lear, but in the extremity of his own pain, he too makes discoveries about man's responsibilities to man. Giving his purse, the last of his wealth, to a poor man, he says:

> Heavens, deal so still!
> Let the superfluous and lust dieted man,
> That slaves your ordinance, that will not see
> Because he doth not feel, feel your power quickly;
> So distribution should undo excess,
> And each man have enough.   (IV. i. 66–71)

It is the same challenge to the human imagination and to the social and economic order as issued from Lear. The one confirms the other – and Gloucester is *not* mad. When Lear is arraigning human justice (so-called justice) and, by demonstrating the universality of guilt, is asserting the universality of innocence, he is speaking to Gloucester, the adulterer:

> Thou shalt not die: die for adultery! No
> The wren goes to't, and the small gilded fly
> Doth lecher in my sight.

And again:

> Thou rascal beadle, hold thy bloody hand!
> Why dost thou lash that whore? Strip thine own back;
> Thou hotly lusts to use her in that kind
> For which thou whipp'st her.   (IV. vi. 162–5)

Lear is spitting sick at the spectacle of hypocrisy – another mode of man's ignorance of himself and indifference to his fellows. Judging is rooted in hypocrisy; forbearance in self-knowledge and charity. 'Judge not' is written over this play, for if you judge, you will judge with the blindness of Lear and Gloucester; should your eyes open, you will exonerate all.[1]

---

[1] 'Judge', here, has reference to rewards and punishments, not assessment and recognition. Contrast, I. iv. 279–81.

But something else is written across the play, and it might be poetically expressed as 'Vengeance is mine, saith the Lord'. Man is, metaphorically speaking, judged by the inevitable processes of cause and effect. Our actions have their consequences and bring their rewards and punishments in the nature of things. This is how things are, and the whole of Shakespeare's work is an exploration of this 'how-things-are'; what men, what actions, what situations can lead to happy 'endings' – or tragic 'endings' given a universe in which every cause has its effect according to its own nature. Not that the most terrible consequences of error are felt by those who commit the error: Macbeth's sin is visited upon the innocent Lady Macduff and all the widows and orphans of his victims, as well as upon himself. So, too, with Lear. But is there no remission, no redemption? Try forgiveness, said the mad Lear – and Shakespeare dwelt on the thought for many a long day.

The mad Lear is recaptured by the retainers of Cordelia, who has come from France to rescue her father. The language in which Cordelia is described at this point leaves no doubt of her function in the play:

> Thou hast one daughter
> Who redeems nature from the general curse
> Which twain have brought her to.   (IV. vi. 206–8)

Does 'general curse' mean The Fall of Man, original sin, or simply the turmoil of the kingdom and the suffering of a people? It is a question *we* may ask: to the medieval mind it would have been hair-splitting, or meaningless. Shakespeare is betwixt and between, but no Elizabethan would be troubled by the question. Who are the 'twain'? Adam and Eve, or Goneril and Regan? This is a rich ambiguity. The word 'nature' has general application, but it is Lear's nature that we hope she will 'redeem'. Redeemer she is, but no allegorical figure: it is the redemptive powers in breathing human life and love that she displays. Her own words recall the heavenly harmonies opposed to the jar of disproportion'd sin, but the voice is the voice of human love and care:

O you kind Gods,
Cure this great breach in his abused nature!
Th' untuned and jarring senses, O! wind up
Of this child-changed father.   (IV. vii. 14–17)

Meantime, repose, 'our foster-nurse of nature', is restoring
Lear to health. Cordelia is by his bed, and when he wakes, the
images of her life and his are in his words:

Thou art a soul in bliss; but I am bound
Upon a wheel of fire, that mine own tears
Do scald like molten lead.   (IV. vii. 46–8)

But this is in part retrospective. 'The great rage is killed in
him'; he is gentle and tractable, but weak and helpless – a child,
no longer childish, but perfectly child-like. He is haunted by the
memory of his suffering, but in all the words, the whispered
words, of the scene there is relief as well as sadness. He is vastly
changed. Even in his bewildered state his own distress is felt as
if it were that of some other:

I should e'en die with pity,
To see another thus.

This is very different from the self-pity of earlier scenes: it is not
centred in himself, but transformed by his thought of others. He
has also learned humility, and, bewildered as he is, he knows
himself better:

I am a very foolish fond old man.

He asks, not as formerly for recognition, but for mercy:

You must bear with me:
Pray you now, forget and forgive: I am old and foolish.
          (IV. vii. 83–4)

He clings to Cordelia, and from this time to the terrible end of
the play he is wholly devoted to her. Or perhaps that is not the
right term, for the total lesson of love is not to be learned at
'fourscore and upward' by one whose whole life up to that time
has been lived in self-love. The old possessiveness is still there,
just as from the embers there come momentary flashes of the old

dominance and vanity. Through his terrible suffering he has learned to feel with and for others, but the fullness of self-sacrificing love would be too much to expect. He is born again, but a new-born child, however innocent, is not more than a beginner in love. Devouring self-love has given way to devouring love. Altruism has been born, and it appears and disappears, but there is no time for its flowering. Altruistic love is an opposite of possessiveness.

'By experience,' Hardy quotes from Roger Ascham, 'we find out a short way by long wandering.'[1] And Hardy adds, 'Not seldom, that long wandering unfits us for futher travel.' So it is with Lear: the 'old man' of his original sin has been burned out of him on the purgatorial 'wheel of fire', but so has his grandeur, his magnificence, his energy. And that is not the worst. He is contrite; redemption has begun; so now we want all to go well with him. We have long forgiven him. Cordelia's love is such that forgiveness is irrelevant, or rather was immediate. But in the nature and process of things there is that 'even-handed Justice' whereby the terrible consequences of a wicked deed or of a wrong choice must be worked out to the bitter end. Men must forgive: fate does not. What Lear has done, and what Gloucester has done, cannot be undone, and though Lear is transformed and might now set in motion a beneficent train of cause and effect, the former causes must work. Work they do, overwhelming not only the sinner himself, but the innocent Cordelia and the loyal Kent (to the horror and scandal of Dr. Johnson, who demanded poetic justice).

The play has shown the possibility of change, the manner of it, and the price of it. In demonstrating the possibility of change for the better, it gives cause for hope, but it offers no facile promises of wish-fulfilment or poetic justice. It does not propound a doctrine: it explores a process. Shakespeare is not an optimist, or a pessimist; he is, in this sense, a realist. This, he shows, is the nature of the moral order, as undeviating as Natural Law.

Shakespeare, looking at man, sees a being to whom harmonious relationship is all important, yet in whom there is an

[1] *Tess of the D'Urbervilles.*

31

individual will that, while it imparts a certain grandeur and majesty, in the long run makes of him either a cruel monster or a contemptible object – a Goneril or a Tom o' Bedlam. Harmony is to be established, love is to be learned, altruism is to be achieved only by the chastening of this individual will, and the way in which this happens in King Lear is through suffering, the harsh teacher of Lear and Gloucester. Yet suffering teaches only because the seeds of altruism are already there and because each needs the love and loyalty of true and faithful ones. Shakespeare sees man, in *King Lear* and in other plays, as a growing and changing being, complex in his own impulses and responses, and set in the larger complex of Heaven and Earth and Chaos and Hell and Purgatory, and the lesser complex of kingdom, society and family. Universal laws permeate the whole, and of these the ones that hold Shakespeare's attention are the moral laws. Man makes moral choices, and whether they are conscious and deliberate and premeditated like Macbeth's, or impulsive and unpremeditated like Lear's, they have their inevitable consequences of good or evil. Lear, as Shakespeare's Man, moves between images of the forces of good and evil, between Order and Chaos, between love and hate, between kindness and cruelty, between angels and beasts, between harmony and disharmony; and in moving he must make his choices and take their consequences, and witness their consequences on others. He can learn from his experience, but learning from experience is slow; he can change, but change may be catastrophic; and there is much waste. That is the tragedy.

CHAPTER TWO

Any God of Power

THE first 'thought' in *The Tempest*, uttered by a blunt and sturdy commoner in a storm at sea, recalls King Lear in the storm on the heath:

What cares these roarers for the name of king? Kings have been held sacred, bearing God's warrant, high in the great Chain of Being, but Alonso, King of Naples, in a ship-wrecking storm has less authority than his bos'n and is less important than the meanest sailor who can 'hand a rope'. A 'dreadful pother' in the heavens and a tempest in the mind teach King Lear the equality of king and beggar. Lear has that in's face that makes men of heroic mould fain to call him master – authority. 'Use your authority,' says King Alonso's bos'n, 'if you cannot, give thanks you have lived so long, and make yourself ready in your cabin for the mischance of the hour.'

Poor, helpless Richard II, trying to reassure himself, cries:

> Not all the water in the rough rude sea
> Can wash the balm from an anointed king;
>
> (III. ii. 54–5)

That is one mood, but later his nerve breaks and he reflects bitterly and cynically on truths that King Lear learns to feel with all the profundity of his being:

> for within the hollow crown
> That rounds the mortal temples of a king
> Keeps Death his court, and there the antic sits,
> Scoffing his state and grinning at his pomp,
> Allowing him a breath, a little scene,
> To monarchize, be fear'd, and kill with looks;
> Infusing him with self and vain conceit,
> As if this flesh, which walls about our life
> Were brass impregnable; and, humour'd thus,
> Comes at the last, and with a little pin
> Bores through his castle wall, and farewell king!
>
> (III. ii. 160–70)

33

King Lear in self and vain conceit, monarchizes, is feared, and kills with looks, but, contrary perhaps to what usually happens in life, he himself has to suffer such tyranny as he once exercised, and it is then he discovers with shame and fury that the thunder will not peace at his bidding. Thunder is the voice of the heavens:

> 'He hath put down the mighty from their seat,
> and hath exalted the humble and meek.'

The boatswain's rhetorical question recalls Shakespeare's earlier explorations of the nature and limits of power, and through Prospero as father, as schoolmaster, as ruler and disposer of events, Shakespeare has something more to say about it. Prospero as magician has power over the elements; he is an exploiter of nature, a scientist, or 'a mighty god' as Faustus would have it. As ruler, whether father, schoolmaster or god, he has power over men; but power for their good – the power to bring about a happy ending.

Our age has a disposition to take tragedy more seriously than comedy and to take comedy more seriously when it is satirical or when we see life's ironies in it. It is easier to believe in man's capacity to bring about unhappy than happy endings. We long for happy endings, but when we are presented with them we fear we are being offered 'dreams to damnation', that our sense of reality is being obscured by wish:

> Such tricks hath strong imagination
> That, if it would but apprehend some joy,
> It comprehends some bringer of that joy;
> (*A Midsummer-Night's Dream*: V. i. 18–22)

For some reason we fear this more than the opposite trick of imagination:

> Or in the night, imagining some fear,
> How easy is a bush supposed a bear!

Even children, nowadays, will express disapproval of a play merely on the ground that it has a happy ending – *therefore* it cannot be credited.

From *Henry VI* to *Timon of Athens* Shakespeare's histories and tragedies affirm and reaffirm the Duke of York's moral in *Richard II*:

> But by bad courses may be understood
> That their events can never fall out good.
>
> (II. i. 213–14)

Most terrible is the story when the bad courses are pursued by the most generous and best intentioned of men (Hamlet, Othello) and when their evil 'events' fall upon the most innocent and most noble (Ophelia, Desdemona). We tremble at the fragility of goodness and the destructive power of evil, but the causal laws have operated; we feel the inevitability, and we are convinced.

For some reason we do not assent so readily to the converse of York's proposition. If we say, 'For by *good* courses must be understood that their effects can never fall out *bad*', doubts arise. In the limited context of 'this earthly world', we lend a ready ear to Lady Macduff's complaint:

> But I remember now
> I am in this earthly world, where to do harm
> Is often laudable; to do good sometimes
> Accounted dangerous folly.   (IV. ii. 73–6)

On the short view, bad causes often seem to turn out good, and good causes turn out bad. Ours is an age of short views. Like Malcolm, we have a disposition to believe that the cards are packed against goodness:

> Though all things foul would wear the brows of grace
> Yet grace must still look so.   (IV. iii. 23–4)

A good man cannot be a deceiver, but a deceiver can appear good. Should evil appear to be good, evil gains the advantage; should good appear to be evil, evil still gains the advantage. We are apt to find Shakespeare's tragedies more convincing than his comedies, to recognise the truth in his representations of good exploited and thwarted by evil to a tragic end. But the opposite may be equally possible, as even Dogberry's muddled

35

honesty illustrates, and there are twin virtues that can cut across the causal nexus of evil deed – evil consequence and replace it by gentle deed – happy consequence.

Those virtues are Mercy and Forgiveness, whose quality Shakespeare weighed in *The Merchant of Venice* and *Measure for Measure*, and to which he gave central place in his last plays. Not that the causal chain can be broken: the deed, once done, cannot be undone; and, as we are shown in *King Lear*, the consequences of an evil deed, or a mere error, follow inexorably; but some consequences that might be expected to follow can be prevented by forgiveness, and some can be diminished or cancelled by the new chain of cause and effect that the act of forgiveness begins. Lear injures Cordelia. The expected consequence is resentment and retaliation. But Cordelia does not retaliate, and consequently Lear is spared a measure of the suffering that would otherwise have fallen upon him, and a special gift of love and joy is given to him that, for the brief period that it lasts, does redeem all sorrows that ever he has felt. To all Shakespeare's audiences this gift continues to be a thing of inexpressible worth, not transitory in man's thought, though transitory in the particular event. This, if anything in human experience, could make happy endings; and henceforth when Shakespeare wants to create a play with a happy ending, forgiveness is of special importance in the story.

The last plays, especially *The Tempest*, rest upon insights that Shakespeare gave to Lear both before and at the time of his reconciliation with Cordelia. Lear, as he learns about himself, loses all patience with the kind of justice that consists in issuing rewards and punishments, and affirms that true justice is the recognition, both in feeling and act, of the equality of human beings:

> O! I have ta'en
> Too little care of this. Take physic, Pomp;
> Expose thyself to feel what wretches feel,
> That thou mayst shake the superflux to them,
> And show the Heavens more just.
>
> (III. iv. 32–6)

Smart 'humane' men of to-day will quibble over what is meant by the superflux – but Lear strips off his clothes. Of course, he's mad – as the world goes! In the course of the rewards-and-punishments kind of justice none of us, said Portia, shall see salvation,

> And earthly power doth then show likest God's
> When mercy seasons justice:

But in the madness of Lear and the wisdom of Prospero justice and mercy become almost indistinguishable: there is only one way to a just, 'even', aequal[1] end for man and that, paradoxically, is for all to take the rewards and for the powerful to forgo the punishments. 'Judge not', says Lear, 'because you cannot; you're not fit.' You may say with the Bible, 'All have offended', or with Lear, 'None does offend', but men are alike in their guilty innocence and the only way to make a human law-court just is to subvert its so-called justice – by bribery for example:

> I'll able 'em
> Take that of me, my friend, who have the power
> To seal the accuser's lips.   (IV. vi. 170–2)

Recognise yourself in beggar and criminal and you will dispense succour and forgiveness. You will also seek forgiveness.

What if a man of power, driven from his kingdom, should recover his power and find all his former enemies at his mercy? Vengeance is possible and tempting. But reprisals add suffering. It depends what end is sought. Even the ruthless Henry Bolingbroke, trying to establish an ordered kingdom, sought to make friends of some of his old enemies by clemency; and his son, Henry V, pointed out that 'when lenity and cruelty play for a kingdom, the gentler gamester is the soonest winner'.[2] Even to such as they, mercy could *sometimes* be seen as the best policy. But suppose our restored king to be one who had thought long and deeply and one who, like Lear, had been chastened by

---

[1] 'Aequus' better conveys the final mood of *The Tempest* than 'happy': a delicate balance between good and evil, joy and sorrow, hope and fear is achieved, and a sober calm pervades the close.

[2] *Henry V:* III. vi. 116–18.

suffering. Such a one would want a happy ending not only for king and beggar, but also for criminal and judge.

How would he achieve it, assuming he had the power? What are the conditions of happiness – men being what they are? A play attempting an answer to that question would necessarily be a study in morals, for what is morals but a science of happiness? *The Tempest* is that play.

The question how to achieve happiness, or conversely how not to, necessarily occupies a serious writer of plays that have happy or unhappy endings, especially if, as in Shakespeare's case, the characters very closely resemble real people. If he is to generate happiness in his audience, he must carry them through imitations of events and situations in which, and from which, happiness seems possible, and he must introduce them to imitation people who seem to possess qualities that make for happiness. This Shakespeare has done over and over again. But in *The Tempest* it almost appears as if he wanted to outline and underline his findings on the subject, for he recalls with intense concentration most of the major themes and characters he has previously explored in depth; and he creates one mysterious central figure, Prospero, whom he endows with magical powers, and whose purpose it is to establish the harmonious order which constitutes the happy ending of the play.

Prospero is not a character in the sense that Lear or Hamlet, or Leontes, or even the Duke of Vienna or Hermione are characters. His voice is often the voice of a tender father, or a gentle or a harsh master, or a man of troubled mind or a competent organiser, or a dignified ruler; but we are aware of him rather as an all-pervading Presence. This impression is achieved partly through Ariel's words and actions, partly through Prospero's own, but also by the simple fact that he is a magician – we know a magician's powers – and, above all, by the fact that he is so often actually present on the stage, invisible to characters in the foreground, who thus become as it were reduced in size. The interesting suggestion (quoted in the Arden Edition, p. 155) that Prospero's appearance 'on top' in the banquet episode is 'not . . . essential to the action' misses the point: it is essential to the meaning of Prospero and to the meaning of the play. It is particularly important since it gives a special quality and a special force to the words of Ariel, to which reference is made below (p. 44). If, as is suggested, Prospero is 'on top' so that the actor playing the part can 'co-ordinate the complex display going on below him by transmitting cues to the musicians behind him who in turn provide cues for stage hands and the prompter', we have a remarkable example of Shakespeare's dramatic economy, and of the way genius can exploit stage paraphernalia for a much larger purpose. This spectacle strongly reinforces the sense of the mysterious presence with his command of spiritual forces for the admonishment of men. For Christians the analogy is inescapable; an audience giving general acceptance to the Christian faith would feel the numinous quality, where a sceptical and materialist audience might see little more than stage tricks and, at best a disturbing, at worst an amusing spectacle.

The God whom Shakespeare's audience knew is almighty. This does not mean, however, that his power at any moment is unlimited. On the contrary, it is limited by the nature of things which he himself has established. At least that is generally true, though there might be particular exceptions, mighty interventions like the Incarnation, or minor ones such as miracles. One element in the nature of things as God has willed it is man's power to choose, which in one major respect is inviolable even by God himself, God having willed it so: man may choose whether to love God or to reject him.

In some respects Prospero is like God. He can raise a storm at will by reason of his control of the elements and the spirits that inform them, but he cannot by waving his wand change the nature of a man. That can be effected only according to the laws and agencies of change, which include the man's own choice. In many plays Shakespeare has explored the laws of change, and especially the power of suffering to establish at least the conditions for transformation. Lear is transformed for the better, Macbeth for the worse. The difference lies in the degree of self-discovery and awareness of reality, and in the preceding and the sequent choices.

Prospero's benevolent 'project', which is to establish a

harmony and begin a new dispensation in which there will be the possibility of happiness and betterment for all, requires the transformation of King Alonso of Naples, and either the training or at least the restraint of others: Ferdinand, Antonio, Sebastian, Caliban, Stephano and Trinculo. Prospero's power – one might say his technological skill – must be used to this end. It might have been used to quite other ends, such as the destruction of his enemies in acts of vengeance; but Prospero is the ruler who will prosper and under whose beneficent ordering all may prosper.

However, endowing Prospero with God-like power raises a difficulty, the difficulty that faced Milton in *Paradise Lost*. The-Nature-of-Things is inexorable; it, or its Creator, if presented as a character in a story will appear tyrannous and cruel, even capricious and arbitrary – as a person, objectionable. Hence the sympathy of many for the rebel Satan. Hence, too, the fairly common dislike of Prospero, who at times may appear a self-righteous bully or a bad schoolmaster. The problems of the humane exercise of power over men, men being what they are, are not shirked by Shakespeare. In Prospero's harsh language to Ariel and Caliban and Ferdinand, the ugly face of power too clearly shows. Especially in the case of Caliban, which is considered below.

The problem is most vividly presented in Miranda's first speech:

> If by your art, my dearest father, you have
> Put the wild waters in this roar, allay them:
> The sky, it seems, would pour down stinking pitch,
> But that the sea, mounting to th'welkin's cheek
> Dashes the fire out. O, I have suffered
> With those that I saw suffer! a brave vessel,
> (Who had, no doubt, some noble creature in her,)
> Dash'd all to pieces. O, the cry did knock
> Against my very heart! Poor souls, they perish'd!
>
> (I. ii. 1–9)

The tenderness for all who suffer; the images of cruel power which by a strange ambiguity show the rebellion of the sea against the cruelty of the sky; the cry from Miranda's heart harmonising with the cries of the drowning; the admiration of the beauty of the thing destroyed and the horror at its destruction; the tender relationship of father and daughter on the one hand, and the acknowledgement of his terrible might on the other; all these and more, in this miracle of exposition, prepare for the challenge of the succeeding lines in which Miranda, with the firmness we always find in Shakespeare's tender heroines (here, as in *The Winter's Tale*, done in a flash), raises the problem of power in the way that Christian doubters raise it: if God permits such suffering and destruction, how can he be both almighty and all-loving?

> Had I been any god of power, I would
> Have sunk the sea within the earth, or ere
> It should the good ship so have swallow'd, and
> The fraughting souls within her.   (II. i. 10–13)

Power should be gentle, and should save, not destroy.

Prospero reassures Miranda that the tempest which looks like an act of vengeance on his enemies is to be no less that the means of their salvation, by an act of reconciliation with him and the beginning of a new order and a new life for Miranda herself, and for all. It is impossible for Christians to miss the analogies with their own myth, but it is not only Christians for whom the issues are important. How shall benevolence deal with the murderer who thrives in evil? How shall benevolent power deal with those who thirst for its overthrow and the advancement of their own personal power and material advantage? What is the nature of the true ruler?

The ghosts of Richard III and Don John, of Iago and Edmund, walk in this play in the persons of Antonio, Prospero's brother, and Sebastian, King Alonso's brother. Antonio urges Sebastian to supplant Alonso by murder:

SEBASTIAN: I remember
  You did supplant your brother Prospero.
ANTONIO: True;
  And look how well my garments sit upon me.
  Much feater than before: my brother's servants
  Were then my fellows; now they are my men.

SEBASTIAN: But for your conscience.
ANTONIO: Ay, sir; where lies that? if 'twere a kibe,
  'Twould put me to my slipper: but I feel not
  This deity in my bosom: twenty consciences,
  That stand 'twixt me and Milan, candied be they
  And melt, ere they molest!

(II. i. 265–75)

Such men, such minds do not make happy endings either in life
or in art. They may die quietly in their beds having enjoyed a
prosperous life (though there is no image of this in Shakespeare's
plays) but

'all the plagues that in the pendulous air
Hang fated o'er men's faults'[1]

attend the deeds of such and often fall on innocent heads such
as Desdemona's, or on whole nations, like Macbeth's Scotland
or Richard's England. Or on the child Miranda, cast from
Milan in the 'rotten carcass of a butt'. With such men in the
play (or in life) how is a happy ending to be attained?

On the long view none is happy unless all are happy, and
virtue is that which would make all men happy. Unfortunately,
it is the short view that appeals to the so-called 'practical' man,
who will settle for the immediate advantage which seems easier
to calculate. In this Antonio stands four square with Falstaff,
and with Falstaff's shadow in *The Tempest*, Stephano: there is an
illuminating parallel between Stephano's and Antonio's
respective assessments of Caliban:

STEPHANO: If I can recover him, and keep him tame, I will not
  take too much for him: he shall pay for him that hath him,
  and that soundly.

(II. ii. 78–80)

ANTONIO: one of them
  Is a plain fish, and, no doubt, marketable.

(V. i. 265–6)

Antonio embodies that in man which cannot or will not feel and
act on the long view, but is bent on immediate interest. If the

[1] *Lear:* III. iv. 67–8.

stories of Richard III and Macbeth and Falstaff are anything to go by, this is the way to ruin.

Fortunately there is the contrary impulse, which we see in Miranda. Different situations, different culture patterns, may foster one of these impulses and inhibit the other. Ceremonies, traditions, social orders exist to reinforce man's flickering altruism or inhibit his egoism, or both. Civilisation is a standing recognition that man's long-term interest lies in deferring personal and immediate satisfactions, and at least behaving as if he loved his brother as himself. Hence the importance, or sacredness as in Shakespeare's plays, of the bonds 'of nature and of nations'. Antonio and King Alonso broke the bonds of family and commonwealth when they supplanted Prospero. Antonio and Sebastian would do the same, by the murder of Alonso. Prospero is the great civiliser, who will renew the broken bonds, educate or re-educate those who have broken or would break them, and strengthen by loving care and by severe trials those on whom their preservation most depends. His function is to preserve the values embodied in Miranda against the values of Antonio and Stephano, and to guide Alonso and Caliban to reject the latter and adopt the former. Even Antonio and Stephano themselves are to be moved towards change.

The transformation of Alonso follows the pattern of Lear's. It is given in outline and given in such a way as to have the explicitness of moral precept. Alonso's ship of life is wrecked; he is subjected to the elements; he loses his children; in his sufferings he remembers his treachery against Prospero and is filled with remorse. It is at this point that Ariel, Prospero's spirit-agent, agent of what he calls 'the powers' and of Destiny, delivers his warning to sinners. What Ariel has to say here has quite different force from anything that is spoken by a regular Shakespearean character. When Hamlet says, 'There's a divinity that shapes our ends' we may say he speaks in character, that is, the words evoke a mood out of which, together with elements previously established, our sense of a particular, seemingly living person is being built. No so with Ariel when he accuses Alonso, Sebastian and Antonio, when he torments them with hunger, fear and grief, or when he makes the deep and dreadful organ-pipe of thunder pronounce the name of Prosper in their guilty ears. He is not a person speaking 'in character' but an admonishing angel, the agent of Prospero who is a supreme presence in the scene. He, as well as Prospero, is an image of unseen realities: he is the voice of reason, of remorse and of conscience in the 'three men of sin', of doom in all, and of wisdom in Gonzalo. There is no scene in which the sense of mysterious powers both within man's mind and in the whole universe is stronger than it is here for an audience capable of feeling the symbolic force of the spectacle. And consequently the words of Ariel admonish the audience no less than the characters in the story. Shakespeare is making explicit what has in former plays been implicit:

> The powers, delaying, not forgetting, have
> Incens'd the seas and shores, yea, all the creatures,
> Against your peace. Thee, of thy son, Alonso,
> They have bereft; and do pronounce by me
> Ling'ring perdition – worse than any death
> Can be at once – shall step by step attend
> You and your ways; whose wraths to guard you from, –
> Which here, in this most desolate isle, else falls
> Upon your heads, – is nothing but heart-sorrow,
> And a clear life ensuing.   (III. iii. 73–82)

'heart-sorrow, And a clear life ensuing' – suffering, contrition and repentance were shown in *King Lear* to be chief factors in the process of change for the better, the conditions of such happiness as erring man may hope to achieve. Lingering perdition, step by step, attended Macbeth and his ways: Shakespeare showed every step. Macbeth suffered the unfruitful agonies of Hell, for he could not repent, could not turn to a 'clear life':

>   I am in blood
> Stepp'd in so far that, should I wade no more,
> Returning were as tedious as go o'er[1]

Macbeth's hope that there is another shore to the sea into which

---

[1] *Macbeth:* III. iv. 135–7.

he is wading is vain. King Claudius, even as he prayed for
forgiveness, knew better:

> But, O, what form of prayer
> Can serve my turn? 'Forgive me my foul murder!'
> That cannot be; since I am still possess'd
> Of those effects for which I did the murder –
> My crown, mine own ambition, and my queen.
> May one be pardon'd, and retain th' offence?[1]

Alonso will be different: he follows Ariel's precept and, recovering his senses, greets Prospero with:

> Thy dukedom I resign, and do entreat
> Thou pardon me my wrongs.   (V. i. 118–19)

For Alonso is like King Lear, whose sufferings were the fruitful
sufferings of purgatory, leading to 'a heavenlier heart'[2] and the
possibility of happiness.

But the achievement of happiness requires more. Not only
must there be a Cordelia to forgive, rather than to resent, but
also there must be no Edmund powerful enough to kill Cordelia
and start a new chain of evil events. Cordelia's personal act of
forgiveness was unconditional and immediate:

> No cause, no cause.   (IV. vii. 75)

but if Lear had not repented there could have been no reconciliation. Prospero has so great care of his 'enemies'

> that there is no soul –
> No, not so much perdition as an hair,
> Betid to any creature in the vessel
> (I. ii. 29–31)

but in preparing the final reconciliation he reaffirms Ariel's
precepts by stating the condition:

> they being penitent,
> The sole drift of my purpose doth extend
> Not a frown further.   (V. i. 28–30)

The words may at first give the impression that he himself is
laying down the conditions, as if he will continue to frown upon

---

[1] *Hamlet*: III. iii. 51–6.   [2] *Felix Randal*: G. M. Hopkins.

them unless they repent. Cordelia never frowned on Lear. As the words of an injured man about his personal enemies, they may sound grudging, condescending, self-righteous. However, such words from one in authority, and not himself personally injured, are commonly accepted, as in parents, teachers, or priests, like Chaucer's humble and saintly parson:

> He was to synful man noght despitous,
> Ne of his speche dangerous ne digne,
> But in his teching discreet and benygne.

> But it were any person obstinat,
> What-so he were, of heigh or low estat,
> Hym wolde he snibben sharply for the nonis.
> A bettre prest I trowe that nowhere noon is.[1]

Prospero's words, and Chaucer's, remark the inescapable fact that the impenitent do not accept forgiveness, and where forgiveness is not accepted there can be no reconciliation and no truly happy issue. At the best the malignant can be merely restrained, but that is an unhappy state of affairs. Prospero's 'frown' was intended to prepare the 'three men of sin' for the moment of acceptance and reconciliation; but they may reject.

Prospero's role at this point of the play (Act V. Sc. 1) gives the words the force of unalterable law. It is true that he is touched with feeling and talks as a human being to the non-human Ariel:

> and shall not myself,
> One of their kind, that relish all as sharply
> Passion as they, be kindlier mov'd than thou art?

but this is Act V and his commanding position in the act confirms and strengthens all the associations with magic or divine power, with Fate and Destiny that, sometimes fitfully, sometimes firmly, collocate about Prospero.

The good old lord, Gonzalo, suffering with the 'three men of sin' prays:

> some heavenly power guide us
> Out of this fearful country.

[1] *Prologue to The Canterbury Tales*: 516–24.

We already know that it is Prospero who will guide them.
Alonso says:

> And there is in this business more than nature
> Was ever conduct of: some oracle
> Must rectify our knowledge.

Prospero, we know, has conducted the business, and is the
oracle. Alonso asks about Miranda:

> Is she the goddess that hath sever'd us
> And brought us thus together?

But they have been severed and brought together by Prospero.
Ferdinand replies:

> Sir, she is mortal;
> But by immortal Providence she's mine;
>
> (V. i. 187–9)

We have seen that she is his by Prospero's providing. Gonzalo
pronounces a blessing:

> Look down, you gods,
> And on this couple drop a blessed crown!
> For it is you that have chalk'd forth the way
> Which brought us hither.

It is Prospero who has chalk'd forth the way that brought them
to this happy ending.

These and other even more powerful suggestions make the
play seem at one and the same time a map of the universe, a
chart of human life, and a plan of the human psyche. For
Prospero is not merely an allegorical representation of God or
Reason or Authority. It is Fortune, his dear lady, that brings
the ships to the island just when his 'zenith doth depend upon a
most auspicious star'. He and Miranda were carried to the
island 'By Providence divine', assisted by the charity of Gonzalo. Above all, the language Shakespeare gives him is the
language of a living man, though almost always with the dignity,
the detachment or the authority of a ruler or a god. Nowhere is
he more human, however, than in the imperfection, or seeming
imperfection, of his dealings with Caliban.

CHAPTER THREE

I, Thy Schoolmaster

MENTION of Caliban shifts the angle from which we view Prospero; but it does not remove our attention from the problems or the meaning of responsibility, authority and power, or of forgiveness, transformation and redemption. These are no less pointedly illustrated in the life of a schoolmaster than in the life of a king.

Prospero, by nature a scholar, by accident a duke, has no alternative but to become a schoolmaster, He has two pupils. With the progress of the one, Miranda, he has reason to be satisfied:

> and here
> Have I, thy schoolmaster, made thee more profit
> Than other princes can, that have more time
> For vainer hours, and tutors not so careful.

> MIRANDA: Heavens thank you for't!   (I. ii. 171–4)

With the other, Caliban, he has failed; for Caliban has had much time 'for vainer hours' and is not disposed to relinquish them or subject himself to rule:

> all the charms
> Of Sycorax, toads, beetles, bats light on you!
> For I am all the subjects that you have
> Which first was mine own king: and here you sty me
> In this hard rock, whiles you do keep from me
> The rest o'th' island.   (I. ii. 341–6)

The twentieth century takes all the force of that word 'sty', and that word 'hard', and that claim to prior possession. We sympathise, all having been stied in the hard rock of school. Prospero loses favour.

When Prospero, the colonist, first arrived on Caliban's island, there was a genuine exchange of knowledge and experience, and of affection, a two-way process of education:

I, THY SCHOOLMASTER

When thou cam'st first,
Thou strok'st me, and made much of me; would'st give me
Water with berries in't; and teach me how
To name the bigger light, and how the less,
That burn by day and night: and then I lov'd thee,
And show'd thee all the qualities o'th' isle,
The fresh springs, brine pits, barren place and fertile:

(I. ii. 333–40)

This ideally educative situation, with its high degree of motivation by affection and altruistic drive on both parts, could not
live in the teeth of emulation. Each assumed himself the
superior. Caliban, first 'king' of the island, knew nothing of
conscience – nothing, that is, of the restraints of immediate
appetite that civilisation demands. To him Prospero's daughter,
being lovely, was a dainty morsel to be enjoyed forthwith, and
a means to ensure the succession to his kingdom:

I had peopled else
This isle with Calibans.

Similarly Prospero assumes Miranda to be his, and his means to
ensure the succession to the duchy of Milan and later to the
kingdom of Naples. She is not, of course, to Prospero an object
of immediate appetite, nor indeed a mere object at all, but a
person whom he loves and to whom he has responsibilities.
Prospero is civilised. Prospero makes the assumption of the
civilised colonist, and of the average schoolteacher, that it is his
duty as well as his right to exercise authority over the savage,
or the untaught, and to control or restrain where inner control
and restraint are lacking; for were not the Roman swords the
'best teachers of civilitie to this and other Countries'?[1]

Prospero's magic power is his 'sword'. He controls Caliban
by corporal punishment: cramps and side-stitches. To Caliban
he is a usurper exercising arbitrary power, and must be resisted.
To himself he is the agent of higher powers and subject to
superior laws, to which Caliban also must be made subject. His
kindness from the first was condescending; Caliban's was
impulsive. Each feels injured when the bond of kindness between

[1] Strachey: See Arden Edition, p. 140.

them breaks, Caliban because he is subjected to rule and punishment, Prospero because his good offices have been rejected.

This is where Prospero appears a bad schoolmaster. If we accept that his 'civilitie' is superior (as we do) and that his duty is to raise Caliban to his own levels of love and honour and grace, then how are we to condone his irritation with the bad boy who persists in breaking the rules? His first failure with Caliban has caused him to give up all hope of success:

> Abhorred slave
> Which any print of goodness wilt not take,
> Being capable of all ill!   (I. ii. 353–5)

Every speech of Prospero's in this first exchange with Caliban has a touchy self-righteousness, an air of injured vanity. He is the teacher who, having failed, blames the pupil, and does not question his own methods or theory of education.

And, within the play, his methods are being called in question. He is quite wrong about Caliban, and the exposure of his error contributes materially to the mood of quiet hope in which the play ends:

PROSPERO: He is as disproportion'd in his manners
  As in his shape. Go, sirrah, to my cell;
  Take with you your companions; as you look
  To have my pardon, trim it handsomely.
CALIBAN: Ay, that I will; and I'll be wise hereafter
  And seek for grace.

                                        (V. i. 290–5)

No attentive reader of Shakespeare's last plays can miss the force of that last word: it implies precisely the miracle of change that Prospero has thought impossible. In a modern production a distinct gesture of surprise and joyous hope from Prospero is essential to explain the point for readers unfamiliar with Christian language.

In the earlier scenes Caliban's reaction to what he feels as injustice and to the 'stripes' he has to suffer is precisely what we should expect: Prospero's claims are resisted to the limit of endurance, and what Prospero has tried to teach is either rejected or perverted:

I, THY SCHOOLMASTER

You taught me language; and my profit on't
Is, I know how to curse. The red plague rid you
For learning me your language!   (I. ii. 365–7)

Prospero's remedy is to apply the treatment that has been in part the cause of Caliban's virulence:

If thou neglect'st, or dost unwillingly
What I command, I'll rack thee with old cramps,
Fill all thy bones with aches, make thee roar
That beasts shall tremble at thy din.

Their first affection gave place to emulation, emulation to domination by Prospero, and thence a vicious circle of repression and hate in which it is impossible for Caliban to learn any lessons but hate and the urge to gain power by violence. These are the lessons he does learn, and that he seeks later to teach Stephano. Not that hate and cruelty have been *implanted* in him by repression, for from the first his nature 'had that in't which good natures could not abide to be with', but repression confirms these vices – as his foaming curses show. The virulence of Caliban's hate then makes Prospero feel that he has been too gentle, not too severe:

therefore wast thou
Deservedly confin'd into this rock,
Who hadst deserv'd more than a prison.

and he threatens still more savage punishment, closing the vicious circle of harshness and resentment. What calls in question Prospero's wisdom is that his action not merely confirms Caliban in his special vices, but also neglects the rudiments of virtue – that is of love – that Caliban showed in their first relationship. It is interesting that the only words Prospero speaks to Caliban which have in them any hope of reconciliation or any suggestion that Caliban may have virtuous potential ('as you look/To have my pardon') are followed immediately by Caliban's resolve to change for the better, to seek for grace through willing *service*, not to be the 'poisonous *slave*' that Prospero has persistently named him. Caliban may be a devil born

51

but it is not true that on his nature nurture can never stick, nor is it true that all Prospero's pains, taken as he says humanely in the education of Caliban, are lost, though it is true that the 'stripes' inflicted upon him in the way of vengeful punishment have been worse than useless, indeed contrary to any humane purpose other than mere restraint – and *that* in the short-term only.

The point is of major importance, for it sharpens the point of a central statement of the play:

> the rarer action is
> In virtue than in vengeance:
>
> (V. i. 27–8)

The word 'virtue' is used, not the word 'forgiveness'. It affirms the positive element in forgiveness, and in the situation of the play. Prospero, refusing to look back over the crimes of his former enemies, looks forward to some positive good. His purpose is creative. Similarly, in the previous line:

> Yet with my nobler reason 'gainst my fury
> Do I take part:

'Reason' and 'virtue', the positive elements in forgiveness, are opposed to fury and vengeance here at the end of the play, as they were certainly not shown to be in that first altercation with Caliban, or indeed in any treatment of Caliban before that one encouraging remark of Prospero's.

There is certainly nothing 'rare' in Prospero's action and speech against Caliban in Act I, nor is it of the same order as his severity to either Ariel or Ferdinand. It shows an attitude that Prospero later rejects as an unworthy reaction to the pain of being struck to the quick by high wrongs. Moreover, it is an attitude that increases hostility and could not lead to the play's happy ending.

Yet Prospero does play a vital part in leading Caliban to the beginning of wisdom, not by instructions and injuctions, not by precepts or behests such as Miranda or Ferdinand might respond to, but by setting him free to learn his own lesson. Much as Milton's God sets Satan free to 'Heap on himself damnation',

Prospero sets Caliban free, but not to the same end. Prospero, like God, sets limits to the freedom of his subject, or Caliban would indeed damn himself by the murder of Prospero; but there are other limits, such as the limitations of Stephano and Trinculo, which are not artificial impositions but are there in the given situation. Yet Prospero's purpose is not shown to be redemptive until that final remark: 'as you look/To have my pardon'. On the contrary, to the last he affirms that this demi-devil cannot be redeemed but is a 'thing of darkness' 'as disproportioned in his manners as in his shape'.

And all the time Shakespeare has been warning us that Prospero is wrong. The warnings are in the quality of language that Shakespeare gives to Caliban. Attention has often been drawn to his cultural richness as a child of nature and of the senses, even in his curses:

> All the infections that the sun sucks up
> From bogs, fens, flats, on Prosper fall, and make him
> By inch-meal a disease!   (II. ii. 1–3)

and his terrors:

>   then like hedge-hogs, which
> Lie tumbling in my barefoot way, and mount
> Their pricks at my footfall; sometime am I
> All wound with adders, who with cloven tongues
> Do hiss me into madness.   (II. ii. 10–14)

but much more in his enthusiasms and his wood-craft:

> I prithee, let me bring thee where crabs grow;
> And I with my long nails will dig thee pig-nuts;
> Show thee a jay's nest, and instruct thee how
> To snare the nimble marmoset;   (II. ii. 167–70)

(Note: 'Show thee a jay's nest' is the voice of appreciation, not of depredation.) Then there is the famous speech in which he appreciates the wondrous music of the island. It is one respect in which his animal judgement shows wiser and better than that of many men. Music in Shakespeare's work is the image of the heavenly harmonies, and we feel that Caliban can appreciate these as Stephano and Trinculo can not. It is not to be expected then that he will be long deceived into taking Stephano for a god. But there is something else in the speech, something we have seen in Caliban from the beginning, namely aspiration.

The instinct for betterment, the root of moral worth, may be perverted into lust or greed, but where it is strongly present we are aware of high human potential:

> Sometimes a thousand twangling instruments
> Will hum about mine ears; and sometimes voices,
> That, if I then had wak'd after long sleep,
> Will make me sleep again: and then, in dreaming,
> The clouds methought would open, and show riches
> Ready to drop upon me; that, when I wak'd,
> I cried to dream again.   (III. ii. 135–41)

Caliban does not suffer from that atrophy of the fancy and the imagination that accompanies the limited materialist view in which Stephano and Trinculo are damned – hence his exercise of judgement when his 'god' is diverted from the serious purpose in hand by gewgaws and trinkets. In that episode (IV. 1. 221–65), Caliban has three speeches, separated not merely by the words of his companions, but by ridiculous by-play with the garments. Caliban will not join in the 'fun':

> Let it alone, thou fool; it is but trash.

Let it alone, thou fool; it is but trash (the 'fool' is Trinculo):

> The dropsy drown this fool! what do you mean
> To dote thus on such luggage?

But the 'god' Stephano does too: Caliban alone preserves the sense of realities:

> I will have none on't.

What matters in this scene is what takes place in Caliban. It is hinted at in his speeches quoted here, but clearly indicated by the difference between his speech of worship immediately before the discovery of the 'frippery' and his final words in Act V:

I, THY SCHOOLMASTER

and I, thy Caliban,
For aye thy foot-licker.
What a thrice-double ass
Was I, to take this drunkard for a god,
And worship this dull fool!

Failure on the part of actor and producer to convey the fullness of this realisation, in Caliban's silences as well as his words in the 'frippery' episode, eliminates one of the most powerful impressions that contribute to the sense of opening wisdom and hope in the final act and the epilogue. Alonso's awakening is a recovery; Caliban's is a discovery. They are complementary, and Caliban's the more moving since he has been thought irredeemable and since in his case Prospero has erred. Alonso's reconciliation with Prospero is a meeting of equals at the *end* of a transformation and at a moment of final acceptance. Caliban on the other hand is at the *beginning* of a process whose discipline is to be the willing service he has hitherto repudiated; his change therefore leaves us with a question and a hope that reach out beyond the end of the play.

Caliban has learned, not from a teacher's words, but by living through an experience. However, had not his teacher been present throughout to set limits to Caliban's malicious activity and to arrange situations like that of the 'frippery' in which it is possible for him to learn, Caliban would have committed murder, and subjected himself (and Miranda) to worse slavery and misery than he suffered in his rock sty. In short he would have re-enacted, in unheroic terms, the story of Macbeth.

And here Prospero appears as a wiser sort of teacher. Now, he is not the one who lectures and prescribes or scolds and punishes; he is the one who arranges situations in which his pupils can learn for themselves. He leaves them free to explore. He interferes only to save them from destroying themselves – not to save them from hurting themselves or making mistakes: these are essential to the process of learning. When he inflicts pain, as in the hunt, he does it (as Portia does) to prevent a murder, but the pain simulates that which would in the nature of things *follow* such a deed. Better be hunted into Prospero's cess-pool by Prospero's hounds, than hunted into the cess-pool of misery and moral degeneration by the dog-faced Erinyes. This is not punishment to revenge; it is the severity of training. The one may often masquerade as the other in the family, the school, or the law court, but the difference between them is great. In human situations vengeful punishment is destructive. Imposed severity with the aim of educating is not the ideal, but when, like Prospero, the teacher has failed to apply the disciplines of affection it may be a necessary, perhaps even a good, second best. It is better for Caliban to take a comparatively harmless dose from the 'poisoned chalice' than to have to drink it all as a consequence of having delivered it to another:

> But in these cases,
> We still have judgement here; that we but teach
> Bloody instructions, which, being taught, return
> To plague th'inventor: this even-handed Justice
> Commends th'ingredience of our poison'd chalice
> To our own lips.[1]

But in this play Prospero is not merely man, teacher, father, ruler: he is a complex symbol stimulating reflections not only on human situations but on the realities that underlie them. Joy, excitement, anticipation, appreciation, access of power are elements in the learning process, as Caliban's own words have suggested; but so too are pain and loss: 'You have learnt something,' says Andrew Undershaft to Major Barbara. 'That always feels at first as if you had lost something.' A clearer judgement can only come at the expense of a cherished error. 'Civilitie' implies the suppression of impulse, service the denial of sloth and self-will. The pain and loss inflicted by Necessity, rather than by a person, we accept. Prospero and Caliban, it has been said, convey reflections upon Art and Nature.[2] So they do. They also stimulate reflections upon many other elements in human experience, Necessity and Freedom for example. Prospero, in the play's dialogue and action, is frequently associated with Fate and Destiny. In some respects he *is* Necessity, as here with Ariel leading the dance of the hounds. The scene should be

[1] *Macbeth:* I. vii. 7–12.
[2] See Arden Edition: Introduction by Frank Kermode.

played as a dance of the Furies, a ritual imitation of their terrors, which does actually prevent their real terrors, since it prevents the evil deed and confirms Caliban's clearer judgement.

In the images of vengeful harshness in Act I Scene II Prospero's treatment of Caliban is different from his treatment of Ariel and Ferdinand. In these later scenes, however, Prospero is doing what *must* be done; the same applies to his disciplinary action with Ariel. Ariel is not a victim, as Caliban at first appears to be. Ariel serves under a free contract, though the contract has arisen out of an obligation following Prospero's act of mercy in releasing Ariel from the pine. Ariel, forgetting his obligation, finds the contract irksome. Prospero has already promised to release him from it one year before his time is out:

> thou didst promise
> To bate me a full year
>
> (I. ii. 249–50)

and Prospero will keep that promise, but there are still some vital days to run. Generous master that he is, Prospero will not even insist on these (I. ii. 423–4), but Ariel is 'moody' for his liberty. The situation is, on the one hand, one between a lord and his man, but on the other, Ariel being no man but a power, it is the necessary one between a Will and a Means to execute that Will. There is here no question of education; Ariel is not subject to change. However, by analogy, we attribute human qualities to the 'element' of air: we say 'as free as air'. So Ariel images the passion for freedom which has to be disciplined to service, if good ends are to be achieved. Hearing and seeing Ariel, we reflect on freedom, as we do also when Caliban makes his bid for freedom. One of the proper limitations of freedom is contractual obligation; another is the bending of faculties (such as fantasy or imagination or technological skill for example) to the fulfilment of a beneficent purpose.

The question whether Shakespeare was consciously allegorising is not perhaps the most important one. The most important is whether such meanings as these are implied in Shakespeare's text and suggested by the acted scenes. Readers and audiences have felt them.

Prospero's harshness to Ferdinand is different again. Here we know precisely his benevolent purpose and we feel sure from the beginning of its happy end. But the gift that Prospero has to offer to Ferdinand is so delicately fragile that it may easily be damaged by the receiver's too eager grasp. Indeed it cannot be received except by one who is more eager to give than to receive: grasping destroys it; vanity or violence destroy it. Hasty desire must be allayed: Ferdinand's 'sword' must fall till he shall have become fit to give and to receive on that day

> When I shall think, or Phoebus steeds are founder'd,
> Or Night kept chain'd below.

It is a recurring theme of fairy-story and romance, and its sexual symbolism is confirmed when Prospero finally bestows Miranda on Ferdinand:

> Then as my gift, and thine own acquisition
> Worthily purchas'd, take my daughter: but
> If thou dost break her virgin knot before
> All sanctimonious ceremonies may
> With full and holy rite be minister'd,
> No sweet aspersions shall the heavens let fall
> To make this contract grow; but barren hate,
> Sour-ey'd disdain and discord shall bestrew
> The union of your bed with weeds so loathly
> That you shall hate it both: therefore take heed,
> As Hymen's lamps shall light you.[1]
>
> (IV. i. 13–23)

But the fairy story theme is not a sexual symbol only; the sexual element is itself symbolic of a more fundamental truth.

[1] There is a danger of reading this passage as if it were a personal threat. Such a reading is not consistent with the play as a whole. The passage (together with 51–56 and 86–101) is a statement of the conditions of happy marriage, for Ferdinand to accept or reject. Prospero at this stage has withdrawn his magic power, and the choice and responsibility rest with the young couple. Whether the strong feeling of lines 19–22 springs from Shakespeare's personal experience or his sense of guilt is not relevant, and is in any case not known.

I, THY SCHOOLMASTER

No delicate and beautiful thing, whether in nature or in art can be received but by the humble and self-disciplined. The avid and the confident will devour, as Caliban would have devoured Miranda; the possessive will crush. Miranda is a flower that Prospero has cherished and cultivated – to give to Ferdinand. But it must be proved that Ferdinand is also a giver, who can cherish Miranda. Prospero's treatment of Ferdinand is not so much a training as a test. True, by patience and endurance Ferdinand is to learn to value Miranda rightly:

> this swift business
> I must uneasy make, lest too light winning
> Make the prize light. (I. ii. 452–4)

But the pains and humiliations he has to endure are not needed to teach him how to love and serve: he has already learned: if he had not, he would not have submitted to them, as he does – for Miranda's sake. Prospero's doubts are allayed:

> all thy vexations
> Were but my trials of thy love, and thou
> Hast strangely stood the test. (IV. i. 5–7)

In the stories of Caliban, Ariel and Ferdinand the themes of freedom and service predominate. Caliban, wanting absolute freedom, wants the impossible, and, when he believes he has got it, makes a fool of himself and subjects himself to worse slavery. Stephano's alcohol gives Caliban immediate pleasure and the illusion of freedom and transformation. The one who has given it to him must then be a true god and fit master – unlike Prospero. Conscience Caliban experiences no more than Antonio: he is in that primitive or immature state in which punishment alone deters. Such rudimentary reason as he seems to possess does not at this time carry him beyond immediate interest or satisfaction. Prospero has been all the Reason and Conscience Caliban has known, and he has hated Prospero's authority. He will be free of them, free from duty, free from care. The new god and the magic bottle will free him. He leaps and dances – headlong into misery:

No more dams I'll make for fish;
  Nor fetch in firing
    At requiring;
Nor scrape trenchering, nor wash dish:
  'Ban, 'Ban, Cacaliban
Has a new master: – get a new man.

(II. ii. 180–85)

Prospero has called him 'poisonous slave'. He repudiates the slavery. So would Ferdinand have done under the same conditions (See III. 1. 61–3). But what is the difference between slavery and service? This is what Caliban discovers when, having realised the difference between Prospero and Stephano, he goes *willingly* to tidy Prospero's cell: then, through service, he seeks the perfect freedom of 'grace' (V. i. 294–5).

Unwittingly Caliban hiccoughs a pun: 'ban' is to curse. But the curse is upon himself: his new master is the Lord of Trivialities. The 'god' proves the inferior of the worshipper. They end in a cess-pool, image of the puddle in their minds and of the consequence of evil. It is the proper end to this episode, but, as we have seen, not final for Caliban. The story of Caliban and Stephano is a parody of the story of Antonio and Sebastian, a parody of the story of 'killing the king', which has been a recurring theme in Shakespeare's plays. It is the murder, or the attempted murder of responsible authority, of social order, of world order, and of the heavenly harmonies. In *The Tempest* the plotters fail. Failure is Caliban's salvation: we have seen how his animal impulse gives way to reflection, self-will to self-criticism:

What a thrice-double ass
Was I, to take this drunkard for a god.

(V. i. 295–6)

We see him growing towards the realisation that

'the nature of man as respecting self, and tending to private good, his own preservation and happiness; and the nature of man as having respect to society, and tending to promote public good, the happiness of society . . . do, indeed, perfectly coincide; . . . they mutually promote each other'[1]

[1] Bishop Joseph Butler: Sermon 'Upon Human Nature'.

which is also the unifying theme of the play. Seen from opposite angles in the stories of Miranda's marriage and Antonio's treachery, it finds its summing up in the comic irony of Stephano's drunken cry, which, be it noted, receives all the emphasis of a striking entry line:

> Every man shift for all the rest, and let no
> man take care for himself;   (V. i. 256–7)

It is as important in reading Shakespeare as in reading Shaw to remember Shaw's warning:

> Whenever you find a joke, search it for
> a hidden truth.

Stephano in his drink may say the opposite of what he intends, but his line chokes the laugh it first arouses, and sharply points the moral of the play. It is idle, given the form and subject-matter of this play, to pretend that it has no moral.

In the harmonious order of the play the pathetic comedy of Caliban's bid for freedom, wildest and saddest moment, is followed by the most delicately restrained and beautiful scene. Caliban has refused to carry logs and wash dishes and takes this as the measure of his freedom. But now Ferdinand, the prince, is bearing logs, doing Caliban's menial chore because

> some kinds of baseness
> Are nobly undergone;

For Miranda's sake is Ferdinand 'this patient log-man':

> The Mistress which I serve quickens what's dead
> And makes my labours pleasures: (III. i. 6–7)

There is no equivocation in the word 'serve' in this motive from old romance: there are no glorious exploits or exciting adventures for Ferdinand – only a menial task. And there is no sentimentality in the language by which Ferdinand offers his love and service to Miranda. He employs the poetic convention of the heart leaving the body and taking rest in the body of the loved one. It is revealing to contrast his use of it with Orsino's in *Twelfth Night*. The lovely and witty figures employed by

Orsino are all self-directed and convey the impatience of his desire, not the lineaments of true devotion:

> CURIO: Will you go hunt, my lord?
> ORSINO: What, Curio?
> CURIO: The hart.
> ORSINO: Why, so I do, the noblest that I have.
>   O, when mine eyes did see Olivia first,
>   Methought she purg'd the air of pestilence!
>   That instant was I turn'd into a hart,
>   And my desires, like fell and cruel hounds,
>   E'er since pursue me.   (I. i. 16–23)

Ferdinand is no proud huntsman, nor yet a pitiable victim; nor is there any effect of cleverness in his words:

>   Hear my soul speak:
>   The very instant that I saw you, did
>   My heart fly to your service; there resides
>   To make me slave to it; and for your sake
>   Am I this patient log-man.   (III. i. 63–7)

The effect of the conventional image is to make Ferdinand the courtier; the impression of the last line is to establish him a true man. The combination expresses the innocent idealism of youth, and the language, even that of the conceit, sounds plain and real. Yet by contrast with Miranda's it seems elaborate. Hers is totally unspoiled by any hint of sophistication: it seems pure, natural frankness and innocence, but it has the grace of 'civilitie' and testifies to the quality of her education. It is the perfect blend of nature and art. So perfect is the 'decorum' of it that to describe Shakespeare's skill here is to describe Miranda's character. The encounter is at its most 'rare' in the culmination, where Shakespeare distils the essence of the courtly tradition and again gives it reality by the plainness of the diction:

> MIRANDA: Hence bashful cunning!
>   And prompt me, plain and holy innocence!
>   I am your wife, if you will marry me;
>   If not, I'll die your maid: to be your fellow
>   You may deny me; but I'll be your servant,
>   Whether you will or no.

FERDINAND :   My mistress, dearest,
And I thus humble ever.
MIRANDA: My husband, then?
FERDINAND: Ay, with a heart as willing
As bondage e'er of freedom: (III. i. 81–9)

'As bondage e'er of freedom' – we are reminded here, at the
end of the scene, of Caliban. Love, freely offered and received,
freely exchanged, is service freely undertaken, and is joy. Love's
service is perfect freedom. This is not an argument: it is the
tune Shakespeare plays on his words.

Both Caliban and Ferdinand are in bondage to Prospero; the
one can accept his servitude, the other can not; the one,
devoting himself to love and service is made free and joyous; the
other, rejecting service and embracing hate is made miserable
and finds himself in tighter bonds. To express the subtle relations
between freedom and service, and the shifts of meaning of both
these chameleon words, is an exercise for specialists in theology,
philosophy, psychology and linguistics. Presented in art, however, as in these adjacent scenes from *The Tempest*, they are
received as known, 'felt in the blood and felt along the heart',
recognised as elements in the world and in our own being.

'Whose service is perfect freedom' – Biblical and liturgical
phrases recur to the mind, and *The Tempest* reads almost like an
experiment of the Baconian kind (let us see what happens if . . .)
to see how these Christian ideas work. The enigmatic Father-
figure of Prospero is present as usual, watching with quiet joy
the scene he has carefully prepared. He pronounces a blessing
on the couple, using that very special Christian word that
is recurrent in recurs in Shakespeare's late plays, 'grace':

                    Fair encounter
Of two most rare affections! Heavens rain grace
On that which breeds between 'em!   (III. i. 74–6)

It has been felt by some that Prospero's magic staff is too
mighty in the play, that we are not held in suspense, for we
know the great magician will arrange things as he wants and
that the characters are puppets that he manipulates. Prospero
certainly wields great power. But the power he exercises is a

power over the event and the situation, not over the person. This must be qualified. Prospero has physical power, technological power, power to raise a storm, to sink a ship and recover it, to preserve garments, to quell the sword, to inflict physical pain. Only through such indirect means can he exercise power over people. He does not control their minds. Situations can be arranged in which Alonso, Antonio and Sebastian can be brought face to face with themselves and made aware of their guilt. But they do not react to the situation in the same ways. Splendid garments can be laid to entrap Stephano, Trinculo and Caliban, but Caliban would not have been trapped by them. Ferdinand cannot by any means be changed in mind by the pains inflicted on him: his mind is sound. Nor can Caliban be changed by his cramps and side-stitches, though he can be made to work. We have seen that he is changed by being placed in situations where he must exercise his own judgement, and the voluntary nature of his final choice and resolution could not be more strongly emphasised than it is by the fact that Prospero, even in the preceding speech, has no hope of his reform:

> He is as disproportion'd in his manners
> As in his shape. (V. i. 290–1)

Attention has been drawn above to the limits of Prospero's power and to the parallel with the Christian idea of God. Prospero's power is limited in precisely the way in which God is said to limit himself, and also in the way that the laws of cause and effect seem to be limited by the special energy of Choice.

In experience, if one who exercises unusual power is not to be a tyrant he must limit himself or be limited by others or by the nature of things. In practice, everyone who has power, however slight, must, if he is not to be domineering or cruel, withhold his power or even relinquish it – a father or a teacher must at some stage refrain. Herein lies the difference between education and brain-washing. Both are modes of conditioning and the dividing line between them is not easy to locate. But the essential difference is that the educator must constantly withdraw and suspend the conditioning process. He must be open to rejection at every point. There will have to be periods in which he is not in fact rejected and, in any teaching process, those periods must be long enough to establish continuity and stability, yet not long enough to remove the possibility of rejection. The brain-washer does not withdraw until the identity of the recipient has been submerged or replaced by a new identity that cannot reject what it has been conditioned to 'know'. The idea is central in Christian theology, where the Almighty God deliberately limits his own power over his creatures so that they may love him; for love implies freedom, and the freedom to love implies the freedom not to love. It is an image of a reality we all experience.

And so is the breaking of Prospero's staff. Power, if it is to be benevolent, must be renounced. The great speech in which Prospero renounces his power is recapitulatory. It gives a special instance of what has been happening throughout. Prospero has never done more than arrange situations and propound the conditions of happiness: contrition, repentance, service, the healing of broken bonds, the appreciation of mysterious harmonies. No one's choice has been made for him. Tenderness for people who are suffering is the immediate motive for the speech of renunciation: in the long run, only altruistic feeling can prevent cruelty in the exercise of power. Prospero takes the part of his 'nobler reason' against his 'fury', but this follows because having taken the eyes of his victims he can weep their fortunes: he sees, 'feelingly'.

> and shall not myself
> One of their kind, that relish all as sharply,
> Passion as they, be kindlier mov'd than thou art?

There can be no redemption, no transformation, no growth, no reconciliation until his former enemies are truly themselves:

> My charms I'll break, their senses I'll restore,
> And they shall be themselves.   (V. i. 31–2)

The point being of such central importance, Shakespeare makes it even more explicit in Prospero's renunciation of all magic power. The speech of renunciation must be *heard*. The strength of Prospero's resolve is in the sound of the final lines as well as in the images of his magic power that precede. The passage has always been considered of major importance; it is surprising that its deepest meaning in relation to Prospero's 'project' and to the main ideas of the play has so often been missed:

> I have bedimm'd
> The noontide sun, call'd forth the mutinous winds,
> And 'twixt the green sea and the azur'd vault
> Set roaring war: to the dread rattling thunder
> Have I given fire, and rifted Jove's stout oak
> With his own bolt; the strong bas'd promontory
> Have I made shake, and by the spurs pluck'd up
> The pine and cedar: graves at my command
> Have wak'd their sleepers, op'd, and let 'em forth
> By my so potent Art. But this rough magic
> I here abjure; and, when I have required
> Some heavenly music, – which even now I do, –
> To work mine end upon their senses, that
> This airy charm is for, I'll break my staff,
> Bury it certain fadoms in the earth,
> And deeper than did ever plummet sound
> I'll drown my book. (V. i. 41–57)

By the breaking of the staff, the drowning of the book and the freeing of Ariel, the characters in the story, including Prospero himself as mere man, are left fully responsible for what shall happen in Naples, that is, in their everyday lives in the future. What will Miranda be when the 'brave' world is no longer new to her? Sebastian and Antonio, though they have been 'distracted' by the realisation of their crimes and by the fear of retribution (which they would have resisted with their swords), speak no words of repentance or reconciliation with Prospero. Prospero has believed them penitent, but will they repent in the full sense of change for the better? Or will they gnaw once again at the bonds of family and commonwealth that uphold Prospero's harmonious order?

The play is open-ended. It has restated the conditions for happiness that Shakespeare has explored in former plays, but the final emphasis is laid on responsibility and freedom of choice. To be happy and human man must be free, free therefore to choose unhappiness. No matter what laws or circumstances may establish the context in which man makes his choices, the responsibility of choice remains with him, and upon his choices the future depends.

CHAPTER FOUR

T'Excel the Golden Age

THE ending of *The Tempest* is not merely happy. The con-
cluding harmony has not been achieved by unaided man,
magic power has been necessary, and without the magic power
or the guiding hand of Providence there is no guarantee that
such harmony can ever be achieved, let alone preserved. If we
assume that there is no such thing as either magic or Providence,
and that Shakespeare assumed the same, we may be unable to
resist the temptation to cut the last five lines of the epilogue and
end on the word 'despair'. Yet, even if we hold that man makes
the gods in his own image, we are asserting that the qualities
attributed to Providence are qualities in man, actual or potential. And then we see that Shakespeare has envisaged a possible
harmony which if it is ever to be achieved must be achieved by
'the audience', who must forgive and be forgiven, and whose
hands and breath must transfer the dream to reality (Epilogue).

Within the last twenty-five lines of the final act we have four
strong images of hope and resolve and future possibility. There
is Caliban's resolve to serve and his hope of grace. There is
Prospero's hope,

<blockquote>
to see the nuptial
Of our dear beloved solemnised;   (V. i. 308–9)
</blockquote>

a line that requires a regrouping of the actors to make Ferdinand
and Miranda once more the centre of attention. There is the
sailing of the ships across calm seas, wafted by auspicious gales
to the renewal of life in Naples. There is the exhilarating – and
tender – image of the release of Ariel:

<blockquote>
My Ariel, chick
That is thy charge: then to the elements
Be free, and fare thou well!   (V. i. 316–8)
</blockquote>

Given these images and the tone of these final words, it seems

68

astonishing that anyone could describe the play as despairing, cynical or pessimistic.

However, there are other moods. Two great central speeches have had overtones of sadness, though one, as we have seen, places faith in human freedom and is spoken in an act of benevolence,[1] and the other is spoken to cheer, not to depress.[2] A journey into a new life may be a source of fear as well as hope, and Prospero's pronouncement,

> Every third thought shall be my grave,   (V. i. 311)

brings sadness at his passing. He was wrenched from studious retirement by Antonio; he will now retire once more, to meditation and contemplation. Antonio and Sebastian are still dark presences on the stage. The mood of the play is not pessimistic, but neither can it be called optimistic. Shakespeare is not an optimist or a pessimist: he is an explorer by creative experiment of the human situation, and especially of human behaviour and the movements of the human mind. He does not, at the end of *The Tempest*, say all will be well, any more than he says all will not be well; he says all will be well if . . . , and 'my ending is despair, Unless . . .' All depends on men's actions and attitudes towards one another.

The epilogue brings together the hope and the fear, but it ends with the hope. Prospero, all his charms o'erthrown, cannot any longer arrange a harmonious order for the audience or create a real world consistent with our dreams. Actor and audience must return to reality: the hands and breath of the audience break the spell of the theatre and prepare for the street and the everyday world. There is the fear of loss and change, and there is the passing of a benevolent protector. But applause is a bond between actor and audience, between dramatist and audience, and this bond is what the tone of the speech expresses most strongly.

The bond is confirmed in three ways: the hands and 'breath' of the audience applaud the play; the applause is an answer to the actor's prayer that his bad workmanship be forgiven; actor

[1] See pp. 65–6.
[2] See Chapter Five.

69

and audience together plead for forgiveness before the Mercy-
seat. These are the given images. No Christian who acknowledges his crime despairs of forgiveness, and just as forgiveness
has been a chief means to happiness in the play, so the Christian
takes it to be in life. Few in Shakespeare's audience would not
call themselves Christians; few would not be habituated to
Christian modes of thought. Even if the epilogue received no
better response than sanctimonious nods and amens, a bond
would be established and faith, hope and charity be uppermost
in men's minds, the last two having been strong motives since
the very opening of the play. Fear and sadness are there in the
image of the good master divested of his power, but he was only
an actor after all, and this was only a play; he is teasing now:
the fear itself provokes the smiles, and is a foil to brighten the
hope. The epilogue is the fitting end to a tragi-comedy, happy
and hopeful, but mindful of the fear and the sadness.

The renewal of interest in pastoral tragi-comedy and the
coming of the masque must have been a god-send to Shakespeare. Pastoral poetry, masque, and spectacle, traveller's tales
and speculations upon the origins of man, but above all the
fairy-tale gave him the opportunity, or stimulated him, to
reach a third stage in his diagnosis of man. Shakespeare began
by exploring situations in history and manipulating situations
in comedy. He moved from history to tragedy, concerning
himself less with political situations than with the inner experience of men. There is a corresponding change in the comedies
with the increasing interest in character. In his final phase he
exploited the new dramatic forms for symbolic presentation of
the underlying Forms, the principles, the structural sinews of
life and mind, the Laws of behaviour and of being, especially as
these relate to what concerns us most, namely human good or
human happiness.

When a clever critic[1] tells us that *The Tempest* is 'only a
rather simpler story' of Shakespeare's than usual, we question
the meaning of 'simpler', and quarrel with that most blasphemous of all four-letter words, 'only' – a belittling and desecrating word and a common inhibitor of critical thought. And

[1] Professor E. E. Stoll: *The Tempest*, P.M.L.A., vol. xlvii (1932).

when the same writer describes the play as 'a sort of glorified fairy-tale', it is only the pejorative qualifiers that mislead. A fairy-tale is no triviality and may be a profound and many-sided image of the human mind. The effect of Shakespeare's 'simpler story' with its 'dreamy spirit' has been to lay the emphasis, not on the immediate event or situation, but on the general and universal meaning, not on one particular life, but on the laws of life. And since the play has a happy ending (however we may qualify the term) and since we all desire happy endings, and since we see a very unhappy story turned into a happy one by the operation of certain attitudes and modes of behaviour, it is borne in upon us that those attitudes and modes of behaviour are being commended to us. The play has serious moral purpose; it is a chart for the treasure of happiness. It implies action in 'real' life.

To those for whom the magic island and the here and now are unrelated things *The Tempest* is a problem, and the argument rages whether the play is a 'pure' fantasy. In fact the play charts the human situation both as it is and as it might be. It is an island of thought or dream in which discoveries are made about ourselves. It is a play in which life is 'acted out'. It is a place of preparation and discovery. The 'inner' life of the mind underlies and conditions the 'outer' life of society and event. Action is prepared in the play-island of thought and dream, and still more at those deeper, unconscious levels from which stories of magicians and magic islands also arise. What happens in Prospero's island prepares for the return to Naples. What happens in the inner life prepares or should prepare for what happens in the external world. Imagination, says one of Bernard Shaw's characters, is a faculty whereby we know things as they are without having seen them.[1] What happens in a play, which is itself an island of dream, of thought and of art, is, or can be, a kind of preparation for life. But it can be so only in so far as it is an image, not merely of what life is or has been but of what it may be and perhaps should be. Taking its material both from what is and what is dreamed, *The Tempest* is a vision of happiness that may be – but on hard 'realistic' conditions.

[1] *Back to Methuselah*, Part IV: **Act II.**

All men want to be happy; even crime is committed in the pursuit of happiness. The difference between the saint and the criminal lies in their relative awareness of the conditions upon which happiness is to be attained. Caliban sees the clouds open and riches descending upon him: his vision of heaven is such as he is capable of. The desire for a better life may express itself in ways that do not in fact lead to happiness, such, for example, as the murderous attempts of Antonio and Caliban; or in ways that do, such as Caliban's final resolve to serve. The goal is the same. Failure to attain it is due to limited awareness.

Limited awareness produces aberrations of perception. Antonio, able to grasp his own interest only, persuades himself by a perversion of the imagination that what he wishes true is true:

> like one
> Who having into truth, by telling of it
> Made such a sinner of his memory
> To credit his own lie, he did believe
> He was indeed the duke; (I. ii. 99–103)

People tend to see what they want to see, or what they expect to see, or what they are capable of seeing; but some men have better vision than others. Shakespeare was familiar with the conflicting views of travellers returned from the New World. When the shipwrecked Lords arrive on Prospero's island, they see according to what they are. Or we may say Shakespeare establishes what they are by the way he makes them see:

ADRIAN: The air breathes upon us here most sweetly.
SEBASTIAN: As if it had lungs, and rotten ones.
ANTONIO: Or as it were perfumed by a fen.
GONZALO: How lush and lusty the grass looks! How green!
ANTONIO: The ground indeed is tawny.
SEBASTIAN: With an eye of green in it. (II. i. 45–53)

One would think there would at least be agreement about smell and colour. There is clearly *some* agreement about the green, but the jaundiced eye sees little, the sanguine much. Is Gonzalo a foolish optimist and Antonio a phlegmatic realist? Antonio and Sebastian certainly adopt the latter pose, and, with all the confidence that such a pose seems to engender, they mock Gonzalo and Adrian, who see 'blessings spread around them' even in the midst of misfortune. Does beauty lie in the eye of the beholder? And is there, then, no knowing the truth about the scene? Can we ask, who is right? Gonzalo or Antonio? Shakespeare adjudicates: Gonzalo is right:

> GONZALO: ... our garments, being, as they were, drenched in the sea, hold notwithstanding, their freshness and glosses, being rather new-dyed than stained with salt water.
> ANTONIO: If but one of his pockets could speak, would it not say he lies? (II. i. 59–64)

Antonio sounds like a man deferring to the fact, yet it is he, not Gonzalo who 'doth but mistake the truth totally', for Ariel has informed the audience:

> Not a hair perish'd;
> On their sustaining garments not a blemish,
> But fresher than before: (I. ii. 217–19)

Gonzalo, then, sees better: Antonio and Sebastian are men who will turn a blessing to a curse, or who are so cursed in their own natures that blessings fall upon them as curses. These 'realists' are not in touch with reality. The contrast between their limited awareness and the insight of Gonzalo is marked throughout the scene. Gonzalo is counting blessings in an attempt to cheer Alonso, whose grief he senses and tries to relieve. Antonio and Sebastian see, but do not feel, Alonso's grief:

> SEBASTIAN: Sir, you may thank yourself for this great loss . . .
> The fault's your own
> ALONSO: So is the dear'st o' th' loss.
> GONZALO: My lord Sebastian,
> The truth you speak doth lack some gentleness,
> And time to speak it in: you rub the sore,
> When you should bring the plaster.

Sebastian's telling of this 'truth' at this time shows his unawareness of the more important truth, that of Alonso's suffering – a truth that can only be 'known' to the extent that it is shared, and if it is shared will evoke words and behaviour such as

73

Gonzalo's, not such as Sebastian's. Sebastian does not see, because he does not feel. Such men are often mockers, and the generous and charitable are commonly their target. Goodness would never have made Antonio duke of Milan; therefore goodness is a fool. Gonzalo's visions of goodness, whether in the surrounding landscape or the future of mankind, are matter for contemptuous wit.

Gonzalo has a day-dream 'T'excel the Golden Age' (II. i. 138–60). If I could colonise this uninhabited island and had the power to establish a new social order, Gonzalo asks himself, what would it be like? First, he says, it would be as different as possible from our present one: no man should prey upon another; hence there would be no property, no trade, no law courts (one hears the voice of King Lear); nor should Adam's curse of work be there, for the island would supply all needs; there would be no strife among the people, 'neither should they learn war any more'. Antonio and Sebastian use a common smear tactic:

SEBASTIAN: No marrying among his subjects?
ANTONIO: None, man; all idle; whores and knaves.

(II. i. 161–2)

Innocence without possession or restriction is something their life-experience has made it impossible for them to contemplate. They are men to whom possession is both goal and criterion. Had they plantation of the isle, possession would be the nettle-seed they would sow it with. The phenomenon of projection whereby we bestow upon others qualities of our own is aptly illustrated in:

GONZALO: Had I plantation of this isle, my lord, –
ANTONIO: He'd sow it with nettle-seed.
SEBASTIAN: Or docks, or mallows.

It is schoolboy wit. However, these two smart ones do mark the inconsistency in Gonzalo's tale:

GONZALO: . . .
   No sovereignty: –
SEBASTIAN: Yet he would be King on't.

ANTONIO: The latter end of his commonwealth forgets the
   beginning.   (II. i. 152–4)

There is no part of the episode that more clearly demonstrates
the relevance of Gonzalo's utopian vision to the play as a whole.
Prospero's aim is to achieve a golden moment, if not a golden
age, something as near to the perfectly happy state as may be
hoped for from erring man. He achieves much – by the power
of his magic staff and books. But such 'kingship' is finally
inconsistent with a community of love. The staff must be broken
and the book drowned. Gonzalo's day-dream, too, begins with
apparent negatives: authority and possession are renounced.
That renunciation, however, is a positive, as Prospero shows;
for it is a setting free of the human spirit – or a recognition of its
freedom. Gonzalo's dream, like Caliban's and like the dream
which is the whole play, is an aspiration, a vision of human
potential. Though the particular form of it is derived from
Montaigne and the current controversies about the state of
Nature and the 'salvage man', its origin in the depths of man's
psyche is testified to by a thousand instances, from the tale of
Eden, through the community attempts of the early Christians,
to the popular song:

> If you were the only girl in the world
> And I were the only boy

and the recurring question, what would you do if you won
£250,000?

Gonzalo's reply to the ever-recurring question has been
accounted foolish, not only by Antonio, Sebastian and Alonso,
but by many readers of the play, notably scholars who have
assumed it to be a satirical comment on Montaigne. These
readers have ranged themselves with the greedy and superficial
characters, perhaps partly because Gonzalo himself is diffident
about his utopia and excuses himself by saying he is giving
Antonio and Sebastian something to crack their jokes on. Yet
the spirit of the day-dream is consistent with Gonzalo's generosity and charity, not with Antonio's meanness. Of course
Gonzalo cannot solve the economic problem of his ideal

community; and of course work can be a virtue rather than the curse of Adam – slavery and service, for example, being opposites; and there is no 'practical' possibility of the golden age being inaugurated yet. No wonder Gonzalo is diffident. But human dreams have been realised, and there will be no change for the better unless more dreams are realised, and the chief of all dreams is the dream of perfect love, which is precisely what Gonzalo's dream is – the kingdom of heaven in which there is no grasping, and where they 'neither marry nor are given in marriage',[1] for all the listening crowds are 'my mother and my brethren'.[2] 'Practical' men, like Antonio and Alonso, can't be bothered with all that: they have business to attend to, ambitions to satisfy, and they have to control people no less preoccupied with immediate self-interest than themselves. Gonzalo cannot answer them. He is not a saint. His disposition is charitable and his faith in some 'heavenly power' that will one day 'guide us out of this fearful country', though fitful perhaps, is persistent; but he is part of Alonso's world. Though he helped Prospero, he did not sail with him or resist the conspirators to the death. He is an image of faith, hope and charity, but a very human image. His vision of love in action cannot be perfect, for his knowledge is limited. Hence, and for other reasons, it can be but imperfectly realised in his own life. Yet even its imperfect realisation is what makes him so far superior to the other 'noble' lords. He cares for Alonso, watches over him, weeps for his sorrows. He is cheerful, encouraging, hopeful in the face of adversity. He appreciates, with the wondering innocence of a child, both the beauties of the island and the grace and gentle-kindness of the spirits; but he assesses with incisive ironic judgement the 'brave mettle' of his mockers, and with a grave wisdom the state of those whose 'great guilt' works in them like poison. Yet he is no less solicitous for the scoffers than for the king to whom he owes, and gives, his loyalty (III. iii. 106–9; V. i. 14–17). Gonzalo's dream is of a piece with his life and action; it is therefore no sentimentality, even though it is not a working drawing for a social order that can be constructed tomorrow.

[1] *Mark:* XII. 25. [2] *Mark:* XIII. 34.

If dreams like this and men like Gonzalo are associated, one may fairly look in the dream, as one looks at the life, for principles upon which a harmonious society may one day be established. This meaning of the passage is not in the least weakened by the fact that Gonzalo is dreaming aloud 'to minister occasion' to Antonio and Sebastian: we know already that nothing is so likely to receive their contempt as hope and charity. In drawing out this contempt by his day-dream of hope and charity, Gonzalo gives them rope to hang themselves. He is playing two games: one the age-old and innocent one of 'If I were king . . .', and the other a cat-and-mouse game with the shallow wits. Both games are consistent with his charitable purpose of keeping the party cheerful; both have even more serious purpose, reaching beyond what man is to what man may be and ought to be. Gonzalo is joking; whenever you find a joke, search it for a hidden truth.

CHAPTER FIVE

Such Stuff as Dreams

DREAMS, drama and life are brought together by Shakespeare in one very striking and puzzling speech of Prospero's. In the fourth act Prospero gives away the one he loves best, but the one who is a thorn in his flesh he must keep: Miranda is bestowed upon Ferdinand, but Caliban remains Prospero's responsibility. The betrothal of Miranda and Ferdinand is celebrated by means of a graceful fertility ritual presented in dramatic form by Prospero through the agency of his spirits. It is a rainbow masque. A rainbow is of the mist as well as of the light, and produced with this in mind, the masque really can be a 'majestic vision'. If the lines are spoken and sung with the incantatory effect of which they are capable, and to solemn and graceful movement, the *vision* is 'harmonious charmingly' – it casts a spell. That is what it is designed to do, both upon Ferdinand and Miranda and upon Shakespeare's audience. It is a dream within a dream. Ferdinand and Miranda are enraptured by it, as the audience must expect since it symbolises and expresses anew the dream of love and marriage which in their case is also the most important and most immediate reality. It confirms the ideal as they themselves have conceived it and as Prospero has expressed it for them.

An ideal, until it is realised, is a vision of a possible future or of a present reality only to be fully grasped in the future. With or without a note of contempt, an ideal is often called a dream. The masque is a representation of a marriage ideal, and by its formal and symbolic harmonies 'gives a very echo to the seat Where Love is throned'.[1] But it is harshly interrupted. No wonder Ferdinand is dismayed: the dream, so real to him because it is the imaginative expression of the reality of his love, is shattered. That which held the meaning of love and fruitfulness and the promise of new birth fades in images of fear and

[1] *Twelfth Night:* I. iv. 20–21.

78

death when the approach of lust and murder in the shape of Caliban and his confederates drains away Prospero's gentler magic, and the spirits 'heavily vanish' to a strange, hollow and confused noise. Prospero is passionately angry, but though 'distemper'd' himself, is more concerned about Ferdinand's dismay:

> You do look, my son, in a mov'd sort,
> As if you were dismay'd: be cheerful, sir,
> Our revels now are ended. These our actors,
> As I foretold you, were all spirits, and
> Are melted into air, into thin air:
> And, like the baseless fabric of this vision.
> The cloud-capp'd towers, the gorgeous palaces,
> The solemn temples, the great globe itself,
> Yea, all which it inherit, shall dissolve,
> And, like this insubstantial pageant faded,
> Leave not a rack behind. We are such stuff
> As dreams are made on; and our little life
> Is rounded with a sleep. Sir, I am vex'd;
> Bear with my weakness; my old brain is troubled:
> Be not disturb'd with my infirmity:
> If you be pleas'd, retire into my cell,
> And there repose: a turn or two I'll walk,
> To still my beating mind.
> FERDINAND and MIRANDA: We wish your peace.
>
> (IV. i. 146–63)

Prospero then turns to the pressing business of thwarting Caliban's conspiracy.

This famous passage could very easily be cut, from 'Our revels now are ended . . .' to 'We wish your peace'. Its omission would in no way affect the plot. If it had not been written we should still have had from elsewhere a strong impression of the reflective solemnity of Prospero, and he would still have been a mysterious presence in the play. Yet the passage never is cut, and if it were, all those who know the play would miss it, for it is among Shakespeare's most famous passages. The fact that it could easily be cut is particularly noteworthy since *The Tempest* is a highly concentrated play. The fact that it never is cut shows its importance to the total effect of the play, or testifies to the powerful impact the words make, or both. If Shakespeare had been writing 'only a rather simpler story of his than usual' it is hard to believe that he would have written it, for it urges reflection. It is certainly not merely a decorative piece. It is the speech of a person we know, human and vex'd, but solemn and embracing the whole universe in his thought. It arouses personal sympathy, and it strikes with awe. It comes as if from some mysterious depth, and in a moment it is gone, leaving us disturbed and questioning. Like Prospero, we try to shake off the burden of the mystery; the escape route is a very familiar one:

> Sir I am vex'd;
> Bear with my weakness; my old brain is troubled:
> Be not disturbed with my infirmity:

But the mystery remains and haunts the memory.

This passage, which Shakespeare need not have included for story purposes, colours our response to the whole play, and to the central figure. And it has this effect long before we start close reading, let alone analytical study. That is one reason why we may feel impelled to look more closely at it. Another is that the play has to be produced, and the speech can be spoken in different ways, some of which may be wrong or inadequate. A third is that, being an apparently separate piece in one sense, yet strongly influencing our response to the whole play, it may be a passage in which Shakespeare is expressing some central meaning.

Even in this play about strange and magical beings and events there is no passage that gives so strong a sense of the unknown, the unseen and the uncertain as this one; and because the mind has moved into this experience a deeper awareness of the meaning of Prospero's speech of renunciation and of the epilogue with its adventure into Naples or into life is possible. A pessimistic, materialistic, sceptical and cynical age may hear nothing but despair in Prospero's words, and the passage we are examining may then be spoken in a tone of world-weariness, tired cynicism or dignified contempt. At least it may if *the context of the speech is ignored*.

Part of that context is an audience with Christian habits of thought and Christian assumptions, including a general confidence that life does not end with death. Perhaps only in the light of this is it possible to understand the relation between the main body of the speech and its opening, where Prospero's purpose is stated. His purpose is to reassure Ferdinand.

Christians often reflect on the transitoriness of human life but always in the context of eternity, which means on the one hand a joyous destiny and on the other a present responsibility. To read 'We are such stuff as dreams are made on' as if it meant 'We all die soon; so why bother?' is to neglect the mood and ideas that predominate in the play.

Whether Shakespeare was a Christian believer is not in question, but interpretation must take account of the context of thought habits in which the language, ideas and form of the play take shape. Otherwise we might make the mistake of interpreting solely within the context of our own thought habits – as bad a fault as to interpret solely within the context of 1611. A work of art, if it has universality, may give expression to truths implicit in beliefs that have become open to doubt.

Apart from the one word 'beating' which conveys the throbbing head, the hammered thought and the distressed heart, the speech begins and ends with everyday kindness and courtesies; the language is colloquial, the tone familiar and fatherly. Near the end of the speech there is the passage already quoted in which there is the sudden shift from the general to the personal:

> Sir, I am vex'd;
> Bear with my weakness; my old brain is troubled:
> Be not disturbed with my infirmity:

It is an apology: Prospero has lost command, not only of the situation, but also of himself. He is at fault; that is why Ferdinand is asked to bear with his weakness. Caliban is out of hand – and that is not merely a description of the situation, but of Prospero's disturbed mind: evil has the upper hand in one who gives way to 'anger so distemper'd'.

Pertelote dismissed Chaunticlere's dream, saying dreams

arise from bodily disorders, in this case the weaknesses of age. But Prospero is not light-minded, neither are Ferdinand and Miranda. Nor has the masque been merely light entertainment. Whether Prospero's thoughts on art and architecture, on drama and dream and life are weak or suggest weakness we have yet to consider. There is one sense, however, in which Prospero has shown weakness: he has allowed Caliban and the conspirators to slip from his mind, thus neglecting his major responsibility and endangering the happiness of all; and then he has lost his mental or emotional balance, giving way to 'anger so distemper'd' that Miranda has never seen the like of it before. The word 'vex'd' is frequently used by Shakespeare in the modern sense of to irritate or annoy, where some outside agency producing the irritation is implied. Of the four instances of the special use of the word to mean mental disturbance given by C. T. Onions in *A Shakespeare Glossary*, only one does not clearly imply agitation by some external agency. Caliban is the external agency here. Caliban and all that he stands for is the cause of Prospero's vexation, and Prospero's anger is the immediate cause of Ferdinand's dismay. Prospero has lost command of himself and of the situation. He is at fault; that is why Ferdinand is asked to bear with his weakness.

Prospero's lapse, like all lapses, is followed by a further temptation, the temptation to despair. As part of this tempta-tion, the first pangs of despair are actually experienced. Prospero suffers these pangs and we feel them in the speech; but in the speech also is that which dismisses the pangs. Having felt them, however, is part of the wrong that he has to be for-given. What Prospero is guilty of is a momentary lack of faith. If we ask, 'faith in what?' the simplest answer is 'faith in the power of good to overcome evil'. We have already seen this lack of faith in his dealings with Caliban.

There is nothing in the least disproportionate about Pros-pero's distress. To him, as to the Christian, evil matters; and here, in the shape of Caliban, it seems irredeemable. Like the medieval Christian, and the modern psychologist, he longs for the salvation of the Devil: is there not some way of integrating 'this thing of darkness' into society or into the personality so that its 'evil' quality becomes 'good' as part of the whole? At this point of the play there seems to be no hope: Prospero is merely repressive. Hence the anger, impatience and something near to despair.

But the despair in Prospero's speech contains its own denial. The point has been made that the general effect is to convey a sense of the unknown. But this is conveyed in a number of different ways that may be resolved into two. There are the images of dissolution and insubstantiality, but there is also a distinct shape. That shape is a globe. The globe is first mentioned as dissolving, but the mind's eye sees it, and before the verbs 'dissolve' and 'faded' disperse it into cloud rack, the images of all that inherit the earth and all their architectural wonders arrange themselves upon and around the image of the globe. Human life, human achievement and the round earth are associated in one shifting image that has none the less a distinct geometry. What is that which surrounds both life and earth? The expression

> our little life
> Is rounded with a sleep

has finality: in the middle of a line it ends the main part of Prospero's speech, and it is followed by a sharp change of tone. For the visualiser it reshapes the circle that momentarily dislimned to less than a rack of cloud. The participle, 'rounded', produces this effect. At least, it does for those who have not been misled by footnotes that would have the word mean little more than 'ended', which implies a linear time. The revels came to a stop in linear time, so Shakespeare said they 'ended'. But here he does not say 'ended' – which would have served his purpose for the metre, though not for the sound-pattern. There is much more in it than that. Dr. Onions in *A Shakespeare Glossary* gives as the first meaning of the verb 'round', to finish off. But he gives *only one* example of its use in that way – namely this passage. He gives four examples of its use to mean surround, encircle, encompass, and two others that imply circularity. Of his instances of the substantive use, all of which imply circularity, two indicate movement and one means 'the earth' – a common use since the Middle Ages. N.E.D.[1] gives only one instance before 1674 of the meaning 'to finish off'—once again this passage from *The Tempest*. This is not surprising since Dr. Onions may well have been responsible for this entry also. However, there is in N.E.D. a significant addition to the meaning given: 'To finish off, bring to completeness or *to a perfect form*'. For centuries the circle had been accounted not only the perfect form, but also the symbol of eternity. Eternity embraces time and mortality but is itself unchanging and incorruptible; so that in eternity all transient things, this 'great globe' and 'all which it inherit', are *present* at once. With this image of the perfect form Prospero concludes his solemn reflection. If he is sad it is because we are yet mortal and imperfect, incomplete by reason of the evil that dissolves us 'into heaviness'; but he is offering Ferdinand the source and ground of cheerfulness, the faith in and the hope of perfection. Another interpretation of 'rounded' well supported by Shakespearean parallels[2] is that it suggests 'crowned'. This too is consistent with the ideas of completion and perfection and with the ideas and impressions of eternity. However, neither the image of the circle nor the associations of one word would be sufficient to establish Prospero's meaning and the tone in which the lines should be spoken, were it not that both are used in a passage where life is viewed against the background of unimaginable time, which itself in the popular Christian mind is 'like an evening gone'. Prospero's speech is a reminder of the fragility of beauty and majesty in *human* life and works; but his vision itself is majestic and harmonious. Its tone is serene and its imagery of air and earth, wide-ranging, large-scale and shadowy, inspires calm acceptance of the mystery rather than world-weariness, an awed humility rather than despair or cynicism. The shadow of doubt gives way before the image of faith, and sleep is not an end. The audience has neither motive nor time for losing hope. Prospero's fury precedes the speech, and immediate action follows it; and Prospero is still the great magician, who has to complete his project of harmony.

[1] *New English Dictionary*, Oxford.
[2] See *The Tempest*: Arden paperback, p. 104. (Note on line 158.)

The speech, then, with all its solemnity, has a cheerful purpose. To say we are such stuff as dreams are made on would be depressing if it meant that we are essentially meaningless, and to say that our little life ends in death is neither encouraging nor very perspicacious. Neither the content nor the images themselves permit such interpretations. What is intimated in Prospero's words is what is intimated by the play as a whole and by the dreams and day-dreams and visions in it, that the boundaries between dream and waking are indefinable and mysterious. There is sleep, there is fantasy or imagination, there is thought. Thought, however logically consistent, is constantly accompanied by a bewildering play of images and associations related to sensory stimuli both immediate and in memory. Our little consciousness is rounded with a plethora of dreams into which and out of which consecutive thought shades and passes. We really are such stuff as dreams are made on, and our clearest consciousness is not so easily distinguished from dream as we should like to think. Chuang Tzu went to sleep and dreamed that he was a butterfly; ever since, he has been wondering whether he is Chuang Tzu who once dreamed that he was a butterfly or whether he is a butterfly now dreaming that he is Chuang Tzu.

We may hold that dreams are insubstantial, or we may believe, with the medieval alchemist – and perhaps with Shakespeare's audience, that they are material;[1] but whichever view we take, we now know of their importance to us in ways definable and indefinable. Even technical investigation has now shown that a person can be driven to the borders of insanity by simply preventing him from dreaming. On the other hand the 'madman' seems to us like one in whom dream has usurped the function of consciousness. Shakespeare's rational man saw madman and poet alike in this respect[2] and Prospero links dream and drama. It is now being discovered, however, that a madman's dreams make sense, and that when the sense is found the madness can sometimes be exorcised – ancient notions

[1] See W. A. Murray 'Why was Duncan's Blood Golden?' Shakespeare Survey 19, 1966. p. 40.
[2] *A Midsummer Night's Dream:* V. 1. 4–8.

proving less erroneous than was once thought, and the ancient function of interpreter being vindicated. The dreams of the poet have always made sense, though there have always been those who feared and mistrusted them.

The Tempest is about drama. Prospero is a great producer – dramatist, not only in presenting the masque, but in disposing the scenes on his island. Both the epilogue and this speech affirm the common substance of drama and dreams and life. N.E.D. explains the noun 'stuff' as 'substance or material (whether corporeal or incorporeal) of which a thing is formed or consists, or out of which a thing may be fashioned'. It also shows, however, that at least as early as 1557 the word could indicate 'solid qualities of intellect or character; capacity for achievement or endurance; the makings of a future excellence'. Such associations as these are the ones most consistent with Prospero's other words and his images, and an examination of Shakespeare's use of 'dream' and 'sleep' gives further confirmation that Prospero is commenting not upon the meaninglessness, or worthlessness of drama and dreams and life, but on their meaning and worth.

When we come to observe Shakespeare's references to dream, we find many literal, some contemptuous, but more in which dreaming is taken seriously. It is noteworthy that contemptuous uses are most often on the lips of shallow, mocking or villainous characters, or limited men of the world like Theseus and Henry V, and that the events and outcomes of the plays show a serious treatment of dream rather than otherwise. Music of the spheres lulls Pericles to sleep; Diana appears, enjoins penance upon him and a duty like the Ancient Mariner's and promises happiness. She is leading him to the renewal of life and love with his wife and daughter.[1] In *The Winter's Tale* Antigonus dreams of Hermione

> in pure white robes
> Like very sanctity,   (III. iii. 22–3)

[1] Pericles (V. i. 225–47).

She gives commands on which the happy outcome of the play depends. Antigonus says:

> Dreams are toys:
> Yet, for this once, yea superstitiously,
> I will be squared by this. (III. iii. 39–41)

Against his 'better judgement', he believes – but the point is that his 'superstition' is right.

All four of Shakespeare's late romances have a dream-like quality in their action and setting and spectacle. All four contain dreams and visions, and in all four the dreams or visions are prophetic of future happiness. At least once in each play dreams are spoken of as flattering or otherwise deceptive; in three of them it is the central dream that is proved true by the events. In *The Tempest* we have Gonzalo's dream of a golden age and Caliban's dream of riches, but we have also this speech of Prospero designed to cheer Ferdinand with serious reflection on the nature of human life and the nature of dreams.

It is very interesting that the play in which there is the greatest number of references to dream, and in which dreams play a great and very important part is *Richard III* – so early a play. Here dream is not merely prophetic but the expression of conscience. Richmond, whose conscience is clear and whose future is assured, enjoys

> The sweetest sleep and fairest boding dreams
> That ever enter'd in a drowsy head.[1]

The dreams of Richard and Clarence, however, have all the violence and all the terror of conscience repressed. Clarence experiences 'the worm of conscience' working in the 'kingdom of perpetual night' in the hidden deeps of the mind's ocean, and both he and Richard experience the tempest in the soul when the images of former cruelties return and presage the horrors of hell. Richard speaks contemptuously of dreams, but in dream the meaning of his life is shown: *Richard III* has more references to conscience than any other play except *Henry VIII*, and every reference has powerful meaning. The contempt of

[1] *Richard III*: V. iii. 227–8.

conscience most like that of Antonio (*The Tempest* II. i. 270–6) is Richard's:

> Conscience is but a word that cowards use,
> Devis'd at first to keep the strong in awe.[1]

and the fearful working of a contemned conscience, symbolised in the storm and the banquet of *The Tempest*, has full melodramatic horror in Richard's dreams and their waking affect.

Men of the world with a strong grasp of the surface of things and of immediate interest, or for whom the long term does not extend beyond one life or beyond the confines of one society, whether they are the ones who overreach themselves like Richard or those who master their narrow world, like Bolingbroke, may deserve the title 'realist' as popular usage bestows it; but in Shakespeare's plays they stand condemned against a standard of reality embodied in dreams. Shakespeare's plays take dreams seriously and Bottom's comic misquotation of Scripture is felt to have more of wisdom in it than the cleverness of Theseus. Scripture reads:

> But, as it is written, Eye hath not seen, nor ear heard, neither have entered into the heart of man, the things which God hath prepared for them that love him.

> But God hath revealed them unto us by his Spirit: for the Spirit searcheth all things, yea, the deep things of God.[2]

Bottom, awaking from his wondrous vision of the Fairy Queen, says:

> The eye of man hath not heard, the ear of man hath not seen, man's hand is not able to taste, his tongue to conceive, nor his heart to report, what my dream was. I will get Peter Quince to write a ballad of this dream, it shall be called Bottom's Dream, because it hath no bottom:[3]

Whether the dream that Shakespeare includes in the action of a

[1] Ibid., 309–10.
[2] *I Corinthians:* II. 9–10.
[3] *A Midsummer-Night's Dream:* IV. i. 210–20.

play be of the fairy kind or a classical omen or the visitation of a god, or whether it be the welling up of past experience, like Lady Macbeth's, it always has truth in it, is always closely representative of the minds and deeds and inner lives of men and, in short, is of the very 'stuff' of which men are made.

A careful study of sleep in Shakespeare confirms that Prospero is no nihilist. Sleep is not death, but 'death's counterfeit' and death itself is not an end. Villains like Antonio may *call* it so, but they usually avoid the words 'death' and 'sleep' in favour of euphemisms like 'the perpetual wink'. Sleep is rest and refreshment, 'Nature's soft nurse', 'chief nourisher at life's feast'. 'Sleep' may sometimes be used contemptuously to imply dullness or inattention, but it is more often an image of calm or peace or innocence. In sleep come visions of gods and truths about the inner life, and out of sleep men rise, like Lear or Pericles, changed or renewed.

Everything points to an interpretation of Prospero's words that confirms the meaningfulness of dreams, questions popular notions about appearance and reality, and looks beyond the individual consciousness for the meaning of life.

In spite of all our increase in knowledge and technical skill, our age is the age of what has been called the 'box-camera mind': we have lost the capacity for long-range focus. Shakespeare lived in an age when men planted and tended oak-trees that would take four hundred years to mature. Today in our planting and our building and our manufactures and our exploitation of natural resources we seldom look beyond a life-span, and usually not beyond a decade, often not beyond the next election. Still less do we concern ourselves about dimensions of human experience not obviously related to £.s.d. or to solid matter; or if we do, we split them off from everyday experience as if they were not part of our normal existence. We have grown up thinking of matter and non-matter as sharply distinguishable, and of present, past and future as clearly separate and distinct. Now that we are becoming less confident about those distinctions there is some hope that we may be able to recover the point of Prospero's words.

However, we do not know past or future except in the

present. One *was*, the other *will be*; but both *are*. Past and future are in our present consciousness, modifying our attitudes and influencing our behaviour. Our moral and aesthetic judgements are profoundly affected by the range of our vision, but those judgements and the actions that follow from them are present and future. Historical and linguistic studies of Shakespeare have been and are immensely fruitful, not merely in the sense that they have piled up information, and not at all in the sense that they have pushed Shakespeare back into his own time, but in the sense that they have shown the miracle of Shakespeare to be even more miraculous than we thought. Their value is not in establishing what Shakespeare *was*, but in demonstrating that knowing more of what he was makes us more aware of what he *is*. However concerned we may be to know just what he wrote and to divine what he intended, what matters most is the plays and poems we have and what they mean now. To establish that Shakespeare thought highly of dreams is of antiquarian interest; but to find in *The Tempest* insights into some of the most important preoccupations and supposed discoveries of our own time is to be made aware of past and future 'in the instant'.

Part of the co-operation that art requires is the bringing of our own experience and wisdom to the appreciation of the artist's work. In the case of Shakespeare, it means relating the life and mind of our time to that of his. Modern psychology has become more aware of the meaning and importance of dreams in our everyday life, modern philosophy and science more aware of the importance of imagination in scientific inquiry.[1] Hence the possibility of a new appreciation of Shakespeare's insights, and more particularly a rediscovery of the meaning of his reflections on dream.

The somewhat shifting use of the word 'dream' in this chapter does not arise from carelessness, but from the impossibility of making sharp distinctions between the experiences referred to by the various literal and metaphorical meanings of the word. There is the constant or almost constant and apparently random flow of images unshaped or half-shaped, moving

[1] See P. B. Medawar: *The Art of the Soluble*, 'Two Conceptions of Science' and 'Hypothesis and Imagination'.

across the mind or before the mind's eye too swiftly for definition. It is not easy to be sure whether these are all fragments of
memory, though in this particular period of history we tend to
assume so. Then there are the recognisable fragments of memory,
flashes from our own past, but these are shaped and re-struc-
tured, highly selected and notoriously unreliable as *records* of the
past. There are the much more highly wrought and re-worked
daydreams, either castles-in-the-air or forebodings. The dream
proper, which seems to structure itself in sleep, is either ordered
and arranged by a different mode of selection or remembered
on waking as if it had some shape or order, albeit of a kind that
usually seems very different from the arrangements of phenomena in waking life. Nor is it easy to distinguish any of these
from the casting about in thought that precedes and accompanies directed thought, the fishing around, the catching up
and rejecting, in search of the next piece in a logical structure.
If a dividing line could be drawn anywhere it would be easiest
to separate off that basic, apparently random flow out of which
all the rest *seem* to rise, rather than to mark off any of the
structured forms from the so-called rational, supposedly fully
conscious, thought processes; for these all have structure and
selection in common.

However, the distinction we try to make is less usually
between structured and unstructured mind-processes than
between those that *common* sense calls 'real' and those it calls
'unreal'. Hence stories, though highly structured and consciously wrought, are often equated with dreams. Shakespeare
names one of his plays a dream and makes Prospero speak of his
masque as a dream and a vision. In this chapter *The Tempest* is
spoken of as a dream partly because it has the quality that
Freud and Jung have discovered in dreams, namely the
presentation in images of elements of the human psyche,
though it is unlikely that any actual sleep-dream would exemplify so many of those elements in such an ordered form, or at
any rate that any dreamer would so remember them on waking.
It is also called a dream because, as in other plays too, the events
in it would not be expected to happen just like that in what
unthinking man calls 'real life'. Shakespeare's challenge to

popular notions of real and unreal and his attempts to penetrate beneath shows and seemings, to distinguish substances from shadow especially in the moral and psychological spheres is now so widely recognised as to need no comment here other than that it has been repeatedly illustrated in these pages and is particularly evident in Prospero's speech on dreams.

Somewhere among our dreams lie the springs of action. *The Tempest* is about action – action towards integration of the psyche, order in society, and harmony in the universe. It is a dream or vision of what may be, of what *must* be if man is to be happy. It does not look towards a static or closed universe; its harmonies are not final in that sense. There is still everything for Miranda and Ferdinand to do and much for them and for Prospero in his retirement to learn and to prepare for. A new life is opening for Caliban too. The process of integration does not end with the play. 'Happy-ever-after' as we have seen does not fit the end of *The Tempest*: a new cycle is beginning. The events of the play have their consequences beyond the play. And similarly the play as a whole begins a movement in our minds that has a particular direction, a tendency towards a particular kind of action consistent with attitudes that have formed under its spell.

The play itself has a cyclic movement. Prospero's story begins with study and withdrawal: it ends with his retirement

> where
> Every third thought shall be my grave.

Reflection – action – reflection is one way of indicating the pattern; reflection, as has been suggested, having much of the quality of dreams, and of imagination. The end is a new beginning, but it is not a mere return to the original beginning. This is not a pointless cycle. Prospero's preparation for death must be understood in the context of such ideas as we find in Macduff's homage to Malcolm's sainted mother:

> the Queen that bore thee,
> Oft'ner upon her knees than on her feet,
> Died every day she liv'd. (IV. iii. 109–11)

That is, the Queen, each day, cleansed her soul in preparation for death, that great occasion that was for her both an end and a beginning. The Christian literature of the art of dying well was considerable in Shakespeare's day. Preparation for death was the theme of a thousand sermons. Disease and violence made death an ever-present reality: each person's chance of dying young, and horribly, was high. Christianity is a redemptive faith; that is, like *The Tempest*, it is all about turning evil to good. Suffering and death are opportunities for glorious life. Even pagans, atheists, renegades and traitors could prove this; Shakespeare celebrates them in his plays. How much more then should Christians do so? Preparation for death can be a means to a noble end for Christian and non-Christian alike, and being so is part of a noble life. Death is not merely a biological event: it is a great idea that profoundly influences a person's way of life. To prepare for a noble death, one must live a noble life. Prospero will not be sunk in apathy for his remaining days. His final period of meditation and contemplation will be more purposeful than was his first retirement to the study.

Prospero, from the beginning, was concerned with the meaning of things, always wanting to know; but he lost his grasp of the relation between thought and action, or rather he did not discover it till the world had cast him out. There is a kind of dream that, instead of containing the springs of action, is a substitute for action, negative, debilitating, escapist, and ultimately destructive. Study or 'the liberal Arts' divorced from action-in-the-world is that sort of dream. Swift illustrates the comic horror of it in his account of the academic researchists of Lagado in Book III of *Gulliver's Travels*. The projectors of Lagado do act, it is true, but solely in terms of their theory and with the utmost contempt for common experience. Hence they make their land barren and the people miserable, while they retain complete confidence in their own wisdom and importance and continue to spin out their webs of the kind of dream stuff that has caused men to be so suspicious of dreams. However, it is wrong to blame the dream: it is the correlation between dream and action that has failed.

Prospero took mere study as a badge of dignity, what we now call a status symbol:

> ... Prospero the prime duke, being so reputed
> In dignity, and for the liberal Arts
> Without a parallel; (I. ii. 74)

and he despised government, which was his major responsibility:

> those being all my study,
> The government I cast upon my brother,
> And to my state grew stranger, being transported
> And rapt in secret studies. (I. ii. 74–7)

This is what John Donne called an hydroptic, immoderate thirst for human learning and languages. It is a 'disproportion'd sin' that Milton avoided by serving in government, because he knew that, if a man is to be a poet, his life must 'be a poem' and that action in the world bears a necessary relation to great art, as well as being part of a harmonious and integrated life-pattern.

Yet Prospero's study did prepare him for his great action. Prospero, unlike Lear, was given a second chance. From his great knowledge acquired during the years of irresponsibility came his great skill and power in the years of responsibility. As a means of escape, the study was a dream world divorced from what we might unthinkingly term the 'realities' of Milanese politics. But the 'dreams' became reality when Prospero applied them to the government of the island and thence of Italy. There is an unreality about theorising not subjected to empirical test, and at another stage there is an incompleteness about 'pure' science until it is applied. A day-dream is 'fruitless', as we say, if it does not issue in action, and here too there may be two stages. A day-dream may issue first as a work of art; that is one way of issuing in action. But the work of art, like pure science, is for the appreciator or student another kind of dream whose reality is not established till it has issued in action in the world. This action-in-the-world as I call it is, as in *The Tempest* and in Milton's life, action with and for other men towards the enrichment or the betterment of the lives of all and towards a more complete harmony. Every scientific hypothesis is a dream that looks to a future for its application or its testing; every formulated law is a discovery of the past for confirmation in the present and guidance into the future. Even a dream that looks back with regret or remorse is a dream of potential unrealised; it is a future in the past. A backward-looking guilt may be the foundation of a present or a future virtue. It may on the other hand lead forward into apathy and despair. Either way its meaning and its realisation lie ahead, not behind.

The Tempest is a parable of evils turned to good effect, of which Prospero's original irresponsibility is one. *The Tempest* as a work of art implies further action on the part of those who appreciate it, and it cannot be fully appreciated except by those who take it as a hypothesis and test, in their own active lives, whether evils can be turned to good and whether new good can be achieved by the kind of attitudes and behaviour imaged in the play. This is one of the senses in which every play is a moral proposition. We do not, of course, attempt to discover whether imitating Macbeth will make us as miserable as the play showed him to be. We certainly appreciate the play more if we have already made ourselves miserable by similar processes (as we all have) but the deliberate tests we make of Shakespeare's hypothesis will be 'by contraries'; namely action in ourselves and towards our fellows that is opposite to Macbeth's, to see whether its effects contribute to happiness. In this respect a play that has a tragic or a miserable ending is not different from a play with a happy ending. We do not aim at misery. Our aim in watching the saddest play is to be made happier, wiser or better. Moreover, every work of art *by reason of its form* points to harmony. So does every moral proposition. Each is a dream of perfection. Each may have its own perfection of form, but neither is more than a part of each man's experience, and must be brought into relation with other parts, just as every mind must be brought into relation with other minds and every body with other bodies in action and interaction.

A work of art is an expression of man's desire for order: so is a moral philosophy or a moral code. A work of art is itself an order achieved; it is also a means to the achievement of a larger order that includes the mind and body of the artist, his material, his medium and the minds and bodies of his public and their media of existence. Similarly, a moral code, besides being ordered in itself, is a means to a proportioned interrelation of impulses within a person, of actions and attitudes within a society and of the impulses, actions and attitudes of persons and societies within ever larger and larger groupings, or within the universe. The achievement of a *new* order is man's basic need. Not even the maintenance of an old order can satisfy. Indeed, that word 'maintenance' itself implies renewal, the taking out of the old part and replacing it by the new one. Even if the new part is in some respects identical, it cannot be the same; and even when man 'preserves' the old he must refurbish it, and there is always the impulse to 'streamline' the design. Works of art he preserves as nearly unchanged as possible precisely because they have in them that miraculous property of relating in new ways to new men and new situations, or because new men in new situations find new ways of relating to them. Shakespeare's plays both change us and change with us. But the impulse towards new order ('system' is the fashionable word) is not in man alone and not peculiar to any time or place. Beginning with man, some would say his basic need is food, but this is as much a statement about the universe as about man. This organism, the body, is like other organisms in assimilating items from outside itself into its own complex order and in contributing items from itself to other complex orders. The record of Evolution is the record of the development of ever more complex systems, organic and inorganic. The living and the non-living interact within larger systems according to observable, but not unchanging, patterns. Either this is the case, or this is the way man sees it, or this is the way man makes it. Each way of putting it affirms man's basic need for order. But the need is always for a new order.

In the search for the new order there are always complementary impulses; one of them is to greater complexity, the other to greater simplicity. The simplicity must embrace the complexity. A poet like Wordsworth will experience at one and the same moment the separate being of the 'loose stones that cover the highway' and the 'unity of all things'; a modern systems analyst delights in a system in which he perceives at one and the same time, high differentiation of items and high integration of the whole. The same apprehension of diversity in unity is the mode of our appreciation of *The Tempest* or of any philosophical, ethical, scientific or religious system. The discovery of unity in diversity is the means whereby we perceive. The idea of naïve or innocent observation is philosophers' make-believe, says Professor P. B. Medawar, the biologist: 'In all sensation we pick and choose, interpret, seek and impose order.'

And this is another sense in which we are such stuff as dreams, for the order that we seek is not first perceived: it is first divined or imagined or dreamed. '"Why can't you draw what you see?" is the immemorial cry of the teacher to the student looking down the microscope for the first time at some quite unfamiliar preparation he is called upon to draw. The teacher has forgotten, and the student will soon forget, that what he sees conveys no information until he knows beforehand the kind of thing he is expected to see.' Gonzalo's vision of utopia or Shakespeare's vision of a harmonious order is not different in this respect from a scientific hypothesis. Each is 'an imaginative preconception of what might be true'. Similarly, 'The formulation of a natural law begins as an imaginative exploit and imagination is a faculty essential to the scientist's tasks'.

In the realm of human behaviour the imaginative divination of a possible order is the foundation of morals. Order, like happiness, is a dream we act towards. This is true even when we look backwards to some lost paradise or Golden Age, for then we are dreaming not of something that has been but of something we desire should be. But the impulse to order is not adequately described by calling it a desire; our desires, including the desire for order, are manifestations or attributes or properties of the impulse. Among the desires that the ordering impulse fathers is the desire to finish and to fix. Without it we should never achieve works of art, societies, moral or legal systems, or any of the creations that make us what we are and preserve our existence. Yet this very desire works counter to the impulse from which it sprang, for that impulse is to continuing creation. Old orders must change and give place to new. Works of art that lose their meaning *in new situations* become obsolete: they are 'dated' we say. Only those that change with the changing world continue to be appreciated. Moral codes established in one age may continue to be observed in a succeeding age for which they are quite unsuited. Unlike obsolete works of art, these are dangerous. They become 'rigid moralities of constraint motivated by fear'.[1] They are attempts to preserve the past by a denial of the future and of the present impulse towards the future; they are a denial of man's basic need to create a new order more complex and more varied than the old. Only a morality of co-operation and aspiration mediated by hope can set men free to be men. That is what is meant by Lear's affirmation of equality and the breaking of Prospero's staff. It is what Shakespeare discovers and reveals by his lifelong exploration of the meaning of love, which has its culminating expression, not in Ferdinand and Miranda – they are beginners – but in Prospero.

[1] Jean Piaget.

CHAPTER SIX

The Worm of Conscience

Every cloud-capped tower, every gorgeous palace and solemn temple is the issue of someone's dream and each one testifies to human potential. Playing our parts on the stage of life (a favourite Shakespearean image) means enacting our dreams, or somebody's dreams, and our lives depend on the quality of our dreams. The bricklayer lays his next brick according to his mental image of the walls he is building. A dream of the future is usually much more complex and much less clear-cut than the bricklayer's image of his wall; but, like the dream, the bricklayer's image is tentative and flexible, adjustable according to the exigencies of his material, the site, the structure he is building, and his body position. The experienced bricklayer is the one who in his time has had to make the greater number and range of adjustments and so can make them quickly and efficiently. Unfortunately he is also the one whom repetition has confirmed in a particular set of adjustments. When his idea of bricklaying becomes fixed, and limited to a particular pattern of adjustments, his experience may be a liability. Should circumstances change in the trade he will need to dream again, and if he cannot, he will be 'redundant'. Shakespeare's tragic heroes are men whose dreams do not match their circumstances and in Lear we see the pain and the shattering effect of a drastic adjustment.

But, however far we fall short of fulfilling our dreams, they shape our lives. Shakespeare's King Henry VI illustrates the point. In a world of lust and strife he dreams of love and peace. His dream is as limited as his will is weak, for it takes no account of the natures of the men he is called upon to rule. It is not, like Prospero's, a dream of the integration of destructive elements into a creative pattern. Henry does not conceive a world in which cruelty and treachery can be transformed into creative power and skill; he simply closes his eyes to cruelty and treachery. The poverty of his dream, the incompleteness of his vision, together with the weakness of his will betray him into the very acts of cruelty and treachery he would most avoid, acts committed against his will and conscience in sheer helplessness when confronted with situations he has refused to imagine, situations which, as we say, he has not dreamed of. As king he fails, yet truth to life as well as art requires that Shakespeare add a gentle beauty to his life consistent with his dream of love and peace. It is not weakness that prompts his forgiving spirit. To his enemies at his mercy he says:

> And Henry, though he be infortunate
> Assure yourselves, will never be unkind:
>> (Part II: IV. ix. 18–19)

This is his ideal, not his fear. His noble and courageous death, and his humble and generous prayer for pardon for his murderer as well as for his own sins, are proper fruits of his vision and of the better elements of his life that spring from it. Henry's ideal, like Gonzalo's, is beyond his grasp in the sense that he cannot order a kingdom in which men really live in love and charity with their neighbours; but there are moments in which Shakespeare shapes Henry's personal life in terms of the ideal, and those moments affirm the worth of the ideal, especially when, as at his death, there is a powerful contrast with men and ideas of very different kind – men of the stamp of Richard Crookback.

In his failure to integrate the 'inner' and the 'outer' worlds, Henry brings destruction on the land he would preserve; but when the only action left to him in the outer world is to die, his soul consents; 'inner' and 'outer' are in harmony, and he becomes heroic. At his death his dream of Christian love issues in action and gives a noble and beautiful shape to his life. What has been a mere wish, unfulfilled, now becomes a living reality.

In this metaphorical sense, Richard too has a dream. It cannot be called an ideal, for it does not reach beyond himself. He dreams of personal power, of wearing the crown, not for any purpose whatsoever other than his own aggrandisement or in obedience to some overmastering drive within. Such a drive appears to be his raging lust for vengeance, not upon any particular person or even upon the house of Lancaster but upon the world, including his own family, that has injured and despised him,[1] and upon heaven and nature that sent him into the world 'deformed' and 'unfinisht':

> Then, since the heavens have shap'd my body so,
> Let hell make crook'd my mind to answer it.
> *(Henry VI, Part III:* V. vi. 78–9)

Richard's dream, too, shapes his life. Elizabethans read history to observe moral examples: Shakespeare shows how a deformed mind in a deformed body perpetrates 'unnatural' deeds that lead to a hideously 'unnatural' end:

> Unnatural deeds
> Do breed unnatural troubles:
> *(Macbeth:* V. i. 68–9)

Compared with *King Lear* or *Macbeth* the *Henry VI–Richard III* tetralogy may seem unsubtle, but only compared with those greater works of Shakespeare: the consistency of the lives, actions and attitudes of both Henry and Richard with modern psychological findings is remarkable. These two characters are almost text-book instances of what are now generally agreed to be the effects of deprivation of parental care and affection in childhood. Dr. John Bowlby[2] writes: 'a young child should experience a warm, intimate, and continuous relationship with his mother (or permanent mother-substitute – one person who steadily mothers him) in which both find satisfaction and enjoyment'. Even partial deprivation, he says, can cause permanent disturbance: 'anxiety, excessive need for love, powerful feelings of revenge, and, arising from these last, guilt and depression'. Nervous disorders and instability of character result. An unconsciously rejecting attitude on the part of the mother, even if it underlies a loving one will produce these disorders. 'Leaving

---

[1] The ambivalence of Richard's attitude to his brothers deserves closer attention.

[2] *Child Care and the Growth of Love.* John Bowlby. Pelican, 1965. Chapters 1, 4 and 5.

any child under three years of age is a major operation . . . on no account should a child be placed with people he doesn't know.' Severe deprivation of maternal attachment during the first three years can produce affectionless and delinquent characters. People who have suffered a degree of deprivation will often hide their disturbance even from themselves by an excessive show of cheerfulness and activity, but this defence is in constant danger of cracking and leaving its owner in a state of despair, and even while it succeeds, the press of activity and ability to tolerate frustration are very trying to others.

Development of the conscience depends on continuous and happy relationships. A baby is very largely at the mercy of his immediate surroundings and his power to choose is rudimentary. As the personality develops, we have to learn to think in the abstract, to imagine, 'to consider things other than just our immediate sensations and desires'. Maturity involves the capacity to think ahead, to control the wish of the moment in the interests of more fundamental long-term needs. A mature individual is 'free from the slavery to his instincts and the urge for immediate pleasure' and is more aware of the demands of his environment. One of our 'foremost long-term desires is to remain on friendly and co-operative terms with others' and it is from this desire that conscience seems to arise. In infancy a child's mother is, 'as it were, his personality and his conscience', and this function of the mother as 'organiser' at a critical period of growth is similar to the function of certain chemicals called organisers which influence the child's growth before birth. Deprivation of these chemicals will hinder growth and cause deformities. Deprivation of maternal attachment at crucial times will cause malformation of the conscience.

In his account of maternal deprivation, Dr. Bowlby might have been writing about Shakespeare's Henry VI and Richard III, both of whom have defects of conscience and neither of whom is able to form stable and satisfactory human relationships. The deprivation suffered by Henry, though his mother is not usually mentioned, is an important part of the story as Shakespeare received it. Shakespeare underlines it by making Henry tell us twice that he was anointed king at nine months old, and by showing him in boyhood surrounded by terrible and ruthless lords. We do not see Henry till the third act of Henry VI, Part I. The first three acts present the disintegration of his father's French dominions and the seeds of civil strife at home. The fierce wranglings and over-weening pride of the barons contending for power during the King's minority form the principal subject-matter. The King, in his brief appearances, is on the one hand an ineffectual peacemaker, and on the other a pawn in someone else's game:

> None do you like but an effeminate prince
> Whom, like a schoolboy, you may overawe.
> (Part I: I. i. 35–6)

There is pathos in his language and his situation which is very moving when we contrast what he is with what a king should be – and that is what Shakespeare is concerned with in this dramatic representation of the kingdom's ruin; but neither of his roles is explored in a personal sense: in Part I we are on-lookers, not involved in his predicament. However, he is a figure of great importance, and his importance increases in the second and third parts of the play. He first appears in sharp contrast with his contentious barons:

> I would prevail, if prayers might prevail
> To join your hearts in love and amity.
> (Part I: III. i. 67–8)

Love and amity have not hitherto been seen or thought of in the play, nor will they appear, except by name or briefly shown by minor characters, in the whole tetralogy including Richard III. For Henry himself, showing the characteristics of one deprived in childhood, cannot love. When we first see him, he is a boy, but he expresses the child's suffering in the presence of wrangling adults:

> O how this discord doth afflict my soul! –
> Can you, my Lord of Winchester, behold
> My sighs and tears, and will not once relent?
> (Part I: III. i. 106–8)

In deference to his childhood appeals, the quarrelling lords make a show of reconciliation, but are not reconciled. When Henry reaches man's years the proud barons show no deference; for Henry, who has known only discord from his infancy, surrounded by strange and monstrous men, never attains maturity. Sighs and tears and pitiful appeals remain his only means of influence, and he is among people with whom these do not avail.

The world of this tetralogy is a world without love. Characters in it long for love, but the longing remains unsatisfied. In the second and third parts a powerful element in the plays' impression is the contrast, indeed opposition, of the figures of Henry, the ineffectual peacemaker, and Richard, the effectual destroyer. Inattentive reading suggests that here we have an exposure of the weakness of Christian charity in the face of ruthless self-interest. Part III ends with the murder of Henry by Richard, and that scene undoubtedly symbolises the defeat of gentleness and innocence by conscienceless malignity. Even on a fairly superficial level, however, there remains a doubt. In *Henry VI, Part II* we have seen the conscienceless Cardinal Beaufort of Winchester triumphant over the only firm and loyal baron at the court. Beaufort, successful in treachery and murder, dies in the torment of terrible dreams and visions and the certainty of hell. The scene is hideous and unforgettable. The comment of the Earl of Warwick is already in the minds of Shakespeare's audience, who expect history to point this kind of moral:

> So bad a death argues a monstrous life.
> *(Part II :* III. iii. 30)

But Henry's final word is a warning that Beaufort's end may be ours:

> Forbear to judge, for we are sinners all.

Henry himself dies with patient heroism, and the following are his final words to his murderer:

> O, God forgive my sins and pardon thee!

These words identify Henry with Christ crucified, as Richard, at the opening of the scene, and throughout it, is identified with the Devil. But, perhaps in part because the Christian myth is itself an illuminating record of human psychology, there is much more to be observed than this apparently simple opposition between Richard and Henry.

Children deprived of love may react in apparently opposite ways, and the effects of their reaction may persist through life. One way is by violence, destructiveness, active hostility, open resentment and cruelty. The other is by withdrawal, dependence, apathy, depression. Both are symptoms of the unsatisfied, often unsatisfiable, hunger for love. Both are usually accompanied by an inadequate sense of identity. Henry and Richard are alike in their disease: neither can love. Yet they appear opposites: Henry sentimental; Richard coldly materialistic: Henry the manipulated; Richard the manipulator: Henry self-effacing; Richard hysterically egocentric – and so on.

I have said that neither has a healthy conscience. Henry is frequently referred to as a saint: Shakespeare could take that from the tradition. But Shakespeare's Henry is not of the stuff that saints are made of. He appears first as the peacemaker and the wise child out of whose mouth cometh forth the wisdom that the great men of the realm will not learn (Part III: III. i.). As in the scene of his death he represents a Christian ideal. Yet from the first there are lines, like those quoted earlier, that suggest the weakling rather than the saint, and at the end of Part I the Earl of Suffolk finds it easy to tempt Henry, by promise of a beauteous wife, to break his contract with the French King and shame his truest and most loyal adviser, Gloster. He does all this, not having seen the lady, but upon description. We see the immaturity and the weakness, no saintliness.

In Part II this impression is strengthened. Justice, or rather injustice, is an important theme. The treacherous Cardinal's plot against the loyal Duke of Gloster thickens. The name of justice is repeatedly on Henry's lips, but always there is a bitter irony of which he himself is unaware. He knows Gloster to be innocent of the indictments brought against him, yet he hands him over to his murderers, who are acting in envy and malice, but in the name of justice and loyalty. He does not attempt to save Gloster, but he cannot bear to see him accused or even to discuss the case. He leaves the council:

> HENRY: My lords, what to your wisdoms seemeth best
>   Do or undo, as if ourself were here.
> MARGARET: What, will your Highness leave the Parliament?
> HENRY: Ay, Margaret; my heart is drown'd with grief,
>   Whose flood begins to flow within mine eyes;
>   My body round engirt with misery –
>   For what's more miserable than discontent?
>   Ah, uncle Humphrey, in thy face I see
>   The map of honour, truth, and loyalty!
>   And yet, good Humphrey, is the hour to come
>   That e'er I proved thee false, or fear'd thy faith.
>   What louring star now envies thy estate
>   That these great lords, and Margaret our queen,
>   Do seek subversion of thy harmless life?
>   Thou never did'st them wrong, nor no man wrong:
>   (*Part II:* III. i. 195–209)

In these words there is shame and sorrow, but no guilt, no sense of his own responsibility. The stars, the great lords, the queen are to blame, not Henry; and their injustice is not to be resisted. Henry shows neither the negative conscience that would convict him of sin, nor the positive conscience that would urge him to act. There is only withdrawal and the unconscious self-punishment and the ineffectual protest of tears:

> His fortunes I will weep and, 'twixt each groan,
> Say, 'Who's a traitor? Gloster he is none'.
>   (*Part II:* III. i. 221–2)

The psychological accuracy of this portrait of Henry is established in two lines that have in them more pain than all the rest and epitomise his life-situation:

> My body engirt with misery –
> For what's more miserable than discontent?

The word 'body' makes us feel his spiritual imprisonment like a physical pain. The 'discontent' of the envious barons has surrounded and crushed him so that the pain and terror of it make growth and mature action impossible. Full recognition of his personal fault and of the responsibility he has not the strength of character to discharge would add so much to the pain and fear he is already feeling as to be unendurable. His betrayal of his friend is felt as some dreadful misfortune that has come upon him from without and in the face of which he is helpless. Remorse, in our modern sense of the word, he does not feel.

A similar impression is received from that scene in Part III where Henry, driven ftom the battle by his wife and Lord Clifford on the ground that they prosper best of all when he is absent, witnesses the slaughter of a father by his son and a son by his father:

> SON: How will my mother for a father's death
>   Take on with me, and ne'er be satisfied!
> FATHER: How will my wife for slaughter of my son
>   Shed seas of tears, and ne'er be satisfied!
> HENRY: How will the country for these woful chances
>   Misthink the king, and not be satisfied!
>
> (*Part III:* II. v. 103–8)

Again Shakespeare gives Henry shame, or the fear of shame, and self-pity, but not a twinge of conscience either in self-blame or stimulus to action.

The impression Shakespeare gives is not of saintliness, but of weakness. Henry does not love, though his talk of love shows his longing for it. His abject betrayal of his son when he disinherits him in favour of the Duke of York so that he himself may continue on the throne for his lifetime is an act that Shakespeare seems to make as despicable as possible. Here, however, a twinge of conscience has weakened such feeble resolution as Henry has tiied at first to show:

> I know not what to say; my title's weak.
>
> (*Part III:* I. i. 134)

But yet his 'conscience' permits him to cling to the throne on condition that he name York his successor. Were it not that he is so obviously still the helpless child, he would here forfeit all sympathy. The Earl of Westmoreland describes him:

Farewell, faint-hearted and degenerate king,
In whose cold blood no spark of honour bides.

and Henry's words and attitude remind us of his betrayal of
Gloster:

HENRY: Ah, Exeter!
WARWICK: Why should you sigh, my lord?
HENRY: Not for myself, Lord Warwick, but my son
  Whom I unnaturally shall disinherit.
  But be it as it may.

(Part III: I. i. 191–4)

It is as if his 'unnatural' fault were an act of God, outside his
responsibility, will and action. Emotion that does not tend to
issue in appropriate and effective action we condemn as sentimentality, feeling that it is not in proportion to its object. When
Henry betrays Humphrey of Gloster he weeps, but does not act.
In the turmoil after Gloster's death when the nobles are hurling
accusations at one another, what comes from Henry is the
following passage that shows how far his dream of the world is
from the reality, how unrelated his feeling is to action:

What stronger breastplate than a heart untainted!
Thrice is he arm'd that hath his quarrel just;
And he but naked though locked up in steel,
Whose conscience with injustice is corrupted.

(Part II: III. ii. 232–5)

The irony is bitter and makes Henry even more contemptible;
for has not he himself repeated that 'the good Duke Humphrey'
had a 'heart untainted'? Shakespeare has carefully built up the
irony. The Scene in which Queen Margaret and Cardinal
Beaufort first entrap Gloster through the plot against his wife
ends with Henry's words:

And poise the cause in justice' equal scales,
Whose beam stands sure, whose rightful cause prevails.

(Part II: II. i. 199–200)

We know, however, that justice is being perverted to the ends of
plotters. In the hall of justice (II. iii), not only is the loyal

Protector deprived of his staff of office, but we have a parody of trial by combat in which, as it happens, the innocent Peter triumphs over his drunken master, who is killed. The King in full solemnity, and in the same court where he has disgraced the innocent Gloster, says:

> And God in justice hath revealed to us
> The truth and innocence of this poor fellow.
>
> (*Part II:* II. iii. 100–1)

However, when all has been said that can be said about Henry's defects of conscience, of which his sentimentality is an example, he still stands in strong contrast to the truly conscienceless ones: Cardinal Beaufort, Margaret of Anjou, The Earls of Suffolk and Warwick, and Richard Duke of York, father of Richard Crookback. Henry does long for peace and love and justice; he is gentle and forgiving, and urges others to forget and forgive; when he injures another, he weeps; he would cause people to live in harmony if he could – and if it did not cost him too much. He has at least a wish for all these things. In contrast, the primitive, wholly conscienceless state finds expression in speeches like that of the Duke of York when he is being sent on the Irish expedition:

> Now, York, or never, steel thy fearful thoughts
> And change misdoubt to resolution;
> Be that thou hop'st to be; or what thou art
> Resign to death – it is not worth th'enjoying.
> Let pale-fac'd fear keep with the mean-born man,
> And find no harbour in a royal heart.
> Faster than spring-time showers comes thought on thought,
> And not a thought but thinks on dignity.
> My brain, more busy than the labouring spider,
> Weaves tedious snares to trap mine enemies.
> Well, nobles, well, 'tis politicly done
> To send me packing with an host of men.
> I fear me you but warm the starved snake,
> Who, cherisht in your breasts, will sting your hearts.
> 'Twas men I lack't, and you will give them me;
> I take it kindly; yet be well assur'd
> You put sharp weapons in a madman's hands.

Whiles I in Ireland nourish a mighty band,
I will stir up in England some black storm,
Shall blow ten thousand souls to heaven or hell;
And this fell tempest shall not cease to rage
Until the golden circuit on my head,
Like to the glorious sun's transparent beams,
Do calm the fury of this mad-bred flaw.

(Part II: III. i. 331–54)

This unselfconscious grasping is typical of Henry's ruthless barons and makes the 'gentle king' seem almost innocent. Yet somehow it has its own kind of innocence. It is an expression of the kind of uncomplicated, unhesitating self-interest that precedes the development of conscience in the infant. Too often we use the word 'innocent' when we mean simply immature. York's speech expresses such an impulse as the mature and healthy mind may experience only in 'that outer chamber of the brain in which thoughts unowned, unsolicited, and of a noxious kind are sometimes allowed to wander for a moment prior to being sent off whence they came'[1]. It can be paralleled by speeches of Cardinal Beaufort, who, by a reversal, the processes of which Shakespeare does *not* explore, dies in agonies of fear and remorse. But it is more interesting to compare York's speech with the speeches of his son, Richard of Gloster.

York is the 'great opposite' of Henry in Part II and the opening of Part III; Richard is Henry's opposite at the end of Part III and is shown in pointed contrast with him from his first appearance in Part II. Like Henry, Richard always has the sacred words upon his lips – but always in mockery. Irony and bathos are common features of the cynic's wit, and Richard is skilful and deadly with both, especially in repartee:

YOUNG CLIFFORD: And so to arms, victorious father,
    To quell the rebels and their complices.
RICHARD: Fie! charity, for shame! speak not in spite
    For you shall sup with Jesu Christ tonight.
YOUNG CLIFFORD: Foul stigmatic, that's more than thou can'st tell.

[1] Thomas Hardy, *The Mayor of Casterbridge.*

RICHARD: If not in heaven, you'll surely sup in hell.
(Part II: V. i. 211–16)

Here, on his first appearance, is the authentic voice of Richard Crookback. His father, York, has spoken words that more truly describe the son than the father:

> My brain more busy than the labouring spider,
> Weaves tedious snares to trap mine enemies.

Richard's natural gift for trapping enemies appears in this very first example of his repartee, and, together with it, his habitual contempt for sacred things accompanied by a contempt for life. The obvious contrast with Henry is pointed in the next scene when Richard makes his first kill:

> Sword, hold thy temper; heart be wrathful still:
> Priests pray for enemies, but princes kill.
> *(Part II: V. ii. 70–1)*

Richard, then, claims to be by nature a prince, as Henry is by nature a priest. Shakespeare makes the contrast between these two as obvious and distinct as possible. Early in Part II when Queen Margaret complains of Henry's incapacity as a lover and a husband, another aspect of his retarded development, she describes him as follows to her lover, the Earl of Suffolk, William de la Pole:

> I tell thee, Pole, when in the city Tours
> Thou ran'st a tilt in honour of my love,
> And stol'st away the ladies' hearts of France,
> I thought King Henry had resembled thee
> In courage, courtship, and proportion;
> But all his mind is bent to holiness,
> To number Ave-Maries on his beads;
> His champions are the prophets and apostles;
> His weapons, holy saws of sacred writ;
> His study is his tilt-yard, and his loves
> Are brazen images of canonized saints.
> *(Part II: I. iii. 48–58)*

Henry's religion is a dream divorced from action, a means of escape or withdrawal, not the mighty driving force of true saintliness. Richard would like to believe that religion and love and conscience, which would restrain his lust for power, are all rat-holes for shrinking cowards. He is the heroic man of action. Shakespeare gives him one of Margaret's lines:

> Shall we go throw away our coats of steel
> And wrap our bodies in black mourning-gowns,
> Numbering our Ave-Maries with our beads?
> Or shall we on the helmets of our foes
> Tell our devotion with revengeful arms?
>
> *(Part III:* II. ii. 160–4)

Richard is as brave as Henry is timid, as dominant as Henry is submissive, as contemptuous as Henry is devoted. Yet in their deepest souls they are alike. Each is isolated and despised, each defends himself by further isolation. Each longs for love, and neither can achieve it.

This last remark requires substantiation in the case of Richard. Shakespeare is most careful to fix in our imaginations the picture of the unlov'd and unlovable child, the monstrous nature of his birth, the fear and loathing of the women who attended at his birth, the sufferings of his mother, and her sense of injury at his very existence:

> Thy mother felt more than a mother's pain,
> And yet brought forth less than a mother's hope –
> To wit, an indigest deformed lump,
>
> The midwife wonder'd, and the women cried,
> 'O, Jesus bless us, he is born with teeth!'
> And so I was; which plainly signified
> That I should snarl, and bite, and play the dog.
>
> *(Part III:* V. vi.)

His mother's own words, designed to throw the blame on him, exemplify the maternal rejection that, according to Dr. Bowlby, can produce the affectionless delinquent:

> No, by the holy rood, thou know'st it well,
> Thou cam'st on earth to make the earth my hell.
> A grievous burden was thy birth to me;
> Tetchy and wayward was thy infancy;
> Thy school-days frightful, desp'rate, wild, and furious;
>
> *(Richard III:* IV. iv. 165–9)

Every word of Richard's to his mother recounts a dreadful history of their relations. He addresses her with a mixture of impatience and ironic contempt, in response to her 'virtuous' admonishment that contrasts so strongly with their mutual detestation. The tone of the first part of what follows is set by that of the last:

> DUKE OF GLOSTER: Madam, my mother, I do cry you mercy;
> I did not see your Grace. Humbly on my knee
> I crave your blessing.
> DUCHESS OF YORK: God bless thee; and put meekness in thy breast,
> Love, charity, obedience, and true duty!
> DUKE OF GLOSTER: Amen! (aside) and make me die a good old man!
> That is the butt end of a mother's blessing:
> I marvel that her Grace did leave it out.
> (Richard III: II. ii. 104–11)

When it serves Richard's purpose to start a rumour that his brother Edward's sons have no right to the throne, he does not hesitate to accuse his mother of infidelity, pointing the slander with a bitter mock.

The desperate, wild and furious boyhood and the 'daring, bold and venturous manhood', exemplify the excessive show of activity that serves as a defence for the emotionally deprived. In Richard, as in the text-book cases, it is frequently combined with excessive cheerfulness and 'harmful-kind' affability. However, the cracks in Richard's defensive façade show through every soliloquy, making him something more than the incredible Devil-figure of pure melodrama. Both the restlessness and the brittle persona are revealed by the Lady Anne, his wife:

> For never yet one hour in his bed
> Did I enjoy the golden dew of sleep,
> But with his timorous dreams was still awak'd.
> (Richard III: IV. i. 83–5)

The difference between Richard's soliloquies and that of his father, York, shows a world of psychological and poetic insight separating them. York is unhesitating, single-minded; Richard is explanatory, self-excusing. Each claims to be ruthless, remorse-less, subtle, treacherous. York claims it as a matter of fact and stern resolve; Richard makes it a hysterical boast. York's lust for the crown is uncomplicated; but Richard's most frequent word is not 'crown' or 'kingdom' but 'I':

> Why, I can smile, and murder while I smile,
> And cry 'Content' to that which grieves my heart;
> And wet my cheeks with artificial tears,
> And frame my face to all occasions.
> I'll drown more sailors than the mermaid shall;
> I'll slay more gazers than the basilisk;
> I'll play the orator as well as Nestor,
> Deceive more slily than Ulysses could,
> And like a Sinon take another Troy.
> I can add colours to the chameleon,
> Change shapes with Proteus for advantages,
> And set the murderous Machiavel to school.
> Can I do this, and cannot get a crown?
> Tut, were it farther off, I'll pluck it down.
>
> (*Henry VI, Part III:* III. ii. 182–95)

But the rhetorical question conveys a doubt, and this vaunting passage follows a remarkable image of himself as a lost creature. It has the air of a dream and is artistically as well as psycho-logically consistent with the dream experiences of *Richard III*:

> And yet I know not how to get the crown,
> For many lives stand between me and home;
> And I – like one lost in a thorny wood
> That rends the thorns and is rent with the thorns,
> Seeking a way and straying from the way;
> Not knowing how to find the open air,
> But toiling desperately to find it out –
> Torment myself to catch the English crown;
>
> (*Henry VI, Part III:* III. ii. 172–9)

This, again, follows a passage in which he tells us what would shake his lust for power if he could have it, namely the 'pleasure of a lady's lap'. At first he speaks of it as a subsidiary lust, a second best to the crown, but as he dwells upon his incapacity

for love-making, the pathos of his deprivation shows through
the bitterness and ferocity of his complaint:

> O miserable thought! and more unlikely
> Than to accomplish twenty golden crowns.
> Why, love forswore me in my mother's womb;
> And, for I should not deal in her soft laws,
> She did corrupt frail nature with some bribe
> To shrink mine arm up like a wither'd shrub;
> To make an envious mountain on my back,
> Where sits deformity to mock my body;
> To shape my legs of an unequal size;
> To disproportion me in every part,
> Like to a chaos, or an unlick'd bear whelp
> That carries no impression like the dam.
> And am I, then, a man to be beloved?
> (Henry VI, Part III: III. ii. 151–63)

Every point of this long soliloquy is concentrated into the more
powerful and even more ambiguous soliloquy in V. vi. 61–93
after he has murdered Henry. The hysteria there is more
intense; the excuses for his villainy are more urgent and defiant;
the affirmation of cruelty is more frantic in the repeated
stabbing of Henry and in the words:

> Down, down to hell; *and say I sent you thither –*

which passionately and defiantly reject Henry's Christ-like
prayer of forgiveness. Love is repudiated with even more violence
and with a lonely agony, and this time the love he rejects is not
confused with lust: it is the love that 'greybeards call divine'.

Among the problems of the child deprived of love, and one
that may remain with him through life, is the problem of
identity. It is the mother's love that makes the child realise that
he is a person. Similarly, it is the love of Solveig that gives Peer
Gynt his identity in Ibsen's play. What we are unsure of, we
feel the need to assert. The frantic boasts of Richard culminate
in his terrifying but also pathetic cry:

> I am myself alone.

This assertion of separateness and special distinction is found in every scene of *Richard III* where he is present. It is in his contempt for every one of the long series of victims, including his confidant Buckingham, whom he over-reaches and destroys. It is also in his furious rages and resentments when he is even temporarily thwarted. It is in his continual histrionics, from the dropping of Somerset's head on the pavement with the laconic,

> Speak thou for me, and tell them what I did,

to the wooing of Lady Anne and his suit for the hand of the princess Elizabeth. Shakespeare simply could not, or would not, write a mere melodrama. All these features of Richard are part of a hard protective shell that cracks and crumbles in Act V. Richard, the bad, comes to no good; the convention is observed. But the convention itself is not a *mere* convention. Melodrama has its truth, though it may present the truth falsely. The truth in it Shakespeare explores in *Macbeth*, where we see just in what senses bad causes lead to bad effects in reality. What he has done in *Richard III*, where melodramatic effects are more prevalent, is similar. People have asked why we sympathise so much with Richard. His wit, like Falstaff's humour, delights us. He is our champion against that bully, conscience. He is able to please himself, as we would like to. No great sympathy is aroused for those he over-reaches: we too have impulses to dominate and assert ourselves. As with all villains of melodrama, we can enjoy the villainy and condemn it at the same time: in the end we, the audience, over-reach even the villain. But there is something more. In every soliloquy the pitiless Richard makes a claim upon our pity. The words 'deformity', 'disproportion' and 'chaos' in the passage quoted above carry ideas of evil for Shakespeare's contemporaries far greater than any they may suggest to us: they establish Richard as Devil. But to any audience, whether of the sixteenth or twentieth century, he is excusing himself; and he does not offer as an excuse or explanation what would not be felt as such. His 'Then' in *Henry VI, Part III*: III. ii. 165 is equivalent to that in V. vi. 78–9:

> Then, since the heavens have shaped my body so,
> Let hell make crook't my mind to answer it.

So as not to go outside the play *Richard III* we might quote a 'therefore' instead of a 'then':

> And therefore, since I cannot prove a lover
> To entertain these fair well-spoken days,
> I am determined to prove a villain.   (I. i. 28–30)

It sounds like a just balance, a fair exchange, and we have no evidence that Elizabethan impulses to demand a tooth for a tooth were less strong than ours. Pity for his deformities may have been less readily shown in those days than now, and perhaps less readily felt, but pity is only one kind of sympathy. What is important about Richard is what we have in common with him, and that is very much the same as saying, what makes him seem human. His repeated appeals for a just hearing have a good deal to do with this. And these appeals are part of his demand to be recognized. In his case this becomes a strident and histrionic egoism, but his cry is heard because we all share the need to be recognised, and because Richard is so successful in establishing and maintaining a strong persona if only by accepting and energetically living up to the bad name he has been given. Every passage of histrionics is punctuated by some blunt or gross or mundane comment, some irony, contempt or cynicism by which Richard shows his 'true' colours; that is displays what appears to be his 'real' identity. But yet he 'doth protest too much'. His hysterical assertion of incredible villainy, over against his hypocritical displays of tender feeling, gives an impression of instability, and there is always the sense of terrible underlying forces and of the fearful turbulence that broke out in his childhood and in the wars. Then again he is always striving, always restless, moving too suddenly and too swiftly for anyone to keep abreast of him, successful in immediate ends but never satisfied. The very fact that he plays so many parts raises questions about the validity of the self he presents to us. Taking an oath before Elizabeth he makes the mistake of swearing by himself. Her answer recalls with dramatic irony all his exaggerated self-assertions:

> Thyself is self-misused.   (IV. iv. 74)

The 'identity' that Richard adopts, and with which he almost, but not quite, convinces us (in this century at any rate) is not really an identity at all, but a persona. It is a mask that represents a man without a conscience. When he is play-acting to deceive other characters, he plays at having a conscience. When he is play-acting in his soliloquies, he plays at not having a conscience. The first he finds easy; at the second he does not succeed, for he is always proving that he *ought* to be bad, either to make up to himself for Fate's injustices, or because the good are contemptible or foolish or a nuisance. 'Ought' implies a conscience. It may be that we today are less likely to notice this implicit conscience. Shakespeare's contemporaries, expecting the reversal in the last act, would be less likely to overlook it. Striving to *be* a man without a conscience, Richard succeeds only in *appearing to be* a man without a conscience. In *Richard III* he is contrasted with Clarence, with nearly every hired murderer, with Edward, even with Buckingham, all of whom are conscience-stricken while he remains unmoved. But Anne mentions those timorous dreams, and the audience know that Margaret's curse will be, and is being, fulfilled:

> The worm of conscience still be-gnaw thy soul!
> Thy friends suspect for traitors while thou liv'st,
> And take deep traitors for thy dearest friends!
> No sleep close up that deadly eye of thine,
> Unless it be while some tormenting dream
> Affrights thee with a hell of ugly devils!
>
> (I. iii. 222–7)

Cardinal Beaufort died in *Henry VI, Part II* tormented by his conscience. Richard's life has been more 'monstrous' even than his. Accordingly the repressed conscience takes revenge. Unable to appear in Richard's consciousness, it appears in his dreams. In public he banishes it with devastating cynicism:

> Conscience is but a word that cowards use,
> Devis'd at first to keep the strong in awe.
>
> (V. iii. 309–10)

but it is the affect immediately following his final and most terrible dream (V. iii.) that is most striking. The dream itself is symbolic in the more limited sense, and formalised, bestowing blessings upon Richmond, curses on Richard. The soliloquy that follows is in the strongest possible contrast with the stylised and ritualised form of the dream. It is also quite different from any other of Richard's soliloquies. He seems for the first time to be really alone, and the words he speaks record, not his thoughts, but his feelings. He is not now addressing the audience, nor is it adequate to say he speaks to himself. He strives for the old, confident persona:

O coward conscience how dost thou afflict me!

and the assertion of identity:

Richard loves Richard; that is, I am I.

but in vain. Both 'I' and 'myself' divide and fall into confusion and absurdity, so that we are aware only of disintegration and uncertain identity. Perhaps we may say the dream has not left him; he is not wholly awake; but the dream has shown him the truth about himself; his 'true' identity is that of a disintegrated person:

What do I fear? Myself? There's none else by:
Richard loves Richard; that is, I am I.
Is there a murderer here? No – yes, I am:
Then fly. What, from myself? Great reason why –
Lest I revenge. What, myself upon myself!
Alack, I love myself. Wherefore? For any good
That I myself have done unto myself?
Oh, no! Alas I rather hate myself
For hateful deeds committed by myself!
I am a villain; yet I lie, I am not.   (V. iii. 182–91)

This speech can be acted only as distraction. It is the nightmare horror still upon him. A similar effect is more subtly and more wonderfully achieved by Shakespeare when Lady Macbeth, asleep, does 'the effects of watching'. *Richard III* is surely the major source document for *Macbeth*. This story of the killing of the conscience and just how it rises up again 'to push us from our stools' needed more careful exploration than it had received even in *Richard III*.

Richard's words show the lack of an integrated personality behind the brittle persona that has now broken and will have to be hastily pieced together when Richard finds an audience again. He tries to recover it:

> Fool, of thyself speak well.

but fails:

> Fool, do not flatter.

We have referred to the uncertain identity. Shakespeare does not use the word, or the word 'mind' or the word 'personality'. The word he uses is 'conscience'. In three parts of *Henry VI* 'conscience' is most frequently used to mean innermost thought. In *Richard III* it usually means that which convicts us of sin and makes us feel guilty. Here the two uses come together. We have heard accusing voices in Richard and *felt* the disintegrating of the false identity or persona. The conscience that has been denied and silenced now delivers all its messages at once:

> My conscience hath a thousand several tongues,
> And every tongue brings in a several tale,
> And every tale condemns me for a villain.
>
> (V. iii. 193–5)

The babel of voices from the innermost mind, though their burden is the same, still suggests the disintegrated personality. In Richard's case, however, it is more appropriate to speak of the unintegrated mind than the disintegrated since, as we have seen, integration has never taken place. He has never been quite a person and his conscience has never matured: out of his birth and childhood and in his thwarted devil-nature no such maturing has been possible. Such conscience as he has now can only punish, and as all its voices cry 'Guilty! guilty!' there is wrung from him once again the cry that was felt rather than heard in the early soliloquies, where it was deliberately disguised as its opposite:

> I shall despair. There is no creature loves me;
> And if I die, no soul shall pity me:

Love alone could save, but one who has not been loved cannot even love himself enough to be an undivided person:

> And, wherefore should they since that I myself
> Find in myself no pity to myself?　　(V. iii. 202–3)

When the others arrive he recovers his former pose. The dreams and voices that were his unintegrated self he calls 'shadows', and he turns to 'practical' affairs – eavesdropping to find out whether his own soldiers mean to shrink from him. He is unregenerate.

The metaphorical and the literal senses in which the word 'dream' has been used in these pages now conflict, for Richard's sleep-dream is in conflict with Richard's life-dream of ruthless power and vengeance. Henry dreamed of being a true king who should order his kingdom in 'love and amity'. He did not achieve this ideal, but the power of his life-dream was such that it shaped his action nobly at the last, even though he betrayed it again and again in life. Richard does not betray his life-dream: every act of his is directed towards the crown, and deeds of cruelty and vengeance accompany every step. But the conscience that has been repressed takes visual shape in his sleep and, for a moment, he is almost deflected from his purpose. At any rate he sees himself differently and, as he himself might have put it, loses his nerve: conscience is for cowards. His use of the word 'coward' is interesting, for Richard is in flight from the promptings of conscience. His first refuge is to go eavesdropping. It is a hasty and pathetic attempt to bolster his confidence, and for the first time makes him contemptible. This, after all, is the meaning of the crown now he has gained it. He has plotted the downfall of others; naturally he suspects that others will plot his. First Buckingham has to be removed; then Stanley, Earl of Derby, and his son are suspected; then every tent may contain a traitor. For, in such cases as Richard's,

> We still have judgement here; that we but teach
> Bloody instructions, which, being taught, return
> To plague th'inventor:　　(*Macbeth:* I. vii. 8–10)

His second refuge is the hurly-burly of war where there is no time for thought, and where, like Macbeth later, he fights desperately to the last. His oration to his soldiers before the battle contrasts with Richmond's. Richmond offers hope, and service in a holy cause; Richard is strident, threatening, and defiant. Richard's lie about the composition of the opposing army, and his foaming contempt are couched in mean and disquieting imagery: they show the fear and hatred in defiance, not the courage:

> A scum of Britaines, and base lackey peasants,
> Whom their o'er-cloyed country vomits forth
> To desperate adventures and assured destruction,
>
> $\qquad$ (V. iii. 317–19)

but in the battle his defiance is as heroic as it is desperate:

> The king enacts more wonders than a man,
> Daring an opposite to every danger.

Richard is nothing if not constant in his desperation:

> Slave, I have set my life upon a cast
> And I will stand the hazard of the die:
>
> $\qquad$ (V. iv. 9–10)

These two issues of the dream of personal power and pride, on the one hand the meanness and triviality exemplified in the eavesdropping and on the other the defiance that springs from the same root, though in some manifestations at least it seems so different, are familiar to us in great literature. Marlowe's Dr. Faustus, who boasts

> All things that move between the quiet poles
> Shall be at my command

wastes his precious years and mighty powers in pointless japes. The heroic defiance of Milton's Satan has won him many admirers, almost disciples, but Satan becomes a spy and a toad, and grovels on his belly as a snake, his angelic accents 'turn'd to exploding hiss'[1] Shakespeare's *Macbeth* shows a dream of personal glory and power turning to dust and ashes, and

[1] *Paradise Lost:* X. 46.

destroying a noble and heroic man and woman who, like Richard, stifle the conscience and act out their ambitious 'dream'.

Henry VI, though he fails to live out his life-dream as he would wish, is ennobled by it. Richard, who lives out his, is both degraded and destoyed by it. Our lives stand in the level of our dreams,[1] but everyone in real life has many dreams to choose from, and a dream can be tested by action that rejects it as well as by action consistent with it. That Richard had a dream of love as well as a dream of hate we have seen, and resentment at not being loved is shown to be at the root of his vengeful ambition. Conscience, says Dr. Bowlby, seems to arise from our long-term desire 'to remain on friendly and co-operative terms with others'. Conscience, had he not repressed it, would have impelled Richard to acts of love and deterred him from deeds of hate. When conscience found its voice, Richard's choice had long been made, the dream of hate had been lived out; conscience could only accuse.

[1] *The Winter's Tale:* III. ii. 80.

CHAPTER SEVEN

This Even-Handed Justice

THE question whether there could ever be a man so resolute in evil as Richard III is raised by Anne's remark about those 'timorous dreams'. Must there not in any real villain be disturbances of mind that make him hesitate? Would he not have moments of horrified realisation? Margaret, as we have seen, has cursed Richard with the words:

> No sleep close up that deadly eye of thine,
> Unless it be while some tormenting dream
> Affrights thee with a hell of ugly devils!
>
> (I. iii. 225–7)

But, until the final act, Shakespeare does not create the inwardness of Richard's life or show whether the curse is being fulfilled. The play affirms that evil deeds produce evil consequences; and, even if we did not know the story, we should foresee Richard's end as surely as we foresee the end of any villain of melodrama. In plays, bad people can always be brought to a bad end. When the play is convincing, the bad end is seen to have arisen directly from earlier events and from the nature of the people involved. If the play is a genuine study of the nature of evil in man, the villain need not die; for, in life, the wicked prosper, or seem to prosper. A play in which poetic justice is meted out cannot be a genuine study of the nature of evil unless there is some sense in which evil does in fact recoil upon its perpetrator. The forces that kill Richard are forces that his own cruelties have raised against him, but then Richard is an extreme villain. Conclusions about the generality of wickedness drawn from the extreme instance may be questionable. The meaning of evil is not most effectively conveyed to an audience by the presentation of a wholly evil being: we are not wholly evil, and cannot identify sufficiently with such a figure, though we can be impressed by the horror of it. It is when evil is seen in one more like ourselves that it convinces most powerfully. We have already seen a number of ways in which Richard *is* ourselves, but it is the sudden appearance of the 'good' impulses, the partial recognition of the truth about himself, and the human fear, all elicited by the dream, that make us feel *within* Richard and that impart tragic awe which his mere death would not impart. We are now no longer merely watching; we are beginning to enter his inner life and thus to experience those consequences of evil that really do seem to be inevitable. In the inner life, we feel, a person is less likely to be able to escape the effects of his own evil choices than in the external world, though he may still remain, at any rate for a long time, unaware of those effects. The revelation of the horrors of Richard's inner world has been prepared, not by the full poetic realisation of his previous inner experience, but by hints of terrible forces within him, by curses and prophecies of dreadful things to come, by the impossible series of wicked triumphs that compels us to expect a reversal, and by the rhythmical iteration of the sufferings of the women, who generate such pity that we come not merely to desire but to expect a terrible vengeance in the soul as well as on the body of Richard.

This is mighty, but less mighty than a comparable realisation of the destructive power of evil in the inner life of one who, like us, has his virtues and his weaknesses, and with whom we can live through the experiences of conscience, of moral choice, and of the raging inner turmoil and the desert of hope and feeling created by deliberate wickedness. Such a one is Macbeth.

At every stage in Macbeth's development, or rather degeneration, we have the experience of choice. Equally, we have the sense of inevitability. This is very true to life, for every deliberate act can be viewed by one philosopher as an act of free will and by another as wholly determined, and the chooser himself can feel about his own choice, not merely in either way, but in both ways at the same time. The witches, the powers of evil, seek Macbeth and prophesy that he will be king. He starts and seems to fear, as if the thought is already in his mind. The uneasy feeling that Macbeth may be doomed has, in any case, started with the mention of his name by the witches in the opening scene. However, when his thoughts are revealed shortly after the prophecy, we find that grammar, rhythm and imagery express his state of indecision. His ambition impels him towards 'the swelling act of the imperial theme', the great drama in which he sees himself as king of Scotland; but his good conscience fills him with horror at the means to the crown which his ambition, stimulated by the witches, has offered:

> This supernatural soliciting
> Cannot be ill; cannot be good:
> If ill, why hath it given me earnest of success
> Commencing in a truth? I am Thane of Cawdor:
> If good, why do I yield to that suggestion
> Whose horrid image doth unfix my hair,
> And make my seated heart knock at my ribs,
> Against the use of nature? (I. iii. 130–7)

Macbeth is a visualiser; the prophecy has brought before his mind's eye the body of King Duncan as if already murdered. Macbeth is not a man whose heart knocks against his ribs at the sight of physical horrors or in the presence of immediate danger. In the thick of battle, when he is fighting honourably and loyally for Scotland and his king, he wades through the slaughter 'nothing afeard' of the 'strange images of death' he makes with his own sword, and freshened rather than dismayed by the sight of enemy reinforcements increasing the already heavy odds against him. To Macbeth

> Present fears
> Are less than horrible imaginings.

But the 'imaginings' that terrify him are not of physical, but of moral and spiritual danger; and, whereas physical danger stimulates him to heroic action, moral horror – the horror of doing a terrible evil – threatens his identity and paralyses him:

> My thought, whose murder yet is but fantastical,
> Shakes so my single state of man,
> That function is smothered in surmise
> And nothing is, but what is not. (I. iii. 139–42)

Such is the power of Macbeth's imagination that the body of
the murdered king in his mind's eye seems more real than the
objects and the people around him. And, for the moment, the
very image that the witches' suggestions have called up deters
him. He seems to put aside the temptation:

> If Chance will have me King, why, Chance may crown me
> Without my stir. (I. iv. 144-5)

Or at least defers the decision:

> Come what come may,
> Time and the hour runs through the roughest day.

When next we see him, an event, the declaration of Malcolm as
Scotland's rightful heir, seems to bring him to the point of
decision; but, even as he makes his resolve, the stars, the light,
and the light of the body, which is the eye, condemn him:

> Stars, hide your fires!
> Let not light see my black and deep desires;
> The eye wink at the hand; yet let that be,
> Which the eye fears, when it is done, to see.
> (I. iv. 50-3)

The expression 'yet let that be' leaves a doubt about the firmness of the decision, and the vivid counter imagery shows a
powerful and living conscience warning him against the deed.
We remain in suspense, for Macbeth has not yet consciously and
irrevocably chosen evil; yet we feel a strong and steady movement towards evil that seems to be bearing him along. The
horrid image now does *not* unfix his hair as it did on first appearance, and, though he fears it will when made flesh, he is already
hardening himself against it.

When the experience of choice is sharpened by indecision,
this is how it feels. There is the sense of great helplessness, the
knowledge that sooner or later the choice will be made, and it
will be made according to which of the forces pressing on the
nervous system will prove most powerful; yet there is also the
weight of personal responsibility, as if 'I', and in the last resort
'I' alone, can regulate those forces, giving the overbalance of
power to one or another. By the poetic realisation of this state

of indecision prior to moral choice, Shakespeare gives us an insight into moral experience and the working of conscience. Richard's immediate and outright rejection of conscience cannot be explored, except by its consequences. The decision itself is a matter of a moment. Only by presenting it, as it were, in slow-motion can Shakespeare live through it and discover its meaning. The more aware the chooser can be of the implications of his choice, the more powerful will be our grasp of its import.

In *Richard III* there is much that stimulates reflection on the *origins* of conscience, whether Shakespeare intended this or not. In *Macbeth* we know nothing of the hero's childhood or family or previous history, and though there are signs of immaturity both in his lust for power and glory and in his dependence on Lady Macbeth, his conscience as a mode of knowledge is highly developed, and as a motivating power by no means undeveloped. The powerful lusts, the touches of weakness and the distinct vision of what ought and ought not to be are given data and together make up the image of a truly human being who, by virtue of his aspiration and his insight, might well have been a very great human being. Macbeth longs to be king, but he also longs to be good; hence his special horror of murder, but not of slaughter in a noble cause. His powerful imagination shows him the horror of evil in visual terms. When we say that Macbeth 'knows' he is doing wrong in murdering Duncan, we do not mean merely that he has thought it out. Shakespeare presents him as knowing it by at least three modes of knowledge: the rational, the emotional and the sensory. In the soliloquy quoted above, the grammar of Macbeth's argument with himself and the objectivity of his self-analysis show him assessing the position rationally. However, the rhythm and the antitheses of the opening altercation with himself and of the final line, 'And nothing is but what is not', convey the emotional tension. The diction and images have powerful emotive force: 'swelling' for example expresses his rising hope and pride as well as intimations of royal grandeur. But every thought and feeling is experienced in his body, not only directly in the unfixed hair and the unseated heart, but through his imagination when the mere image of murder *'shakes'* so his 'single state of man'. We cannot say that Macbeth knows with his 'head' and not with his 'heart' the horror of committing this crime, and therefore lacks motive for rejecting the temptation. Shakespeare makes Macbeth know it with head and heart and body. Unfortunately heart and body also know 'the swelling act of the imperial theme'. This is the dream of grandeur that will require the direct translation into life and act of the daydream of murder, which the head condemns and the body shrinks from.

Probably for everyone 'I ought' or 'I ought not' follows upon some imagined scene in which an obligation to do or not to do is dramatised as in a dream or day-dream, whether or not it is also being reasoned out. Everything depends on how, or whether, we live out the dreams. By the 'horrid image' of murder, Macbeth's conscience warns him against the very evil that it dramatises. Should he act according to the *meaning* of his vision, he would live it out by *rejecting* the image and refraining from the deed. That would be to affirm his rational judgement and accept the warning. In the event, he lives out the murder, which is the 'suggestion' of the witches, and rejects his good conscience.

That Macbeth's conscience is good and not merely a cowardly self-interest set against the self-interest of ambition is shown in his next long soliloquy, where every kind of self-interest, both noble and ignoble, is present. Richard knows conscience only as an interfering nuisance or as a terrifying threat to which only a coward would submit. Hamlet does himself the injustice of stigmatising his conscientious scruples as cowardice. Macbeth is restrained from committing the murder by two kinds of fear: one is fear of being murdered in his turn; the other is fear of doing evil. The second is the fear we find in saints and martyrs, and we do not call it cowardice. Ironically, it is cowardice that finally drives him to resolve upon committing the murder: he is too cowardly to endure the name of coward from his wife. This, however, is only the last straw and is partly occasioned by his unbounded admiration for Lady Macbeth.

It must be noted that, though Lady Macbeth plays on his own weakness by calling him coward when she is pressing him to do the murder and when she is trying to revive his manhood in the presence of Banquo's ghost, this is not how she describes him when she reflects alone upon those qualities that might prevent him from committing murder. These are her thoughts about him:

> Yet do I fear thy nature:
> It is too full o' th'milk of human kindness,
> To catch the nearest way. Thou woulds't be great;
> Art not without ambition, but without
> The illness should attend it: what thou woulds't highly,
> That would'st thou holily; would'st not play false
> And yet would'st wrongly win; thou'dst have, great Glamis,
> That which cries, 'Thus must thou do,' if thou have it;
> And that which rather thou dost fear to do
> Than wishest should be undone. (I. v. 16–25)

Macbeth himself has already confirmed the truth of the last two lines, but it is her description of the nature of his fear that is important in expressing the quality of his conscience. What she knows he fears is 'illness', unholiness and playing false. 'Illness' in Shakespeare's day did not mean sickness, but evil or wickedness; here it suggests the cruelty in murder. And he fears these things because he is 'too full' of positive good. Lady Macbeth, like Goneril, despises this good, but whatever she may think in her barbarous mood, the 'milk of human kindness' is a virtue that life soon teaches her to long for. When Lady Macbeth calls upon the powers of evil to turn her milk to gall, she is not merely repudiating her feminine nature, she is desecrating the most sacred bond of kinship and of tender care, and defiling the very sources of life in her. Her husband, she believes, has not only too much gentleness in him to be a murderer but also too strong a sense of the sacredness of life. If 'kindness' has the same meaning as our word today, then 'milk' will be an intensifier and the worst that Lady Macbeth can be saying is that he has too much kindness to serve his own interests. Those who admire crime will condemn him for it and say that 'milk' refers to cowardice that masquerades as kindness. But the word 'kindness' must, in Shakespeare, have associations with 'kindred' and 'nature' and thus the phrase implies the gentleness that is a bond between man and man. This meaning is confirmed by Malcolm when, pretending that he will be a worse tyrant than Macbeth has become, he says it will be his delight to

> Pour the sweet milk of concord into Hell   (IV. iii. 98)

Macbeth, then, according to his wife is one who feels strongly the bonds between man and man, one who has too much love in him to do a cruel deed – except, as we have seen, in the way of duty to his king and country. What Macbeth fears is to defile these bonds, to do wrong. This is not a personal and immediately selfish fear; it comes from reverence for life and for concord.

In the scene from which these words of Lady Macbeth are taken we are being shown what it is in Macbeth that causes the horrid image of murder to unfix his hair, and the passage quoted is only part of the impression we receive of Macbeth as one in whom the bonds of nature and of kinship are strong. He himself has few words in the scene and the strength of the bond between him and Lady Macbeth is shown more perhaps by her words than by his. Lady Macbeth's dominance suggests a possible weakness in him, a boyish dependence perhaps, but there is also a tenderness. In the passage quoted, Lady Macbeth shows how well she understands him; she has just read a letter in which he has imparted news relating to their secret. His language in the letter is that of a tender sharing:

> This have I thought good to deliver thee (my dearest partner of greatness) that thou might'st not lose the dues of rejoicing, by being ignorant of what greatness is promis'd thee. Lay it to thy heart, and farewell.   (I. v. 10–15)

It is a great mistake to read Lady Macbeth's reflections upon the news in this letter as if she were Goneril, who indeed cannot use the word 'milk' without contempt and who really does despise the 'milky gentleness' of her husband, Albany. There is never any sign of gentleness or love in Goneril nor any real bond between her and any other person (unless her lust for Edmund be cited). Lady Macbeth is all solicitude for her husband. She rejoices in his greatness, and greets him ecstatically:

> Great Glamis! worthy Cawdor!
> Greater than both by the all-hail hereafter!

If he hesitates and has doubts, she will bear the burden of decision and preparation:

> Leave all the rest to me.

Indeed, part of the preparation is her advice and encouragement, in which the tone is one of intimate sharing even in – or rather especially in – its sinister irony:

> Your face, my Thane, is as a book, where men
> May read strange matters. To beguile the time,
> Look like the time; bear welcome in your eye,
> Your hand, your tongue: look like th'innocent flower,
> But be the serpent under 't. He that's coming
> Must be provided for; and you shall put
> This night's great business into my dispatch;
> Which shall to all our nights and days to come
> Give solely sovereign sway and masterdom.
>
> (I. v. 62–70)

There is the possessiveness and solicitous condescension of a mother, the common understanding and the shared aspiration. Her terrible repudiation of her womanhood and all tenderness is already belied by this bond between her and her husband, as it will continue to be belied by subsequent behaviour. The tragic irony of their story is that the gentleness in Macbeth really is killed by the course of action upon which Lady Macbeth urges him, while her own gentleness reasserts itself as the accuser that disturbs her sleep and drives her to suicide. There is a sad contrast between Macbeth's words at her death and his first gentle greeting with its shared secret:

> My dearest love,
> Duncan comes here tonight.

The structure of *Macbeth* is like St. Andrew's cross, with Macbeth moving along one diagonal, Lady Macbeth along the other: their positions are reversed at the end of the play. At the beginning, Lady Macbeth is dominant. Her conscience is thoroughly repressed – that is, like Richard she does not know that it exists – and she has not the imagination to realise either the horror of evil or the probable consequences of murdering the king. These are the lineaments of bravery. Macbeth, on the other hand, is dependent and hesitating, because his vivid imagination and his active conscience make the decision to do evil very nearly impossible, and immediately after it is done drive him almost to distraction with fear and shame. At the end, Macbeth has 'supp'd full with horrors' and has learned by 'hard use' to contemplate them with indifference; his imagination is dead and his conscience hardly speaks. Lady Macbeth, however, is tormented by guilt and remorse to the point of suicide. Virtue repressed – virtue which she thought weakness – takes vengeance upon her. She who has thought that she could dash her baby's brains out finds that she cannot kill an old man because he resembles her father and that she feels so strongly for that old man and for a murdered lady that she cannot cleanse herself of their blood or keep them out of her dreams. Throughout all the period after the murder of Duncan both she and Macbeth suffer bitter remorse, but she suffers in silence and, as before the murder, is solicitous only for him.

> LADY MACBETH: Nought's had, all's spent,
> Where our desire is got without content:
> 'Tis safer to be that which we destroy,
> Than by destruction dwell in doubtful joy.
>
> (*Enter* Macbeth)
>
> How now, my Lord? why do you keep alone,
> Of sorriest fancies your companions making,
> Using those thoughts, which should indeed have died
> With them they think on?   (III. ii. 4–11)

He, on the other hand dwells on his own suffering:

> O! full of scorpions is my mind, dear wife!

Until after the murder of Banquo, however, the bond between them remains tender and strong:

> LADY MACBETH: Come on:
> Gentle my Lord, sleek o'er your rugged looks;
> Be bright and jovial among your guests tonight
> MACBETH: So shall I, Love; and so, I pray, be you.

There is all the tenderness of shared suffering and mutual pity in these lines, as in their first endearments there was the shared hope. But the sharing is to end: Macbeth does not confide to her his secret intention to murder Banquo:

> Be innocent of the knowledge, dearest chuck
> Till thou applaud the deed.

And she can only marvel at hearing from him strange words she does not understand. After the murder of Banquo they still appear at first a perfect team as they pronounce the welcome to the guests, and Lady Macbeth is his 'sweet remembrancer' when anxiety makes him forget to 'give the cheer' to his guests. When the ghost appears, Lady Macbeth is at his side trying to brace his courage by the sharp rebuke that was once so effective in moving him to a determined purpose; but we soon realise that he is hardly conscious of her presence. There is very great pathos in the quiet moments after the 'good meeting' has been broken 'with most admired disorder'. It is as if, after the expenditure of all her strength in his behalf, a great weariness falls upon Lady Macbeth. This is conveyed in two brief replies to questions which Macbeth addresses to her in the midst of broodings that are almost soliloquies:

> What is the night?
> LADY MACBETH: Almost at odds with morning, which is which.
> MACBETH: How say'st thou, that Macduff denies his person
>   At our great bidding?
> LADY MACBETH: Did you send to him, Sir?
>   (III. iv. 125–8)

But Macbeth is brooding deeply on his own fears and upon a new resolve. He hardly seems aware of her presence, but she listens to his broodings and in one single line expresses all her care for him, while the burden of her own suffering cannot be shared:

> You lack the season of all natures, sleep.

He replies to her:

> Come, we'll to sleep.

but his next word is about himself – and it is the resolve to harden himself by further dreadful deeds. The bond is breaking between them, or rather withering on Macbeth's part. We do not see them together again, but when we next see Macbeth he has lost all power of tender feeling. Not so Lady Macbeth! When next we see her the close pent-up guilts rive their concealing continents as she walks in her sleep and relives her experience in nightmare. Even here, apart from the overwhelming and inescapable guilt and remorse, her predominant emotion is solicitude for her husband, still expressed in bracing rebuke. To this are now added agonising regrets that she and her husband have, putting it euphemistically, felt no solicitude for Duncan and Lady Macduff, either in love or in duty. It is this awareness of others that gives pathos to this dramatic re-enactment of their agonies of guilt and fills the audience with tragic pity and fear rather than with mere triumph over a 'fiend-like queen'. She 'did not know what she was doing' when she tried to 'un-sex' herself and dispel all 'compunctious visitings of nature'. Her violated nature, whose disposition was and still is towards love, now reasserts itself to her infinite suffering, self-condemnation and finally self-destruction. Lady Macbeth's tragedy is the waste of love.

We have seen that, unlike Lady Macbeth, Macbeth does know, in at least three senses of the word, what he is doing when he decides to murder Duncan. The divided conscience and the implications of moral choice are yet more fully explored by Shakespeare in the soliloquy of Macbeth at the very point of decision on the night of the murder:

> If it were done, when 'tis done, then 'twere well
> It were done quickly: if th' assassination
> Could trammel up the consequence, and catch
> With his surcease success; that but this blow
> Might be the be-all and the end-all – here,
> But here, upon this bank and shoal of time,
> We'd jump the life to come – But in these cases,
> We still have judgement here; that we but teach
> Bloody instructions, which, being taught, return
> To plague th' inventor: this even-handed Justice
> Commends th' ingredience of our poison'd chalice

To our own lips. He's here in double trust:
First, as I am his kinsman and his subject,
Strong both against the deed; then, as his host,
Who should against his murtherer shut the door,
Not bear the knife myself. Besides, this Duncan
Hath borne his faculties so meek, hath been
So clear in his great office, that his virtues
Will plead like angels, trumpet-tongu'd, against
The deep damnation of his taking-off;
And Pity, like a naked new-born babe,
Striding the blast, or heaven's Cherubins, hors'd
Upon the sightless couriers of the air,
Shall blow the horrid deed in every eye,
That tears shall drown the wind. – I have no spur
To prick the sides of my intent, but only
Vaulting ambition, which o'erleaps itself
And falls on th' other –

Enter Lady Macbeth   (I. vii. 1–28)

As in the soliloquy examined earlier, we see here the form and
grammar of argument suggesting rational thought. At the same
time, nothing could suggest the wish and the fear, the tension
between urgency and indecision, more effectively than the
rhythm and grammatical shape of the opening lines. He speaks
boldly, as if he would risk eternity for the crown, but he
hesitates in fear of more immediate retribution. If this hesitation is cowardice, it is also prudence and, in so far as it shows
a realistic grasp of the nature of things, it is wisdom. The
subsequent course of events confirms the existence of a moral
'law' by which an evil choice does bring evil consequences upon
the chooser – not only the consequences that Macbeth appears
to be thinking of here, but the inner consequences of moral,
emotional and spiritual destruction. Richard would have
despised Macbeth for hesitating to take the risk of retribution
in this life or any other. So does Lady Macbeth in the ensuing
lines. We may approve his wisdom or condemn his fear, or both;
but after line 12 a very different motivation appears and we see
at work what most of us would call a good conscience or a
better nature. For five lines Macbeth thinks only of the bonds
that bind him to Duncan and the obligations that a noble host

and a loyal kinsman and subject would fulfil. Here there is no threat, only the attraction of love and duty. Not that there is any sign of personal affection: that is not the meaning of 'love' in this context. Duty is the formal aspect of love, expressing co-oper-ation and respect within a harmonious social framework – that is how Shakespeare normally uses the word, and the word 'love' often appears with it in the plays to emphasise the strength of the bond. Macbeth's words about Duncan show that he is aware of the bond and values it. Here is the love-conscience working, but without strong feeling for the individual person.

But Macbeth's awareness is wider and deeper than this. Contemplating Duncan's great virtues as a man and as a king, and showing his intense appreciation of them by the degree adverbs, he sees them, and his own projected crime in the context, not of a particular act alone, nor of society merely, but of the universe; and he, like the universe in his imagination, overflows with pity. The pity and the tears are in Macbeth, and so are the angels that plead against the murder: this is *his* vision, and it is decisive:

> We will proceed no further in this business: (I. vii. 31)

Macbeth's conscience, allowing the admixture of selfish fear, may not be perfect, but if the function of conscience is to guide and direct us beyond immediate interest to that 'long-term desire to remain on good terms with others' and beyond that to the achievement or even the preservation of a harmonious order in the universe, then Macbeth's conscience is of a high order and we might well weep with him at the thought of a deed that would run counter to it and bring so much unhappiness.

Very sadly, however, the words in which he first rejects the idea of murder are regretful and indecisive:

> I have no spur
> To prick the sides of my intent,

and it is as if he despises himself for his failing ambition. Lady Macbeth enters: she will be the spur. In the face of her heroic malignity, his conscience is silenced and he makes his feeblest and most contemptible objection:

FULL CIRCLE

If we should fail?

With the disorganisation of his own moral being, he does indeed show the cowardice that Lady Macbeth has accused him of. Here, as earlier, he seems vulnerable to her suggestion. His own kind of courage is now to be replaced by a new kind infused into him by her, which will destroy them both.

> I dare do all that may become a man
> Who dares do more, is none.

gives way to

> I am settled, and bend up
> Each corporal agent to this terrible feat.
> Away, and mock the time with fairest show;
> False face must hide what the false heart doth know.
>
> (I. vii. 80–3)

Rationally, he knows that murder is unmanly and that he will be less than man if he commits it, but lust for 'the ornament of life', fear to be called a coward, and admiration of an intrepid woman overcome both reason and conscience, and he takes his first decisive step on the road to misery and damnation.

His conscience, however, is not silenced. On the contrary it troubles him with added power and in a new way. The attractions of goodness now disappear and only the warning and the threat remain. We have seen the link between imagination and conscience. The horrors of murder that Macbeth formerly saw with the mind's eye now materialise before him in the shape of an 'air drawn dagger' that seems to lead him to Duncan's chamber. It does not lead him: it marshals him the way that he is going. It does not even speed him there, for he awaits the signal to approach the chamber. But, on its blade and dudgeon, gouts of blood warn him that he will be one with murderers and ravishers and the powers of evil. This, the final warning, is by its visual manifestation more vivid than previous ones; but, being a mere threat it is weaker in its effect. The vision of Pity and the attraction of goodness almost deterred him; this horror he sweeps aside contemptuously.

After the deed is done, the conscience that gave warning

against cruel deeds and appealed on behalf of love and duty changes again. Now it becomes the terrible accuser: it condemns and punishes with remorse and guilt, and also with fear of the 'even-handed Justice'. Now Macbeth sleeps in the affliction of terrible dreams that shake him nightly; hands reach from the air to pluck out his eyes, for he has looked on the murdered king; a voice cries 'sleep no more', for he has murdered one who slept; each night, 'on the torture of the mind' he lies 'in restless ecstasy'. The rejected conscience takes vengeance. At the same time, the conscience once rejected is more easily rejected a second time. As Richard suspects his subjects, so Macbeth suspects Banquo. Banquo is murdered – by hired murderers: there is a degeneration even in forms of murder. But Macbeth's visualising conscience is still strong. From his royal banquet one guest is absent. He pays an ironic compliment:

> Here had we now our country's honour roof'd,
> Were the grac'd person of our Banquo present;
>
> (III. iv. 39–40)

At the name, Banquo's ghost appears 'with twenty trenched gashes on his head'. Macbeth is 'quite unmanned' and betrays himself before his guests. Yet, when the ghost disappears, he tries to recover himself with the same vaunting irony. At once the ghost is present again. We know Macbeth as one who has only to think of an abomination to see it. This is the third and last of the visible projections of his conscience, and this time the audience see it too. For Shakespeare's audience this would not be merely a psychological phenomenon: they did not think – and we should be foolish to be confident – that conscience has no origins beyond the mind of man. However that may be, the ghost confirms Macbeth's vision of the angels pleading trumpet-tongued against the murder of Duncan: Macbeth has violated the universal order. Just before the murder of Banquo he has uttered the first of his three invocations of chaos, blood-curdling to Shakespeare's contemporaries:

> But let the frame of things disjoint, both the worlds suffer,
> Ere we will eat our meal in fear, and sleep

> In the affliction of these terrible dreams,
> That shake us nightly.   (III. ii. 16–19)

Ghosts presage disjointing of the frame of things. An audience that feared ghosts and feared chaos, and grasped the link between the two, would be drawn into Macbeth's experience, and feel the power of the accusing conscience, by seeing the apparition that he sees but is not seen by others.

Macbeth can no longer endure the torment of conscience and the fear that 'blood will have blood', his blood. He makes his second major choice and takes an even more firm step down what the Porter euphemistically calls 'the primrose path to the everlasting bonfire'. There have been no primroses on Macbeth's path, and now there is nothing to gain but escape from remorse and escape from the vivid knowledge of his true situation. Twice before, we have been with him in states of acute indecision, living through the experience of choice. In the first he did not choose, but hoped the choice would be made for him (I. iv. 144–5). In the second he made the decision that Lady Macbeth persuaded him to reverse (I. vii. 31). In each, we were with him, hesitating before the act of choice. After Banquo's ghost has disappeared and the banquet has ended in disorder we are taken again into his thoughts for, though Lady Macbeth is present, he seems not to be addressing her but brooding upon his situation. He sees himself standing deep in a river of blood. Should he continue to wade across, or not? This time the decision comes *before* the image of division, and the image is given as the reason for the choice that has already been made. He has decided that conscience must be killed: there must be no hesitation about doing wrong or injuring others:

> For mine own good
> All causes shall give way: I am in blood
> Stepp'd in so far, that, should I wade no more,
> Returning were as tedious as go o'er.
>
> (III. iv. 135–8)

This assessment of the situation is more consistent with his wish than with reality. His subsequent development, if that is the word, will show that he is not in a river or a pond, but in a sea.

There is no wading through to the other side: he will be engulfed. The image of a possible return is a reminder of the only true way to come to terms with his conscience, namely to repent, to relinquish his crown and all the effects for which he did the murder.[1] Externally the penalties would be severe, but the inner life would be redeemed. The possibility is there, but he chooses a different way to quieten the conscience, namely 'by custom of fell deeds':[2]

> My strange and self-abuse
> Is the initiate fear, that wants hard use:
> We are yet but young in deed.   (III. iv. 141–3)

Now Scotland will become a place where

> Each new morn
> New widows howl, new orphans cry: new sorrows
> Strike heaven on the face.   (IV. iii. 4–6)

The innocent Lady Macduff and her children will be slaughtered so that Macbeth may sleep. But what now happens to Macbeth is what he partly foresaw would happen:

> this even-handed Justice
> Commends the ingredience of our poison'd chalice
> To our own lips.

The consequences of his evil choice are first and most terribly experienced within himself.

In *Richard III* there is no such exploration of the experience of conscience and of choice as we have observed it here in *Macbeth*: Richard is an unhesitating sinner. The theme of retribution, however, is common to both plays. In each, usurpation and murder bring the kingdom near to chaos. In each, the usurper is killed by the forces that his own evil deed has roused against him, and peace is restored only after his death. In each, the protagonist suffers the consequences of his evil within himself. The difference lies in the depth to which the inner life is explored.

[1] Cf. Claudius (*Hamlet*: III. iii. 54).
[2] *Julius Caesar*: III. i. 270.

The full effect of inner changes for the worse, brought about by the denial of conscience and the choice of evil can be felt in Macbeth so much more strongly because he is not a villain from the start. He is not, like Richard, a man denied the experience of love and duty; and he is highly honoured by 'all sorts of people'. Though a man of ruthless boldness in fight, he is capable of tenderness and pity and he desires a good conscience and a stainless reputation. All this we have seen. Finer feeling and imaginative realisation strive in him against the murder of Duncan. That murder being committed, the next comes more easily, and the next. At first the powers of evil have to visit Macbeth and urge him on to the evil he has already contemplated or to which his ambition predisposes him; but, after the appearance of Banquo's ghost, he does what Lady Macbeth did at the very first: he seeks the powers of evil, calls upon the witches. The Macbeth who visits the witches of his own free will is already a changed man; there is a wildness and a domineering violence in his speech that were not heard before the appearance of Banquo's ghost, and resemble more his rages in Dunsinane castle during the final war, when it is said of him:

> Who then shall blame
> His pester'd senses to recoil and start,
> When all that is within him does condemn
> Itself, for being there? (V. ii. 22–5)

All *consciousness* of inner conflict has gone, but we have the sense of fearful tensions at play beneath the surface. Yet, after he has seen the apparitions from the witches' cauldron and heard the reassuring (but deceptive) prophecies which convince him that he bears a charmed life, he sees 'no more sights' and is devoid of fear and remorse. No longer does he hesitate to do evil – though he cannot decide whether to put his armour on, and his servants scurry hither and thither in obedience to his violent commands and countermands. None serve him now but 'constrained things, whose hearts are absent'. The honour that he so coveted he must not look to have, nor other rewards of age that might well have been his:

I have liv'd long enough: my way of life
Is fall'n into the sere, the yellow leaf;
And that which should accompany old age,
As honour, love, obedience, troops of friends,
I must not look to have; but in their stead,
Curses, not loud, but deep, mouth-honour, breath,
Which the poor heart would fain deny, and dare not.

(V. iii. 22–8)

The language in which he requests the Doctor to cure Lady Macbeth gives the impression that he himself still knows what it is to suffer from 'a mind diseased' and to bear in the memory 'a rooted sorrow'; but his ungovernable rages alternating with black despair mark the unbalanced mind in which self-awareness is fitful and uncertain.

The final state of mind of one who has made Macbeth's choices and whose conscience has been killed by the 'hard use' of evil deeds is presented in his famous speech on the meaninglessness of life. A cry of women is heard, and we are reminded how the knocking at the gate startled him on the night of Duncan's murder. Now, 'direness', familiar to his slaughterous thoughts, cannot once start him. The queen is dead. Macbeth's comment is

She should have died hereafter:
There would have been a time for such a word –

These terrible words express at once his need to sorrow for another and the horror of his incapacity to do so. They recall a bond that once existed and a shared dream that has not been realised; but neither here nor in the preceding or ensuing lines does Shakespeare give Macbeth one word of tendernesss. In the scorched earth of his mind, love cannot revive: it is his own disappointments on which he dwells, and his bitter contempt for a life that has no hope, no joy, no meaning for him. To Cleopatra, on the death of Antony, 'All's but naught' and 'there is nothing left remarkable beneath the visiting moon'; but Cleopatra forgets herself in thoughts of Antony, and learns love as she has not known it before. Shakespeare fills her speeches with him both at his death and ever afterwards. From Macbeth's speeches, on the other hand, Lady Macbeth is most dreadfully absent. Their final separation is the signal for an outburst, not of grief, but of cynicism, in which his private chagrin is inflated to a solemn affirmation of the worthlessness of life in general:

> Tomorrow, and tomorrow, and tomorrow,
> Creeps in this petty pace from day to day,
> To the last syllable of recorded time;
> And all our yesterdays have lighted fools
> The way to dusty death. Out, out, brief candle!
> Life's but a walking shadow; a poor player,
> That struts and frets his hour upon the stage,
> And then is heard no more: it is a tale
> Told by an idiot, full of sound and fury,
> Signifying nothing.
>
> (V. v. 19–28)

The passage is preceded by a speech of angry defiance; it is followed by a scene of desperate fury. The one who struts and frets and whose life has been full of sound and fury and lunatic violence is Macbeth. The world Macbeth sees and condemns is a projection of himself. His words describe, not the external world or the nature of man, but the last state of one who has lived the life Macbeth has lived and made the choices Macbeth has made. Shakespeare is observing a process – a process human beings have a disposition to ignore. Either, like Lady Macbeth, we lack the imagination to foresee the consequences of evil; or, like Macbeth, we put aside the knowledge. But the process is ineluctable.

Cynicism is a mode of self-defence. If one blames the world, or the nature of man, one need not blame oneself. If one makes a general exaggeration of faults, either in the world or in oneself, one can avoid a true assessment of oneself. One may then, like Jacques or Timon, maintain a pose of superiority even while viewing human nature with *defensive* contempt. Every cynic has, in one form or another, made Macbeth's choice,

> For mine own good,
> All causes shall give way.

He is a disappointed egoist, often one, like Timon of Athens, whose egoism has been disguised as altruism till the counterfeit

144

altruism has ceased to bring in immediately pleasing returns. Cynicism breeds equally in the disappointed idealist and the thwarted opportunist. Macbeth is something of both, and his feeling that life is meaningless is the more intense.

To ensure that we continue to feel Macbeth's fate as to some extent our own, Shakespeare retains our sympathy for him, partly by his desperate bravery to the last, partly by pity as the witches' prophecies fail him, but much more by one moment in which his bravery falters, but his almost obliterated conscience revives in a genuinely altruistic impulse. He meets Macduff, whose family he has slaughtered:

> Of all men else I have avoided thee:
> But get thee back, my soul is too much charg'd
> With blood of thine already.   (V. viii. 4–6)

This and his magnificence preserve a sense of his worth and preclude any acceptance of his own assertion that life means nothing. What Macbeth might have been, another man might be; for different choices can be made. The choice that Macbeth has made leads to despair; but he very nearly made the opposite choice, and here at the end is the voice of the conscience that might have saved him and created happiness through love and duty.

Macbeth has chosen murder, but the life has gone out of *him*. He has practised cruelty and has cultivated indifference, and love has died in him. He has violated the bonds of order, and he himself has become a chaos. He has committed moral suicide, and this one last altruistic impulse is the final gush of his life-blood. All things but one that gave meaning to his life he has annihilated; that one is his dream of the secure enjoyment of 'solely sovereign sway and masterdom'. That dream having proved an illusion, he dismisses life as 'signifying nothing'. But he does not commit suicide:

> Why should I play the Roman fool, and die
> On mine own sword? whiles I see lives, the gashes
> Do better upon them.   (V. viii. 1–3)

His life continues to mean destruction and murder. Yet the

pang of conscience immediately follows these words and reminds us how love and duty once attracted him. His life, that has lost meaning for him, is profoundly meaningful to us.

Macbeth reads like a dramatic exposition of two sayings from Scripture. One is St. Paul's dark summary of the moral law:

> For the wages of sin is death.

The other is in the words of Jesus:

> For whosoever will save his life shall lose it.

But neither of these sayings is complete, and each of them implies its sequel. St. Paul continues:

> but the gift of God is eternal life.

The whole range of the passage from Matthew's gospel reads:

> For whosoever will save his life shall lose it: and whosoever will lose his life for my sake shall find it.
> For what is a man profited, if he shall gain the whole world, and lose his own soul?

Like both these sayings, *Macbeth* affirms the worth of the human soul, and by its terrifying imitation of despair, arouses hope and a longing for abundant life. The hope is encouraged by the spectacle of Macbeth's grandeur – though ruined – and the realisation of human potential conveyed by this and the reappearance of a conscience that could not quite be killed. And hope ends the play, with the return of the rightful king and the beginning of a new order which is also the recovery of the old order.

The question whether Shakespeare intended to deliver a moral exhortation or preach a Christian sermon through the implications of this play is not so easy to answer as was once assumed.

The last statement of the recurring theme that first appeared in the opening scene with 'Fair is foul and foul is fair' has the *form* of a 'moral' pronounced by one who, above all others, should know:

And be these juggling fiends no more believ'd,
That palter with us in a double sense;
That keep the word of promise to our ear,
And break it to our hope.   (V. viii. 19–22)

Though its meaning is not to be summed up by this or any other single quotation, the play is certainly a representation of what happens when a man and a woman hearken to the promises of the 'Fiend'. Shakespeare compels us to identify with that man and woman, even though they be mightier, more heroic, more influential than we. The deeds they do, we probably will not do; but the choice they make we have often made, and may make again. It is true that the play delineates a process; it would be difficult to maintain that it does not also offer an evaluation. An evaluation of a process in which I see myself an actor does in practice imply a prescription or prescriptions.

It will be observed that the sayings of Jesus and St. Paul, quoted above, are not exhortatory in their form: each, whether true or false, is in the form of description, or statement of fact, comparable to 'He who puts his finger in the fire will get it burnt'. The second premise, 'I do not want my finger burnt', or, in the case of *Macbeth* and the two scriptural sayings, 'I do not want to suffer death or despair, or meaninglessness, or an emotional and spiritual desert' can be taken for granted either in this or in its positive form, 'I want my finger painless and healthy' or 'I want life and hope and significance and a "well of water springing up into eternal life"'. The conclusion follows: 'I must not put my finger in the fire', 'I must not live as Macbeth lived' – and so forth. Exhortation, then, is implicit. In the case of the scriptural sayings, everyone would assume this. *Macbeth* has a moral point. It says, 'These are the ways to misery; you do not want misery; so avoid these ways;' or, 'There are numerous indications in the play of a road to happiness that Macbeth did not follow; you want happiness; so take the road Macbeth did not take.'

However, it may be objected, the so-called 'moral' of a play or story may be really a counsel of prudence, not a statement about right and wrong about moral good and moral evil. If the exhortation to avoid Macbeth's ways and follow those he rejected is basically an appeal to our self-interest (because we want happiness, not misery) then it is a counsel of prudence and not strictly a moral exhortation at all, it might be asserted.

The first part of the answer to this is that the play, like the passages from Jesus and St. Paul, does not acknowledge the distinction. In studying the play, we have observed in Macbeth different and conflicting forms of self-interest. Egoism, or selfishness is pleasing oneself in the comparatively short term or in a narrow context and thus regardless of the interests of others. Altruism or unselfishness is pleasing oneself by having regard to the long term and the universal context, and thus of the interests of others, and ultimately of all. In Shakespeare's plays the first is both condemned as bad, at least in many of its forms, and seen to lead to unhappy endings in most, perhaps in all, of its forms. Altruism is both approved and seen to be the means to happiness. We have observed much of the language and the imagery that stigmatises Macbeth's egoism as evil and his altruism as good. This moral approval and condemnation is embodied in a metaphysic expressed in images of a universe in which evil and unhappiness are inseparable and both are pleaded against by angels. The philosopher's distinction between moral and prudential considerations would appear to be inapplicable to Macbeth unless the word 'prudential' be taken to mean 'prudent in the short run or in a narrow context' (i.e. expedient) and 'moral' taken to mean 'prudent in the long run or in a universal context'. Indeed, Shakespeare's plays *as a whole* seem to demonstrate that what is good is also generally advantageous even in the short run and in the individual life; and *Macbeth* shows the destructiveness of evil within the nature of the one who does evil. A Macbeth will bring suffering upon the innocent and the good; a Prospero will save the wicked from the destruction that would otherwise fall upon them; but this does not alter the general Shakespearean picture of the moral and natural order, or the general impression that virtue pays and vice does not.

The second part of the reply to the assertion that in so far as *Macbeth* is exhortatory it urges counsels of prudence, not moral imperatives, would involve a discussion of whether moral prescriptions are not always in some sense prudential. This, however, is not necessary for our purpose, which is to observe that Shakespeare's plays, like the Sermon on the Mount, link goodness with happiness and evil with misery inextricably, and that all these are operative within a context of order and disorder in which the second is evil but subordinate to the first and capable, like Satan, of being exploited to good ends, as in the regeneration of King Lear. That order prevails in *Macbeth* has been obvious since Bradley pointed it out, but from the disruption in the play no good issues. This emphasises how much it is in man's interest to subserve the universal order; and that is also his moral duty.

CHAPTER EIGHT

Both Law and Impulse

Three years she grew in sun and shower,
Then Nature said, 'A lovelier flower
On earth was never sown;
This child I to myself will take
She shall be mine and I will make
A Lady of my own.

Myself will to my darling be
Both law and impulse: and with me
The Girl in rock and plain,
In earth and heaven, in glade and bower,
Shall feel an overseeing power
To kindle or restrain.'[1]

In *Richard III*, Clarence, Edward IV and the Second Murderer
are all, like Richard himself, punished by their consciences.
Unlike Richard, however, each of these is influenced by his
conscience for the better. Clarence prays:

O God! If my deep prayers cannot appease thee,
But thou wilt be aveng'd on my misdeeds,
Yet execute Thy wrath in me alone;

(*Richard III*: I. iv. 69–71)

The Second Murderer refuses his fee for the murder. Edward
really tries to change and to put right some of the wrongs he has
done: he would reconcile his warring kindred and establish a
harmonious royal household for the good of the kingdom, but
he is too late and too weak an adversary for Richard, who disrupts all harmony. By these means and others Shakespeare keeps
our minds on the power of conscience even while Richard still
seems impervious to it. Richard flouts conscience, but we are
being reminded that conscience cannot be flouted with im-

[1] Wordsworth: *Lyrical Ballads*.

punity. At the same time we are given hints of a conscience that can do more than threaten, accuse and punish. Hints only however; for images of the mature conscience we have to look in later plays – including *Macbeth*, where we have already observed the positive conscience that almost saves the hero by directing him towards love and duty.

'Conscience' is another chameleon word and it is necessary to pause and consider ways of using it. Hitherto we have employed it to mean that within us which prompts us to do and to be right – 'right' meaning that which is consistent with love and duty, on the personal, social and universal levels. In this sense, conscience is always beneficent, even when it terrifies or punishes; for it directs human beings to "subserve the universal order", where their interests as well as their moral duties lie. If Macbeth had obeyed his conscience, even on the final battlefield, he would have changed; repentance would have been an affirmation of the worth of human life; and, like the traitor Thane of Cawdor, he would have found meaning in his own life, even at the point of death:

> but I have spoke
> With one that saw him die: who did report,
> That very frankly he confess'd his treasons,
> Implor'd your Highness' pardon, and set forth
> A deep repentance. Nothing in his life
> Became him like the leaving it: he died
> As one that had been studied in his death,
> To throw away the dearest thing he ow'd,
> As 'twere a careless trifle.   (I. iv. 3–11)

Cawdor, having re-entered the social and universal order by acknowledging his error before his king and his God, can perform his final act of life with the nobility, the dignity and even something of the 'honour' that Macbeth dreamed of and lost.

Conscience, in this sense of the word, Richard has contemptuously rejected, but we have noticed the deep division of his mind. We have seen how anxious he is in every soliloquy to demonstrate that he *ought* to do the things and be the person everyone else considers wicked. If we think of conscience, not as that which directs us to right, but that which directs to what we *think or feel* is right, then we observe in Richard two consciences. According to the one, he ought to crush feeble tenderness and importunate duty and take just reprisals against a world that has cursed and tormented him; only thus can he preserve his dignity. According to the other, he ought to be loving and dutiful, merciful and generous. The origin of the second conscience we have already observed. When he boasts,

> I do the wrong, and first begin to brawl.
> The secret mischiefs that I set abroach
> I lay unto the grievous charge of others.
>
> (I. iii. 324–6)

he is describing as 'wrong' the acts that his mother would condemn. His other conscience works within a different frame:

> For I have often heard my mother say
> I came into the world with my legs forward.
> Had I not reason, think ye, to make haste
> And seek their ruin that usurp't our right?
> (*Henry VI: Part III:* V. vi. 70–3)

He is born into a family whose 'right' is power, and his 'duty' is to destroy its enemies, but he personally is the one who leaps into the world to fulfil that duty. The macabre jest is proved by his life to be in deadly earnest, and the condemnation by his mother, glanced at in these lines, where she speaks of his monstrous birth, pursues him through life. Hers is the accusing finger, and when, after his nightmare, his resolution wavers, he is on the point of capitulating to the conscience that derives from her, the conscience that would have him 'die a good old man'. Considered as a betrayal of the other conscience, which urges him to be ruthless, not now for his family's 'honour', but for his own power, this temporary defeat by his mother's values shows, as he says, a loss of courage. But he recovers – and dies under her curse.

Shakespeare's use of Richard's mother as a symbol of what most of us would consider the 'good' conscience by which he is condemned seems natural. But his mother's rejection of him makes his rejection of her, and of the conscience she is associated with, all the more credible. What is extremely striking is the genealogy of that other conscience, the conscience he obeys. Shakespeare, in creating it, is linking together the last three plays of the tetralogy, and gives us another remarkable example of the chiming of his artistic and psychological intuitions. In all three plays in which Richard appears, there is only one person of whom he ever speaks with genuine affection and praise. That is the man whose name he proudly bears, his father, Richard Duke of York:

> EDWARD: How fares my brother? Why is he so sad?
> RICHARD: I cannot joy until I be resolv'd
>   Where our right valiant father is become.
>   I saw him in the battle range about,
>   And watch'd him how he singled Clifford forth.
>   Methought he bore him in the thickest troop
>   As doth a lion in a herd of neat;
>   Or as a bear, encompass'd round with dogs,
>   Who having pinch'd a few and made them cry,
>   The rest stand all aloof and bark at him.
>   So far'd our father with his enemies;
>   So fled his enemies my warlike father.
>   Methinks 'tis prize enough to be his son.
>   (*Henry VI, Part III:* II. i. 8–20)

When the news comes that York is slain, Edward weeps. Richard cannot:

> I cannot weep; for all my body's moisture
> Scarce serves to quench my furnace-burning heart:
> Nor can my tongue unload my heart's great burden,
>   (II. i. 79–81)

The fires of pride as well as of grief are burning in Richard, but pride or grief or vengeance, the passion binds him to his father, both in likeness and in a bond of feeling:

> Richard, I bear thy name; I'll venge thy death,
>   Or die renowned by attempting it.

We have already observed the likeness between Richard and his father, York, as it appears in *Henry VI, Part II* (see p. 109 ff).

The bloodlust and vengefulness in Richard's speeches here are as much a sign of the bond between them as the affection, admiration and grief; for it mirrors his father's ruthlessness. Where a son takes his stamp so strongly from the father, he will often go more than a step beyond his father. In a previous scene Richard has identified himself with his father in the lust for the crown, and Richard's lust, even though on his father's behalf, has appeared stronger than York's. Richard demonstrates how York may break his oath of fealty without being forsworn. York listens, as Richard's mother would never have listened:

> An oath is of no moment, being not took
> Before a true and lawful magistrate
> That hath authority over him that swears.
> Henry had none, but did usurp the place;
> Then, seeing 'twas he that made you to depose,
> Your oath, my lord, is vain and frivolous.
> Therefore to arms. And, father, do but think
> How sweet a thing it is to wear a crown,
> Within whose circuit is Elysium
> And all that poets feign of bliss and joy.
>
> *(Hen. VI, Pt. III:* I. ii. 22–31)

Richard later urges his brother Edward to the throne, but in very different terms. A comparison reveals that Richard's emphasis is still upon his father: Edward should rule to prove he is his father's son:

> Nay, if thou be that princely eagle's bird,
> Show thy descent by gazing 'gainst the sun:
> For chair and dukedom, throne and kingdom say;
> Either that is thine, or else thou wert not his.
>
> (II. i. 91–4)

The identification of Richard with his father, who struck ruthlessly for the throne, will not be complete till Richard himself is on the throne. The artistic pattern shaping here in preparation for *Richard III* is also one half of the psychological pattern of what is sometimes called the internalisation or introjection of parental attitudes in the formation of conscience. Here we see the original, in the father he loved and admired, of the conscience that Richard *did* obey, and had to defend against the other conscience which was associated with his detested mother. Shakespeare maintains the contrast even to the point where Richard is made to suggest his mother's infidelity to his father during the French wars: all that his mother stands for is unfaithful to all that his father stood for. Observing this element in the pattern of the tetralogy, we are perhaps touching upon some of the less obvious reasons why we sympathise with Richard when reason condemns him: we see the father and the father's aspirations in the son; we *feel* the mother's rejection and share, or sympathise with, Richard's sense of grievance.

We have seen that York has something of the unreflecting, unhesitating, conscienceless lust of the infant in that unorganised state when there are only absorbing needs and ungovernable impulses, all self-centred (p. 109). The child at this stage cannot distinguish tasty from distasteful, pleasing from unpleasing, right from wrong, *till after the event*. We have seen from *Macbeth* that a characteristic of evil is that, before the event, it looks desirable, may even 'wear the brows of grace'; only after evil has been done is its hideous quality revealed. On this showing, sin is immaturity, the infant's incapacity to see beyond immediate sensations and desires. A similar observation was made in our study of Lear. In this sense Richard is one stage more mature than his father, maturity being a state in which individual needs and impulses are governed and organised in such a way that they do not destroy the lusting individual himself and in such a way that harmonious relations with one's fellows are possible. Alternatively we might say that maturity is a condition in which altruistic drives, whether rational, emotional or instinctual, predominate over ego-centric drives, but within a harmonious and integrative process, not by repression. This way of putting it may bring to mind the myth of God and Satan, or Shakespeare's myth of *The Tempest*. In succeeding chapters, we shall observe other images of it from Shakespeare's work. Both York and Richard are destroyed by their ungovernable lusts, but we see the derivation of Richard's lusts, and he is driven towards their satisfaction not merely by native impulse but by a conscience. His state is primitive, but less primitive than his father's.

This conscience that impels Richard towards the throne has at least this merit, that it is a positive drive. Richard aspires to the throne and wreaks vengeance upon enemies, not merely because it would seem wrong to do otherwise, but because his 'right' and 'reason' demand that he do thus. The emphasis is on the drive, not on any deterrent element. With the conscience that condemns and punishes, the reverse is the case.

A modern myth of conscience runs somewhat as follows. Parents' prescriptions and prohibitions are internalised by the child, not remembered, but absorbed into unconscious experience and operating 'inside' yet as if they had their origins not in other people but in some mysterious other source which, though 'without', speaks from 'within'. Parental prescriptions and prohibitions, even if for the child's protection, necessarily run counter to his unbridled lusts and impulses. Frustration follows and rage: he would murder his mother and father, who stand in his way. But then mother and father will be gone, and where will he be? Or perhaps they will retaliate and destroy him. Rage, as he knows it, is an ungovernable destructive passion, and his parents' anger or irritation or even mild disapproval may seem to him a world-destroying threat. This is intolerable; to avoid it he must follow the prescription and obey the prohibition. When he does not, even in the absence of the parent, he experiences the terror: the murderous parent, too terrible for conscious contemplation, has slipped into his unconscious and become the commanding, threatening, punishing conscience.

This description of our experience of conscience commands immediate assent as at least part of the truth, and we are not surprised to find the shapes and some of the complexities of it represented in Shakespeare's plays. The virtue that Richard rejects and the innocence that he injures are embodied in his mother and his sister-in-law, Queen Elizabeth. Together they lay curses on him. Henry's queen, Margaret, becomes in *Richard III* the strange and powerful figure of avenging Fate. She curses all, but especially Richard. These three mothers in the ritual drama of Act IV, Scene IV, are more disturbing images of the internalised complex of prescription, prohibition and threat than the images of his murdered victims that condemn him in the final dream; and, were it not for the depths that have been touched by the poetry of these women and the rhythmical patterns of their speeches, the ghosts in the last act would seem raw and unsubtle; for though they are several, they speak with one voice, whereas the internalised mother is a complex more subtly represented by the three voices of the tormented mothers in the play.

The internalised father we have observed; and, opposing mother to father, we have spoken of two consciences. Whereas Macbeth suffers from a divided mind but has a single and fairly highly developed conscience, Richard has two consciences but is single-minded in obeying one of them and rejecting the other. However, the conscience he rejects is not presented as one uncomplicated prompting to virtue. Being rejected, it accuses and condemns with three distinct voices, not counting that of Anne and that of the murdered men. Shakespeare's creative imagination, even in a melodrama based on a conventional moral formula, reveals living complexities that the formula blurs.

If we say Richard has a 'bad' conscience, we probably mean that he has hurt his good conscience and it is hurting him. The conscience he derives from his father we should almost certainly call a perverted conscience, if indeed we do not refuse altogether to name it 'conscience'. The Christian church has taught that it is not enough to have a conscience: what is necessary is to have an enlightened conscience. And, in practice, this is the general view. Richard's very attempts to vindicate his actions by an appeal to justice and fair play imply a standard by which the 'conscience' that urges him to ruthless acts is condemned. Richard is an extreme case of a common and popular error: 'Please sir, he hit me first' is a plea unfortunately not confined to *children* who are 'getting their own back'. Fate hit Richard first, and so did people. He wants to retaliate, and we share his impulse to hit back. But when his hitting back injures someone with whom we identify, we blame him for it: that is, we condemn our own revengeful impulse. He – and we – ought not to hit any more. Conscience has thus received training from judgement and experience. In practice all consciences are modified by such processes, and not always for the better. Between them, Polonius and Laertes and Hamlet so pervert the conscience of Ophelia that her innocent love seems a guilty thing, and in her madness she sings of the deed they have accused her of as if acting the part they have cast her for. Lear's conscience, on the other hand, receives a training for the better under the pressure of painful circumstance; that is, Lear becomes aware of the needs of others, and thus of the cruelty of social institutions and customs that make indifference and injustice respectable. 'Training', however, is not the right word; for it suggests that his conscience is taught to act in clearly specified ways. 'Education' is the better word, for Lear's awareness goes beyond his conditioning. To speak of Lear's experience as the education of a conscience – which it is – is to include in the word 'conscience' what some would wish to *ex*clude, namely the moral judgement. Conscience in this sense is something more than impulse or stimulus. The educated conscience makes lightning acts of moral judgement which are based on established habits of reflection on moral issues within a context of social or metaphysical conceptions. Later we shall observe a Shakespearean image of spontaneous altruism. In Viola of *Twelfth Night*, altruism is instinctual; she stands at the opposite pole to York, for though, like him, she acts upon unreflecting impulse, unlike him, she does what a healthy conscience would command. The regulator of her actions is love.

Conscience as a regulator of impulse and of action may be likened to a system of warning lights and directional guides such as traffic signs, which give information about consequences likely to ensue from their observance or non-observance. Its directions may be accepted or rejected. Conscience implies choice, but it does not choose. In so far as it controls or regulates, it does so by guidance or exhortation: it is open to question and subject to choice. However, like the system of traffic signs, though its dictates can be disobeyed, they are felt as legally binding, and to this extent they predispose to particular choices.

The idea of law, part of our dream of order, has great motivating power. In a community, laws prescribe, sanction and deter; but the importance of law for our survival and well-being gives it a driving or restraining force beyond the power of stipulated rewards and punishments. Were it not that the two major elements in the meaning of the word 'law' are normally present and operative in our minds at the same time, laws would be less effective than they are. A rule established by authority invites rebellion unless it is also felt to be an expression of the regularity in the nature of things. We speak of laws of nature or of the physical world, which cannot be broken and which we cannot defy with impunity. A similar concept underlies most of our thinking, whether common sense or 'scientific', about psychology and morals, though here the inconvenience of the idea of causation produces many a shift to avoid its implications. *Macbeth* is about the inexorability of causal law in moral experience, and the deceptions and self-deceptions that obscure it. The idea of God has embraced and related these various concepts of law, and affirms the yet unexplained mystery of the motivating power of the idea of law. Within *The Tempest*, the figure of Prospero has similar force.

As a system of directional guides and descriptive signs, conscience may be thought of as akin to reason, or as a function of reason; as a motivator it is allied to emotion. The conscience of Richard III is compounded of intelligence and hate; even his love of his father (if 'love' is the right word) directs him to hate. A healthy conscience, one that makes for happiness, is compounded of intelligence and love. The blend of love and reason in characters who create happiness we shall consider further. Of these the chief is Prospero, and the nature of conscience is most effectively represented in an image or symbol like that of Prospero, which has equal reference to the psychological, the social and the universal order; for, just as law is not to be adequately described in terms of human communities alone, so conscience is not to be described in terms of the human psyche alone. As the accusing and admonitory conscience, Prospero works through Ariel; but he himself, as we have seen, presides over, and is thus an important element in, the stage spectacle where he, 'on top', represents Destiny and the wrathful powers, while Ariel is the warning voice that demands 'heart-sorrow and a clear life ensuing'. Prospero himself is accusing and admonitory towards Caliban, and the relation between them almost parallels that between Richard and his mother. On the other hand, Ariel is a protector and a guide as well as an accuser; and the staff of Prospero that orders and regulates, yet is broken so that free choices may be made, is as valid an image of conscience as of benevolent political authority or the providence of God. Prospero as the wise and tender parent and Miranda as the loved child present an image that contrasts strongly with that of the young Richard III and his parents. Shakespeare, however, does not explore the origins and development of the love-conscience as he does of the hate-conscience: there is no account of the childhood experiences of a great creative figure in his plays to set over against the childhood experiences of the great destroyer, Richard.

Wordsworth, searching among his childhood memories, as well as among philosophical and psychological theories, to discover the origins of the creative faculties that make him a poet, does give such an account; and Wordsworth's story is a valuable supplement to the myth of conscience related above (see p. 156):

> blest the Babe,
> Nursed in his Mother's arms, who sinks to sleep
> Rocked on his Mother's breast; who with his soul
> Drinks in the feelings of his mother's eye!
> For him in one dear Presence, there exists
> A virtue which irradiates and exalts
> Objects through widest intercourse of sense.
> No outcast he, bewildered and depressed:
> Along his infant veins are interfused
> The gravitation and the filial bond
> Of nature that connect him with the world.
> Is there a flower, to which he points with hand
> Too weak to gather it, already love
> Drawn from Love's purest earthly fount for him
> Hath beautified that flower; already shades

160

Of pity cast from inward tenderness
Do fall around him upon aught that bears
Unsightly marks of violence or harm.[1]

The emphasis here is on the 'gravitation', the strong tendency
to meet and link with others, both people and objects. The
primary need for mother grows into love, and readily extends
to what the mother loves. *In practice* there is no hard and fast
line to be drawn between 'good', meaning pleasant or desirable,
and 'good' meaning 'right' and implying 'ought': for who shall
parcel out experience

by geometric rules
Split like a province into round and square?
Who knows the individual hour in which
His habits were first sown, even as a seed?

(II. 203–7)

Wordsworth shows how the 'slavery to instincts and the urge to
immediate pleasure'[2] may grow into appreciation, contemplation and love. The long-term satisfactions can be intuited, but
they are often so far beyond immediate perception that motivation by 'ought' is required to keep us in pursuit of them.

It is noteworthy that Wordsworth, like Shakespeare in
Macbeth, makes no clear distinction between moral and prudential considerations, not at any rate either in this section of
The Prelude or in *Lyrical Ballads*, where Nature and the language
of the sense (in which 'the grand elementary principle of
pleasure'[3] is specially important) are recognised as the soul of
all his moral being.[4]

In the psychological history of childhood that Wordsworth
gives us, prescription and prohibition are clear and strong, and
the might of an accusing conscience is powerfully realised in one
of his most famous passages, where the threat of it is embodied,
not in the figure of a person and not in an image of disintegration
but in a huge peak, black and huge:

[1] *The Prelude* (1850): (II. 234–51).
[2] Dr. J. Bowlby, op. cit.
[3] Preface to the *Lyrical Ballads*.
[4] 'Lines written above Tintern Abbey'.

161

> the grim shape
> Towered up between me and the stars, and still.
> For so it seemed, with purpose of its own
> And measured motion like a living thing,
> Strode after me.[1]

The succeeding affect, as in Richard's case, is one of temporary disorganisation, but Wordsworth, unlike Richard, accepts and contemplates the mystery of it, and he records the experience as one of the most formative of his life. From it, and from others like it, comes Wordsworth's insight into the 'unknown modes' of our being. The poetry imparts the awesome experience to the reader, but in that awe the wonder is greater than the terror:

> but after I had seen
> That spectacle, for many days, my brain
> Worked with a dim and undetermined sense
> Of unknown modes of being; o'er my thoughts
> There hung a darkness, call it solitude
> Or black desertion. No familiar shapes
> Remained, no pleasant images of trees,
> Of sea or sky, no colours of green fields;
> But huge and mighty forms, that do not live
> Like living men, moved slowly through the mind
> By day, and were a trouble to my dreams.[2]

'You have learnt something; that always feels as if you had lost something.'[3] Wordsworth, reflecting on this experience of his boyhood, sees it as the work of a creative spirit that intertwined his passions with the enduring objects of nature and made him contemplate with reverence the least motion of a bird or an opening leaf, and recognise 'A grandeur in the beatings of the heart'. Within the context of the love process that he describes, even the shattering power of the threatening conscience is not truly disintegrative, but *confirms* his sense of 'the unity of all things'.

If we were to use the word 'conscience' to mean only the

[1] *The Prelude:* I. 381–5.
[2] Ibid., 390–400.
[3] *Major Barbara:* G. B. Shaw.

threatening, accusing, punishing factor in our moral experience, then clearly we should need some other word for the encouraging, creative factor, and a third for the rational, guiding or dispassionately organising factor which is equally important in our moral growth. As it is, we use the word to mean all these, sometimes separately, sometimes all at once. It is in this larger sense, including accusation, warning, judgement, motivation and organisation that conscience finds symbolic representation in *The Tempest*, not only in Ariel, but in Gonzalo, Miranda, Ferdinand, the Masque goddesses, and above all in Prospero, who embraces the whole, having vision, like Gonzalo, affection, like Miranda, humility and devotion, like Ferdinand, general precepts, like the goddesses, energy, like Caliban, and practical wisdom and skill to bring those under his guidance to the point of renewal and redirection.

Prospero, like the chemical organiser (see p. 102) and like the infant's mother, is both the law and the impulse that order and stimulate growth and foster happy human relationships. If we think of conscience as the whole complex of drives and regulators that urges us to such ends, we see Henry VI and Richard III as moral defectives; but, more than that, we see the incompleteness of the idea of conscience as an avenger and a stimulator to vengeance that we have encountered in *Richard III*. Between *Richard III* and *The Tempest* there is a profound development of moral and psychological insight, which we shall trace through some of Shakespeare's images of love, contrasting these with some of their contraries.

CHAPTER NINE

An Unerring Light

WE have already seen that *King Lear* almost bridges the gap between *Richard III* and *The Tempest*. From infantile egoism Lear grows towards the kind of maturity that is symbolised by Prospero. The fully mature person in this sense will be one whose inner harmony is so complete, and whose vision of social and universal harmony is so strong, that to love his neighbour as himself and to 'seek first the Kingdom of Heaven' are habitual to him. Perhaps no human being as yet achieves this; reaching the moon is doubtless child's play in comparison; but the dream or vision of it is both the occasion and the goal of moral striving.

Henry VI and Richard III were abortive growths, being deprived of love and unable to realise it in their lives. Henry knew his longing for it. *The Tempest* is a vision of the order that Henry longed for and of the sinews of that order. Prospero is Shakespeare's final image of love in action. The word 'love' is more ambiguous than any of the words we have so far reflected on; but, clearly, in describing the mature conscience, we are describing love. The new order that men seek implies love; indeed it is possible to describe the ideal order *as* love, and say it is love that men seek. The river of life that flows from the belly of Krishna, though it divides into a myriad streams recombines into one before returning to its source. We use 'love' to mean the motive, the aspiration and the goal. Prospero's benevolence is love as a manifestation of the will. 'Love your enemies' said Jesus; but an enemy is by definition someone you do not like, someone you have the urge to injure, someone you fear. Loving one's enemy must be an act of will and reason, at least in the first instance, though by habit it may become an established attitude or disposition. In contrast, the love that Henry and Richard were deprived of in infancy is on the child's part a devouring passion, on the

164

mother's a possessive as well as a protective and self-sacrificing urge.

In the sort of maturity that would make possible a harmonious world the primal lust is transformed into altruism and benevolence, so that passion and reason are one. In Prospero the passions are present in the kind of balance with one another and with reason that mystics call detachment, and that is the maturity of love. The point may be illustrated by contrasting Prospero with Theseus in *A Midsummer-Night's Dream*. In common usage both Prospero and Theseus might be described as detached, but in truth there is the strongest possible contrast between their attitudes.

Theseus, like Prospero, is a ruler who is responsible for the well-being of others and brings about a happy ending. He is generous, but also condescending, superciliously indulgent, faintly contemptuous, indifferent. Prospero is commanding and dignified, but deeply involved and passionately concerned. To emphasise that Prospero's detachment is love, not indifference, Shakespeare at times allows passion to break bounds, as for example when Prospero is 'vex'd' and his 'old brain is troubled' by the conflict with evil. His tenderness for Miranda, his severity with Ferdinand, his joy in their union, his affectionate asides to Ariel, his pity for the sufferers, his sadness in departing, all convey impressions of strong feeling. But the feeling never overbears the will. Sufficient passion is displayed to demonstrate Prospero's mastery of his passion, to show that passion has to be mastered, and that, like Caliban and Ariel, it will at times rebel or grumble. Even tenderness, undisciplined, might become sentimentality and be, in effect, unkindness. Benevolence, which is the balance of reason and love, requires severity to Ferdinand and Miranda in their preparation for marriage. In Prospero himself, when passion would be unforgiving, love forgives:

> Though with their high wrongs I am struck to th' quick,
> Yet with my nobler reason 'gainst my fury
> Do I take part: (V. i. 25–7)

The word used is 'reason' not 'love'. Prospero's detachment is the kind in which love and reason prompt in the same way. Reconciliation is the rational end upon which, as we might say, Prospero has 'set his *heart*'.

Bottom, referring to a very different sort of love, the wild 'fancy' of the inconstant lovers of *A Midsummer-Night's Dream*, makes the conventional remark:

> to say the truth, reason and love
> keep little company together now-a-days;

The Tempest brings reason and love together. They are perfectly blended in Ferdinand and Miranda, as well as in Prospero. Mere reason would have saved Ferdinand the trouble of suffering indignities and carrying logs for Miranda; mere passion would have spoiled their happiness by too hasty sexual indulgence. The perfection of happiness is represented as being subject to the perfect balance of love and reason, which results not in the diminution and frustration of either, but in the increase and fulfilment of both. Similarly reason alone might have whispered to Prospero, as it whispered to Richard, 'an eye for an eye, and a tooth for a tooth'; but the 'nobler reason' disciplines the inordinate passion and points to the superior satisfaction of 'love and amity'.[1]

In Theseus Shakespeare kept the balance sufficiently for the purposes of *A Midsummer-Night's Dream*, but the qualities of Theseus are more like those of Henry Bolingbroke and his son than like those of Prospero, and, while they make a good ruler, they do not make the best. Theseus lives with gusto. He has won Hippolyta with the sword, and will wed her with pomp with feasting and with revelry. Desire is strong in him and he is impatient for his wedding night

> but, O, methinks how slow
> This old moon wanes! she lingers my desires,
> Like to a step-dame or a dowager,
> Long withering out a young man's revenue.
>
> (I. i. 3–6)

This image in which he describes his 'love' is in impatience hot

---

[1] *Henry VI, Part I:* III. i. 68.

enough, but in human sympathy cold, and it is a getting, not a giving image. Soldier, seducer, athlete, huntsman, he has a sensuous appreciation of beauty and delights to hear the music of his hounds uncouple in the western valley. But all is enjoyed in the clear light of superficiality, which he calls 'cool reason'. Reason he has, and judgement, and he exercises these for the good of all. He recognises the feelings of the lovers and decisively overrules the prejudice of Egeus so that sensible arrangements can be made for their marriages. He values loyalty and honest compliment from the humblest:

> Love therefore, and tongue-tied simplicity
> In least speak most to my capacity.
>
> (V. i. 104–5)

It is a wise remark, and generous; yet in its context, it smacks of policy rather than of sympathy. The competent ruler is able to distinguish between the sincerely loyal subject and

> the rattling tongue
> Of saucy and audacious eloquence.

His is the coldly judicious wisdom of a ruler of men. A profound evaluation of such love and tongue-tied simplicity as we see for example in Virgilia is not to be expected from Theseus:

> My gracious silence, hail!   (*Coriolanus:* II. i. 166)

Though he is surrounded by mysteries and profundities of which even Bottom is aware, Theseus knows nothing of either. Poetry and dream are lunacy to him; the lover and the visionary are mad. Their language may be entertaining, but it is not comprehensible to 'cool reason', and so can be dismissed with indulgent mockery.

These remarks on Theseus are not to be taken as detracting in any way from his importance in *A Midsummer-Night's Dream*. His cool reason is in perfect contrast to the wayward fancies of the lovers on the one hand and the earth-wisdom of Bottom on the other. My purpose is to illuminate the character of Prospero and show to what extent Shakespeare has blended in him and in *The Tempest* as a whole, reason and love, insight and imagin-

ation, judgement and tenderness and will. Theseus has judgement on the one hand and strong instinctual drives on the other.
His instincts are well regulated by his judgement, but there is no
tenderness, no strong emotion, no *sharing* of experience with
others, no profound sympathy – no love in the sense in which
we find love in either *King Lear* or *The Tempest*. To read the
famous speech of Theseus in the light of Prospero's speech on
dreams is ironic; for Theseus is saying contemptuously what
Prospero says in all seriousness and what Shakespeare has said
profoundly in the scenes of King Lear's madness and other
madnesses in his later plays:

> I never may believe
> These antique fables, nor these fairy toys.
> Lovers and madmen have such seething brains,
> Such shaping fantasies, that apprehend
> More than cool reason ever comprehends.

(V. i. 2–6)

Shakespeare spent half his life exposing the shallowness of
Theseus' 'rational view' of the human imagination. He ended
his life's work with antique fables and with fairy toys, including
The Tempest, and through them gave his audiences the opportunity to apprehand far more than cool reason ever compre-
hends. Among the apprehensibles is this mature human love
which is also 'Reason in her most exalted mood'[1] the perfect
conscience, and the reflection of that visionary order towards
which all aspiration tends.

*   *   *

Though Prospero is descended from a line of Shakespearean
kings and rulers, including Henry V as well as Theseus, and
Duncan as well as Henry VI, what is of at least equal importance is his descent from Shakespeare's earliest exponents of
altruistic love, notably Viola in *Twelfth Night* and Portia in
The Merchant of Venice. Stephano's moral: 'Every man shift for
all the rest' is not only the moral of *The Tempest*; it is the fruit of

[1] Wordsworth, *The Prelude (1850)*: XIV. 192.

Shakespeare's explorations of the meaning and the conditions of happiness pursued throughout the plays. The tragedies show how happiness can be lost; the histories dwell upon the act of order in a peopled kingdom, a condition of happiness that Elizabethans reflected on both with pride and with anxiety; the comedies generate happiness. Shakespeare's recipe for misery and destruction is the failure of love in many different forms; his recipe for happiness is love in action, also in different forms.

In Shakespeare's first five plays it is almost true to say that there is no love. There is whoredom, marital infidelity and rape. There is family solidarity and feud. There is Henry's sentimentality. Love is much mentioned, but little shown. Queen Elizabeth's love for her children and the affection of the princes for each other may be thought exceptions; some might wish also to except Queen Margaret's passion for Suffolk. The first expression of romantic 'love' in the pastoral mode is the following:

> My lovely Aaron, wherefore look'st thou sad,
> When everything doth make a gleeful boast?
> The birds chant melody on every bush;
> The snake lies rolled in the cheerful sun;
> The green leaves quiver with the cooling wind
> And make a chequer'd shadow on the ground:
> Under their sweet shade, Aaron, let us sit,
> And whilst the babbling echo mocks the hounds,
> Replying shrilly to the well-tun'd horns,
> As if a double hunt were heard at once,
> Let us sit down and mark their yellowing noise;
> And – after conflict such as was suppos'd
> The wandering prince and Dido once enjoy'd,
> When with a happy storm they were surpris'd,
> And curtain'd with a counsel-keeping cave –
> We may, each wreathed in the other's arms,
> Our pastimes done, possess a golden slumber,
> Whiles hounds and horns and sweet melodious birds
> Be unto us as is a nurse's song
> Of lullaby to bring her babe asleep.

(*Titus Andronicus*: II. iii. 10–29)

The lover is Tamora, Queen of the Goths, now Empress of Rome and wife of Saturninus. It is not Saturninus she solicits, however, but her murderous servant, Aaron the Moor. This is the scene in which Tamora and Aaron plot the rape and torture of the innocent Lavinia and the murder of her lover and her brothers. Lavinia is to have her tongue cut out and her hands cut off so that she cannot reveal her torturers, the sons of Tamora. The romantic verse is the expression of one devouring lust and the prelude to others. Its beauty is ironic. Shakespeare is not yet writing of love.

What Shakespeare is clearly very much interested in at this period is the dramatic *tour de force*. The wooing of Anne and the suit to Elizabeth are striking examples from *Richard III*. *Titus Andronicus* gives the impression that this young upstart dramatist, 'the only shake-scene in a country', is demonstrating how many separate horrors he can pack into one melodrama. *The Comedy of Errors* touches upon various kinds of love in ways that show the writer's potential, but we have the impression that he is trying just how many comic situations he can concentrate into one play by means of two pairs of twins in a series of misunderstandings. Like a juggler in training, he practises with the device of mistaken identity. As in the later Shakespeare, the stage tricks take on deeper significance; but comic situations predominate.

The Two Gentlemen of Verona is the first play in which Shakespeare attempts to deal directly with love and friendship. The general feeling is that he does not succeed. Ibsen's Peer Gynt spends a purposeless life in self-indulgence and unconvincing self-assertion only to find at the end that there is not enough substance in him to make one bright button on the waistcoat of the world. Yet one thing and one alone makes him worth something: he is the object of the constant and self-less love of Solveig. Shakespeare's Proteus, like Peer, is contemptible in his infidelity to Julia, his inconstancy in both love and friendship, and his dastardly attempt upon Silvia, the lover of his friend; but the wronged lover, Julia, and the wronged friend, Valentine, remain constant and true, and Proteus finds his worth and his heaven and a firm identity in them. Professor J. F. Danby points out that we have, especially in Julia, an image of the pursuing love of God:[1]

> Herein is love, not that we loved God, but that he loved us and sent his Son to be the propitiation for our sins.
>
> (1 John, IV. 10.)

Whether Ibsen and Shakespeare intended it or not, each has recreated this Christian myth.[2] Ibsen does it with great beauty and insight so that we recognise some of its truth about human beings and human life. Shakespeare attempts more and achieves less. He introduces the unselfish friendship of Valentine and does it so unconvincingly as to arouse disgust. There are two important reasons for this. One is that his special gift for characterisation, that is for making images that really do seem like people, conflicts with his use of characters as symbols. The other is that in this his first attempt to explore the nature of love he treats it too lightly in the hasty conclusion of the play. It is not possible to present the Divine Love by a desecration of human love, and his presentation of human love in the earlier scenes has been so moving that his cavalier treatment of the human relationships in the final scene is inconsistent with the symbolic meaning.

Proteus, when found out, says he is sorry. Valentine replies:

> Who by repentance is not satisfied
> Is nor of heaven nor earth, for these are pleas'd;

and Valentine forgives. Shakespeare has here confused repentance and contrition, two very different things. Ariel, in *The Tempest* does not confuse them: 'heart-sorrow' comes first, but 'a clear life' must ensue. We have been given a pretty convincing impression of Proteus as one who cannot be trusted to remain constant (as the name implies). We are now to assume that, having apologised, he will change to 'a clear life', but since Shakespeare has made him seem real, we cannot assume this. Perhaps, given the clues in the lines, Shakespeare's audience

---

[1] *Critical Quarterly*, Vol. II. 1960: 'Shakespeare Criticism and *The Two Gentlemen of Verona*.'

[2] The word 'myth' does not imply error or falsehood.

could accept the 'repentance' for the sake of the story and the Christian idea; and, if we could do so, the scene might not be entirely spoiled by the psychological improbability. What really does make the gorge rise, however, and take all our sympathy from the forgiving Valentine, is that he adds:

> By penitence th'Eternal wrath's appeased:
> And, that my love may appear plain and free,
> All that was mine in Silvia I give thee.
>
> (V. iv. 81–3)

If this is intended to express the meaning of love by an echo of the Christian doctrine that God so loved the world that he gave his only son, it is so far from succeeding as to be almost blasphemous. What we have here is the spectacle of a sentimental and self-righteous young man offering to hand over the girl he loves, and who loves him, to a proven dastard and liar who merely says he is sorry for what he has done. What is worst of all about this, and clearly inconsistent with Christian doctrine, is that the girl is treated as a chattel. Her wishes, indeed her faithful love of Valentine, do not count – except as something to exploit. The point is that, earlier, Shakespeare has made his audience feel about Silvia as if she were a real girl. He cannot then suddenly and without preparation assume that his audience will be indifferent to her personal feelings. It is probably true that he is concentrating in this final scene upon his symbolic pattern, and perhaps elevating friendship above sexual love, but he is doing violence to his own most remarkable gift as an artist, the gift of verisimilitude through characterisation. Valentine treats the lady as an expendable item; Shakespeare has made her a person and now uses her as a property. Here once again, as in *Paradise Lost*, we see the difficulty of allegorising God and his Son by means of characters with recognisably human traits.

Some have said, however, that Silvia is not a person. This comes of not reading the play *as a whole*. It also comes of judging by comparison with Shakespeare's greater plays. A character analysis of Silvia does not yield what a character analysis of Portia or even Olivia yields. Nor can we find much distinctive characterisation in the final scene itself. Furthermore, Silvia has not been prominent *in person* throughout the play. Why, then, this sense of violation at the end? How is it that we feel about Silvia as a person? The answer to the first question lies as much in our feelings about Valentine and Proteus as in our feeling for Silvia, and in the fact that Silvia has been most prominent throughout *in idea*. When Proteus seemed still a loyal friend, Valentine could say,

> Forgive me that I do not dream on thee,
> Because thou seest me dote upon my love.
> (II. iv. 168–9)

This is Valentine placing true love before friendship; that is accounted right. Proteus places false love before friendship, betraying two loyalties; that is wrong, as Proteus confesses. Silvia is thus the token of the constancy of Valentine and the inconstancy of Proteus, and she is much more defiled by what appears the inconstancy of Valentine than by the attempted rape. Even if Shakespeare had deployed his art to make Silvia a distinctly allegorical figure like Griselda, Valentine's act could still not have been a satisfactory representation of unselfregarding friendship; for indifference to one love does not demonstrate the strength or unselfishness of another – quite the contrary. Tacked on to the end of a speech about forgiveness, and sounding like a boy's attempt to be a god, Valentine's act is offensive and so unconvincing that it looks like a mere device of the playwright to bring Julia back into the dialogue.

The fact that we feel towards Silvia and Valentine as persons, in spite of the fantasy situations in which they have appeared and the conscious art of some of their speeches, is partly due to their first appearance together in the play. There Silvia has all the apparent modesty and submissiveness and all the real dominance of a living woman. Her mixture of shyness and boldness in setting the pace of their love affair is not only delicious but also convincing. Shakespeare ensures that it will convince by having Speed present to offset the romantic by the mundane, the sighing by the jest; and henceforth Valentine and Silvia are real persons for us, whatever impossibilities they engage in. In itself this scene might not have been enough, but there is

Julia, a creation of such beauty and such life – as well as symbolic meaning – that in her presence the other main characters remain people. Again, however, everything depends on the early scenes in which she appears, especially the first. The incident of the letter, the pretence of indifference in the presence of her maid, the display of passion in solitude, the subtle changes of tone in the exchanges between mistress and maid, and the authenticity of the language, however consciously shaped, in which the tumult of feeling is expressed, all these make us *know* Julia and like her. The extraordinary beauty and power of her feeling, her practical sense and the firmness of her will in the scene where she resolves to leave Verona and pursue Proteus to Milan move much stronger feelings than liking, which persist in us to the end. Julia is so real that Silvia, closely associated with her, is felt as a person too.

In the final scene Julia has few words to say, but she is a silent presence, injured by Proteus when he pursues Silvia, most injured when he attempts the act of violation. When Silvia is offered to Proteus by Valentine, our attention is on Julia, and would be even if she did not faint. Julia's story is on Silvia's lips when she reproaches Proteus. It is Julia we most care about, for in Julia we have seen the true example of unselfish love which is so falsely and so feebly paralleled by Valentine's renunciation of Silvia.

Julia, disguised as a boy, has carried a message of love from Proteus to Silvia and has not betrayed her identity. The contrast between her act and Valentine's does more than anything to destroy the last scene, for Valentine's looks no better than a bad imitation of hers. The difference is extreme. Julia would help Proteus to win the lady of his desire: Valentine would sacrifice Silvia to the man she detests. Julia is acting contrary to her immediate desire; Valentine is indulging his. Julia is a powerfully effective image of love as something different from and superior to desire and self-indulgence, an image of altruistic love. Julia is at one and the same time both a person and a symbol. The hasty denouement, the unconvincing change in Proteus, the failure of Valentine as an image either of love or of wisdom, or indeed of friendship, the unfeeling exploitation of

Silvia – all these spoil a play that began with great promise;
but the dawning insight into the meaning of love in Julia out-
weighs them in importance even though it does not save the play.

* * *

Since the discovery that leads to the exploration of altruistic
love in *King Lear* and *The Tempest* is made in *The Two Gentlemen
of Verona* why not speak of Julia rather than Viola as the founder
of Prospero's line? We might indeed have done so but for one
imperfection in Julia which is deliberately removed by Shakespeare from *Twelfth Night*. That Viola seems a living person
even more distinctly than Julia is beyond question. The symbol
and the character are so perfectly fused in Viola that, though
she is a representation of ideal love, she does not lose one iota of
humanness and reality. She is a marvellous image of moral perfection in human form – perfection, that is, in one respect,
namely her love. To many people Julia should appear more
credible, for there is a common human weakness in her love
wholly absent from Viola's. Most lovers are unaware that
jealousy and perfect love are incompatible. If A loves B with a
perfect love, then B's interests will be paramount with A, and if
B loves C, then A will desire that C love B. A's satisfaction will
be found only in B's satisfaction. Julia's love is not quite perfect.
She delivers the letter from Proteus to Silvia, and receives
Silvia's picture for Proteus. She is thus faithful to Proteus, but
Shakespeare gives her these words:

> Yet will I woo for him, but yet so coldly
> As, heaven it knows, I would not have him speed.
>
> (IV. iv. 102–3)

'Naturally!' we say, using the word in twentieth-century fashion
as an excuse for human weakness. In the event, Julia does not
plead for Proteus – not even coldly. On the contrary, she lets
Silvia know how faithless Proteus is by telling of the lady he has
deserted. Understandable as this may be, it is a betrayal, and
Julia is thus far from being a perfect symbol of the pursuing love
of God. Afterwards she says,

> I hope my master's suit will be but cold.

175

She studies Silvia's picture, finds the face no more beautiful than her own, and complains that there is no good reason why Silvia should be preferred. This is very far beneath the unreflecting altruism of Viola's passion.

In *Twelfth Night* the situation is complicated by the fact that the Countess falls in love with the disguised messenger. Duke Orsino loves the Countess Olivia. Viola loves Orsino, but she is disguised as a boy and is in his service. She is called upon to plead his love before Olivia, and does so with such sincerity, passion and eloquence that Olivia catches 'the plague' of affection from her and, taking her to be the young man she appears to be, falls in love with her. This intriguing situation Shakespeare did not invent. Among the sources from which he drew his material is *Gl'Ingannati*, an Italian play. In that play Lelia loves Flamminio and takes messages from him to Isabella. Isabella (like Olivia) falls in love with the messenger, Lelia. Lelia, however, is even more 'human' and 'natural' than Julia: her sole aim is to oust her rival if she can. She has taken service with Flamminio to ensure that 'if she doesn't enjoy him, nobody else does either'. She amuses herself by encouraging Isabella's passion for her, but responds to Isabella's advances only on condition that she 'get rid of Flamminio'.[1]

The quality and the importance of the change that Shakespeare made cannot be exaggerated. Viola, brilliant with vitality, intelligence and will, is yet as patiently devoted as Griselda. The duel between Viola and Olivia is both exciting and profound (I. v.). It is a witty and amusing entertainment; but, it is a vision, in most convincing shape, of a moral ideal that is too frequently said to be beyond the attainment of any but the most exceptional human beings. Viola has admitted that her assignment is 'a barful strife', but no bars detain her. She will stand at Olivia's door 'like a sheriff's post, and be the supporter to a bench' till she gains admittance. The mere report of her manner and bearing causes Olivia to break her firm resolution to receive no messenger. The duellists begin confidently, Viola rather pert, but conscientiously acting her part, Olivia con-

[1] Bullough: *Narrative & Dramatic Sources of Shakespeare*, Vol. II, pp. 296–309. Routledge 1958.

descending and mocking. But there is deep feeling beneath Viola's wit:

'by the very fangs of malice I swear, I am not that I play.'

It flashes out in a sharp challenge such as no ordinary messenger would deliver to the countess:

Most certain, if you are she, you do usurp yourself; for what is yours to bestow is not yours to reserve.

This is the first of a series of challenges and rebukes that show on the one hand that Viola is of noble birth, above the station of a messenger, and on the other that she is so passionately devoted to Orsino that denial of his suit makes no sense to her. There is anger in it, too, that Olivia should despise what to Viola is most precious. Viola's proud loyalty and intense earnestness gain the initial advantage, so that Olivia consents to hear the message alone. Then Viola makes her first mistake and loses the advantage to the lady of the house: she asks to see Olivia's face. The difference between Viola at this point and Julia looking at Silvia's picture measures the tremendous leap in Shakespeare's awareness of moral potential since *The Two Gentlemen of Verona*. There is no jealousy, no envy even, no complaint – only unstinted praise, and passionate urgency on Orsino's behalf:

Tis beauty truly blent, whose red and white
Nature's own sweet and cunning hand laid on.
Lady, you are the cruell'st she alive,
If you will lead these graces to the grave,
And leave the world no copy.   (I. v. 223–7)

Olivia too confidently presses home her advantage; she speaks slightingly of her own beauty to mock the awe-inspired young 'man' before her. But in doing so she belittles what Orsino's love has made sacred for Viola, and the passion with which Viola replies removes all the fine-lady airs from Olivia's speech. Olivia's whispered question shows that it is her turn to be awestruck:

How does he love me?

and later

> Why, what would you?

Now the advantage is so firmly with Viola, eloquent in her master's praise but betraying her own passion and devotion, that Olivia can only 'speak in starts', distractedly. Viola's utterly unselfregarding love has won Olivia's heart:

> Methinks I feel this youth's perfections
> With an invisible and subtle stealth
> To creep in at mine eyes.

This perfect blend of intense desire and utter self-forgetfulness which is the paradox of true love is achieved here as nowhere else in Shakespeare's plays, and to it Viola adds elsewhere the patient endurance for the sake of love that Julia claimed:

> I'll be as patient as a gentle stream,
> *(Two Gentlemen:* II. vii. 34)

As the boy, Cesario, speaking of a sister he never had, she tells her own story:

> My father had a daughter lov'd a man,
> As it might be perhaps, were I a woman,
> I should your lordship.
> ORSINO: And what's her history?
> VIOLA: A blank, my lord. She never told her love,
> But let concealment, like a worm i' th' bud,
> Feed on her damask cheek. She pin'd in thought;
> And with a green and yellow melancholy
> She sat like patience on a monument,
> Smiling at grief. Was not this love indeed?   (II. iv. 106–14)

Heaven and earth are one in Viola. She is so convincingly a living girl that the perfection of love in her is seen as a practical reality. Only when the play is over can one begin to question whether it is too good to be true, but by then her love has been seen to be the chief source of happiness in the play, and there can be no doubt about its potential for happiness in life.

> Serene will be our days and bright
> And happy will our nature be

AN UNERRING LIGHT

When love is an unerring light,
And joy its own security.[1]

However, love as a passion is not an unerring light even in this play. Viola is perfect in unswerving devotion of the impulsive or instinctive kind. There is not the slightest hint in her of conscious self-interest. But her judgement is not perfect: she places herself and Olivia in an impossible situation. She is an image of a part of human nature that needs its counterpart to be complete. Sebastian, her twin, is the counterpart, and his coming makes sense of the nonsensical situation in which Olivia seeks to be betrothed to a maid, in which Sir Toby involves the same maid in duels, and in which Orsino pursues a fantasy, though we can see that his real affection and trust are in Viola. Sebastian is not a Prospero but he enters the play as the 'unerring light' of frank affection, rectitude and good sense. Like Prospero, he is the truth-bringer, as well as one who cares. He meets with strange events, and he questions his sanity:

Or I am mad, or else this is a dream,   (IV. i. 60)

but he neither despairs of his reason nor disparages dreams and he guarantees happiness ever after by an affirmation of constancy that shows him the true brother of Viola:

I'll follow this good man and go with you;
And, having sworn truth, ever will be true.   (IV. iii. 32)

Proteus said that if man were but constant he were perfect, and Shakespeare is certainly laying great emphasis on constancy in love as essential to the happy ending; for here once again he diverges from his source-tale, Barnabe Riche's *Apolonius and Silla*, where the counterpart of Sebastian gets the lady with child, then deserts her – the story requiring his absence. In *Twelfth Night* Shakespeare needs Sebastian as well as Viola to represent love as that

ever fixed mark.
That looks on tempests and is never shaken   (Sonnet 116)

Sebastian is committed by will, as Viola is committed by feeling.

[1] Wordsworth: 'Ode to Duty'.

179

Having taken his vow, Sebastian will keep it even if emotion fails. Where we cannot love in feeling, we can dutifully bend to acts of love. If the first part of Wordsworth's verse fits Viola, the second fits Sebastian:

> And they a blissful course may hold
> Ev'n now, who, not unwisely bold,
> Live in the spirit of this creed:
> Yet seek thy firm support, according to their need.[1]

Shakespeare does not use the word 'duty' in the larger sense given to it by Wordsworth, but the concept is implicit in Sebastian's vow, in the rational authority of Theseus and in the benevolent detachment of Prospero.

* * *

The exercise of will and reason in altruistic deeds Shakespeare has thought of in *Love's Labour's Lost*, with the additional idea that a duty faithfully pursued may be a training in love. Four fine gentlemen, warring against their own affections, have forsworn the company of ladies and vowed themselves to an austere manner of life for three years in which they are to devote themselves to study. Their purpose is to win fame and honour with their 'little academe', and their scheme is an idle fancy that overlooks the most immediate practical realities such as that the visit of a princess and her lovely ladies has already been arranged:

> So study evermore is overshot.
> While it doth study to have what it would,
> It doth forget to do the thing it should;
>
> (I. i. 140–2)

These words might have been said to Prospero in his early days as Duke of Milan before harsh trials and the providence of God brought him to his senses. The princess 'on mere necessity' must be received. The real presence of the ladies is too much for the gentlemen: they fall in love, and their vows are broken.

[1] 'Ode to Duty'.

Shakespeare's love stories usually end in marriage; this does not. It ends in severe tests. One of the gentlemen, the king, must for a twelve month endure 'frosts and fasts, hard lodging and thin weeds' observing a hermit's rule more austere than the rule he disobeyed to woo the princess. He and two others have their fortitude and patience tried, to prove their constancy and show themselves worthy of their ladies. The fourth is different. He is Berowne, the cleverest, most witty and most elegantly superficial of them all. The trial that is imposed upon him by his lady, Rosaline, is strikingly different from the rest: not only is it a test of his enduring devotion to the lady, it is also an act of charity and a redeeming discipline. The play is as much a practice-ground for wit as *Titus Andronicus* is for horrors and *The Comedy of Errors* for amusing situations; it is also believed to be a satire on some of Shakespeare's word-catching contemporaries; yet at the end, wit receives as harsh a rejection as Falstaff receives at the end of *Henry IV, Part II* – harsher. Berowne is a man 'replete with mocks', who exercises his wit at the expense of all who lie 'within his mercy'. Rosaline *therefore* commands:

> You shall this twelvemonth term from day to day
> Visit the speechless sick, and still converse
> With groaning wretches; and your task shall be,
> With all the fierce endeavour of your wit,
> To enforce the pained impotent to smile.
>
> (V. ii. 838–42)

Her aim is to weed the wormwood of cold mockery from his fruitful brain and choke the gibing spirit.

> Whose influence is begot of that loose grace
> Which shallow laughing hearers give to fools.

If his 'fault' can be redeemed by cheering those in need, then Rosaline will have him, fault and all; if not, he must reform. Rosaline enjoins a severe training in altruism and also in judgement as a necessary preliminary to the 'world-without-end bargain'.

This final exchange between Rosaline and Berowne makes

the punishment fit the crime, but by no means in the light vein of *The Mikado*. The tone is in stark contrast to the general tone of the play:

> To move wild laughter in the throat of death?
> It cannot be; it is impossible;
> Mirth cannot move a soul in agony.   (V. ii. 843-5)

Berowne is horror-struck, and has no more jests or repartee in the play, only the resolve to 'jest a twelvemonth in the hospital' and a rueful complaint that the ladies might have married them and given the play a happy ending, 'like an old play'. This omission of the usual happy ending is more than a clever variation upon a comic convention: the test that replaces it compels a reappraisal of the values of the play, challenging the clever mockery and affirming two things: human sympathy, with which mockery has nothing to do, and a sense of reality, which is what Berowne himself *seemed* to have at the beginning of the play.

These two qualities of human sympathy and awareness of reality are the same we have observed as love and reason, seen exemplified in Viola and Sebastian, and in Gonzalo and Prospero, and noted as the sinews of conscience. Nothing is more characteristic of Shakespeare than this seriousness in comedy. Sometimes it finds painful expression, as when the popular and jovial Falstaff, lacking both qualities, fails to achieve a happy ending. Falstaff's end is particularly painful to those who cannot distinguish his sentimentalities and hypocrisies from affection, and his cunning and cynicism from awareness. The rejection of Falstaff is as surely a rejection of egotism and lack of vision (i.e. taking the short view) as the disintegration of Richard III or the degeneration of Macbeth. Mention is made here of Falstaff because we meet him in *Twelfth Night* (Sir Toby) and *The Tempest* (Stephano). Falstaff, Toby and Stephano are in strong contrast to Prospero and Viola; for, though they create amusement for onlookers uninvolved with them, they do not create happiness. Stephano's way is exposed in *The Tempest* as a deception, and he shares in the happy ending only by a reversal of his values. W. H. Auden has noticed in Falstaff the state of un-complicated, unhesitating self-interest that precedes the deve-lopment of conscience, a different mode of which we have observed in Richard Crookback's father, the Duke of York.[1] Auden writes:

> Once upon a time we were all Falstaffs: then we became social beings with super-egos. Most of us learn to accept this but there are some in whom the nostalgia for the state of innocent self-importance is so strong that they refuse to accept adult life and responsibilities and seek some means to become again the Falstaffs they once were. The commonest technique adopted is the bottle . . .[2]

That the bottle is not the only technique and that the mani-festations of infantile egoism are not always comic we have seen in the stories of King Lear and Richard III. Richard and Falstaff, both descendants of the medieval Vice, are indeed two faces of the same coin. Even Prospero was once guilty of the refusal to accept his responsibilities: his intoxication was that 'hydroptique immoderate thirst for human learning and languages'.[3] Sir Toby Belch is one of four, or if we count Sir Andrew Aguecheek, one of five inebriates in *Twelfth Night*. Orsino, Olivia, Malvolio and Sir Toby are all intoxicated with themselves. The happy ending involves bringing all of them to their sober senses. Sir Toby, being least self-conscious, may at first appear least egotistical, and his plea, 'Dost thou think because thou art virtuous there shall be no more cakes and ale?' sounds plausible. In fact, and in spite of appearances, his egotism is a much greater threat to human happiness than Malvolio's partly *because* many find him attractive. He is a parasite, and his 'fun' is always at someone else's expense; his contempt for others is but thinly disguised by his hearty word and his play-acting. Every lord of misrule of Toby's kind has something in him of Richard Crookback, though the quality

---

[1] See p. 109.
[2] 'The Prince's Dog' p. 195, in *The Dyer's Hand and Other Essays*, Faber, 1962.
[3] John Donne.

may appear in less *unattractive* guise, or rather in attractive disguise. Humour and mischief in Rosalind are pure virtue – not in Toby or Falstaff; Viola has the virtue of wit, Toby the vice of it. Sir Toby and Falstaff make laughter, not happiness. To fit into the happy ending, Toby would have to be redeemed or, like Stephano, become an unwitting image of redemption. Otherwise he must have his head broken and be pushed off-stage, much as the audience may regret this. Misrule may be great fun, but it is not tolerable for long – even in drama.

Malvolio's egotism is obvious, his vanity is absurd, his censoriousness irritating, his officiousness infuriating. We don't like him; so he can be made a butt for our amusement. But he is not dangerous, and he is a loyal and honest steward; so the jest seems to be carried too far, and this is sad because the uncharity of it mars the final happiness and obscures somewhat the marvellous image of Viola's love. Malvolio, however, is one of those who cannot be forgiven, because he cannot accept forgiveness. Reconciliation is offered him, but he is too preoccupied with his own resentments and spews his malice over guilty and innocent alike:

I'll be revenged on the whole pack of you.

His egotism contrasts with Viola's altruism, his vanity with her humility, his stupidity with her intelligence, his resentment with her patience, but in so far as he arouses pity we are unable to rejoice in his defeat. Had the action permitted his reform and reconciliation with Sir Toby, we could have rejoiced in the true defeat of his vices, and all the more in the triumph of Viola's virtues. But he remains unregenerate, and as with Sir Toby, the happy ending can be achieved only by removing him from the stage.

Sir Toby and Malvolio show opposite kinds of misrule. Sir Toby's is the perversion of fun, Malvolio's the perversion of duty. The proper end of both fun and duty is charity; each is its own kind of service. Fun that hurts is funny only to the cruel and self-righteous, and it is important to note the supreme self-righteousness of characters like Toby. The uncharity of the

officiously dutiful is more popularly detested, for the importance
of duty and its attendant virtues is commonly underrated.
Viola does her duty to Orsino faithfully, but because of her
passion we forget that it is duty and see it only as love. Sebastian's vow to be for ever true shows the risk he is taking: perhaps
Olivia will not always be to his taste. Then feeling may evapor-
ate and duty will be the only mode of love. In Olivia's household, Love would have made impossible both Sir Toby's riot
and Malvolio's officiousness, that is, both forms of contempt;
but so would duty if Sir Toby had been capable of it and Malvolio had not mingled vanity with it. Duty is the mode that love
adopts when knowledge and feeling fail; unfortunately it can also
be adopted by love's enemies, of which egotism as exhibited by
Malvolio is one. Hence Malvolio's failure as Olivia's steward in
spite of his efforts to order the household according to what is
in truth his duty.

Sir Toby's variety of misrule seems simpler, because it is in
open defiance of any kind of order, rule or proportion:

I'll confine myself no finer than I am.

However, he is no less self-righteous in his defence of 'cakes and
ale' than Malvolio is in defence of 'civil rule', and he is equally
incompetent to achieve his aim. What he does achieve is disorder and its consequences, and fortunately (this being comedy)
they fall upon himself. Almost the last word Shakespeare puts in
his mouth is

I hate a drunken rogue.

The comic irony of this is blunt compared with Stephano's
'Every man shift for all the rest', but the point is the same, for
Sir Toby's head is wounded and it is the doctor who is drunk.
In blaming the doctor, as in gulling Malvolio, robbing Sir
Andrew and spoiling Olivia's household, Toby shows his own
lack of the very quality he now needs the benefit of, namely
charity through service.

Sir Toby is a dwindled version of Falstaff, who two or three
years earlier had been Shakespeare's great comic creation. His

reappearance as a comparatively minor figure shows that Shakespeare is aiming at effects different from those that Falstaff achieved for him. True to reality, Shakespeare could not make Falstaff's end anything but a sad one; and Toby's is no better. Shakespeare, creating impressions of happiness, has discarded the Falstaff character in favour of Viola and others like her. Is there then no place for Falstaff and his like in a dramatic vision of happiness, except as a foil to characters capable of love? Among the many distinguished apologists for Falstaff, W. H. Auden is a recent one, and his defence is couched in such terms that his argument demands careful examination in this study; for if the defence holds, perhaps the charge of uncharity against Sir Toby can be refuted or at least mitigated, and he may be seen as a supplement rather than as a foil to Viola. Auden sees in Falstaff 'a comic symbol for the supernatural order of Charity as contrasted with the temporal order of Justice symbolised by Henry of Monmouth'.[1] This is Mr. Auden's answer to the question why, since drunkards are so disgusting, we do not turn our eyes away from Falstaff to the hero prince, indeed why, whenever Falstaff is on stage, we have no eyes for Hal. Auden asserts that qualities such as charity and forgiveness cannot be shown in 'secular' drama because it is not possible in such a way to distinguish the mere act of kindness or pardon from the *spirit* of charity or forgiveness. The only way to manifest charity, then, is indirectly, as in the case of Falstaff where comic villainy (comic because in fact Falstaff does not harm anybody) evokes happy laughter and warm sympathy, and where the subversion of justice and duty, as in Falstaff's recruiting, promotes the satisfaction of both those who are enlisted and those who are not. Again, Falstaff's idleness and drinking, his 'surrender to immediacy' and refusal to accept reality are, as a parable, 'signs for the Unworldly Man' who asserts private concerns as against the public interest and thus in 'the justice of charity' treats each person, not as a cipher, but as a unique person. Furthermore, he 'radiates happiness as Hal radiates power, and this happiness without apparent cause, this

[1] References in this and the following paragraph are to *The Dyer's Hard*, see p. 183.

untiring devotion to making others laugh, becomes a comic image for a love which is absolutely self-giving'.

This amounts to a subtle and eloquent case for that 'state of innocent self-importance' in which people 'refuse to accept adult life and responsibilities and seek some means to become again the Falstaffs they once were', that is the infantile, pre-conscience state which as social beings we find reprehensible if it persists into adult life and which Shakespeare represents as being so destructive in Lear and others.

Will the case stand up? First, are there alternative explanations for the way 'Falstaff affects us as he does'? Auden assumes that everyone delights in him, but this is far from being the case; many are merely intimidated and profess a delight they do not feel. Falstaff, as already mentioned, derives from that popular medieval character, the Vice. Among the reasons we have for liking the Vice or Falstaff are those given earlier for our attraction to Richard: he does what he likes; the rules do not bind him; he doesn't have to consider other people; he gets his own way exactly as we think we should all like to do. His impudent avowal of his own wickedness, or his ironic assumption of innocence, together with his cleverness in overreaching others, whether by word or deed, act as a kind of defence or excuse for our own 'pleasant vices', that is, our own uncharity; so, naturally, we have a fellow-feeling with him. Toby and Falstaff stimulate the imitation charity of boon-companionship and we are only too happy to find excuses for their uncharity since it is ourselves we are excusing. Malvolio, on the other hand, reminds us too much of the rules we want to break.

This can be reversed, however. Malvolio may remind us of the rules we want to keep, and so find approval, or win our pity. We may then feel like suppressing the deviant individual in favour of the rule. Auden sees Falstaff as the affirmation of the importance of the individual life against suffocating social chains and a social order that treats men as things. But this is precisely where the text does not bear him out. Falstaff does treat people as commodities. It is true that he does so in a most engaging way and that his attitude of total indifference to other people, except for the convenience or amusement of the moment, is disguised by wonderful expressions of affection. There never was a false face more calculated to disguise the false heart than Falstaff's. The valid defence of Falstaff would be to point out that his is another case of retarded development. He takes his pleasures as a baby takes milk till the source is exhausted or till he surfeits. His affections are as strong and as delightful as a child's cupboard-love – and as fickle. He cannot be called possessive in the usual sense, because he lives only in the moment, and 'out of sight is out of mind'; yet his affection has all to do with possession – or acquisition. But this is not really to defend, rather to excuse. Falstaff is treacherous and ruthless. Boon-companionship, tavern friendship, camaraderie may be attractive, and are popularly mistaken for the genuine article. Nowhere are these qualities more attractive than in Falstaff; which is as much as to say that Shakespeare extracted as much 'happiness' out of this character as can be extracted. To do so Shakespeare had to make other characters expendable, for example, those 'mortal men' who are 'food for powder' and whom Falstaff leads 'where they are pepper'd'.[1] Mistress Quickly is exploited and imposed upon, but she appears to like it and to be attached to her parasite; so our consciences sleep. Shallow, like the recruits, is an object of contempt. Here, however, is the chief reason why we cannot take Falstaff as a symbol of charity: he cannot be what he is or appeal as he does unless we pretend that his kind of attitude will do no harm, and we cannot pretend that without sharing the *contempt* he has for his victims. The disposition we have to rejoice with him and to excuse him is based on a fundamental uncharity. This is even more clear in the case of Sir Toby, partly because Malvolio is not quite so easily dismissed, and because Sir Andrew's childishness touches pity rather than contempt.

'Fair is foul, and foul is fair.' Shakespeare, dealing with Falstaff, is like Milton creating Satan. To know the Devil one must be fair to him, and he is very attractive. His appearance is false, but it is prepossessing. The Falstaff who, according to Mr. Auden, 'radiates happiness' is confined to *Henry IV, Part I*, however. In Part II, he makes laughter, but it is not the joyous,

[1] *Henry IV, Part I:* IV. ii. 65–7; V. iii. 36.

friendly laughter of Part I; his true colours show, and the logic of his actions is expressed, at the moment when he is licking his lips at the prospect of the largest booty of all:

> 'I know the young King is sick for me, Let us take any man's horses – the laws of England are at my commandment. Blessed are they that have been my friends, and woe to my Lord Chief Justice!'
>
> *(Henry IV, Part II:* V. iii. 131–4)

Here is Shakespeare's recognition of what has become gradually clearer as the play has proceeded, namely that the authentic voice of Falstaff, *as revealed in his actions*, is the voice of Richard III: the childlike exuberance is an imposture.

We have been warned that sometimes when a devil is cast out the place is left clear for seven devils to enter in. When Falstaff is cast out, another devil is already in. He is seven times more attractive to the Elizabethans than Falstaff, seven times more prepossessing and seven times more dangerous. His name is Henry V and his meaning ruthless power. He is heroic, magnanimous, self-sacrificing (within narrow limits), superbly competent – and he is the destroyer of two kingdoms. In the name of that which all men most desire, namely order, he produces its opposite, disorder, 'which oft our stage hath shown' (*Henry V:* Final Chorus. 13). For Henry too, people are expendable. This is his reply to the Dauphin's insult:

> many a thousand widows
> Shall this mock mock out of their dear husbands;
> Mock mothers from their sons, mock castles down;
> And some are yet ungotten and unborn
> That shall have cause to curse the Dauphin's scorn.
>
> *(Henry V:* I. ii. 284–8)

Just as Falstaff looks, at first, like a dispenser of joy, so Henry is taken as the creator of order, and he is called 'this grace of kings'.[1] Later on, Shakespeare uses that word 'grace' more carefully.

When Auden proclaims Falstaff 'a comic symbol of the

[1] *Henry V:* II. Chorus. 28.

supernatural order of Charity'[1] he contrasts him with Henry, who represents 'the temporal order of Justice'. This is consistent with Auden's claim that 'Falstaff's neglect of the public interest in favour of private concerns is an image for the justice of charity which treats each person, not as a cipher, but as a unique person' and that Falstaff, the 'Unworldly Man' contrasts with the 'worldly man' who will 'if it is necessary to the achievement of his end' treat persons as things. There is something more in this than the question already considered whether Falstaff treats persons as ciphers or things. Two orders are set in opposition here: the individual and the general. Although Auden affirms that 'real' laughter is absolutely unaggressive and that when we find things amusing we 'do not desire to change them, far less hurt or destroy them', he seems to see in Falstaff a challenge to 'the temporal order of Justice'. His final paragraph places Falstaff side by side with Christ as one whom 'the highest religious and temporal authorities condemn' as a Lord of Misrule. That this is the gravest possible error can be seen, not only by noting that Christ proclaimed a new order, while Falstaff proclaims no order whatsoever, but by contrasting Falstaff with the mad Lear, who *can* be compared with Christ as a Lord of Misrule very different in kind from Falstaff. All revolutionary movements, Shaw observed in the appendix to *Androcles and the Lion*, attract those who are not good enough for society as well as those who are too good for it. There is not the slightest possibility of a Falstaff asserting any private concerns against the public interest except his own, or of showing any unworldliness other than incompetence arising from the extreme shortsightedness of his moral vision. Lear's attack on temporal justice is very different (*King Lear:* IV. iv). His 'none does offend' is his affirmation of the 'supernatural order of Charity' – indeed of the *natural* order of Charity. Like Falstaff he advocates the subversion of temporal justice: judges are thieves, so he will bribe them to let the thieves go free. But the similarity between Lear (or Christ) and Falstaff is not merely superficial: it is wholly illusory. Lear has discovered other men; Falstaff never discovers others. Lear is attacking hypocrisy, contempt, exploitation;

[1] W. H. Auden, op. cit.

Falstaff is 'a comic symbol' of hypocrisy, contempt and exploitation. Falstaff does not contrast with Hal; he is the satirical
counterpart of Hal. Apart from the uproarious humour, the
difference between them is that Hal is rather less shortsighted
and recognises the importance of the social order, though with an
eye to personal aggrandisement. A truly happy social order
requires much longer sight than Hal possesses. Hal knows that
being generous to people sometimes serves his turn; Falstaff
never thinks of being generous except as far as words go. Happiness is not to be achieved until men realise that private good and
public good 'do indeed perfectly coincide'.[1] Viola acts as if she
knows this; Caliban grasps the point; Prospero, who serves to
the limit of his power but knows when to break his staff, symbolises the ultimate coincidence of private concerns and the
public or universal interest. Lear challenges justice in the
name of love, asserting the worth of every man; Falstaff merely
asserts himself. Lear, when he challenges justice, has grown out
of his all-devouring infancy; Falstaff never grows out of it. The
defence of Falstaff as a symbol of charity cannot hold. He may
be an *object* of charity and, in so far as his engaging ways make
us overlook his vices, he perhaps may predispose us to tolerance
if not to charity; but he is more likely to predispose us to an easy
sentimentality, and there is not the slightest hint of charity in
his own behaviour – only a mocking imitation of it.

Mr. Auden's claim that Falstaff's 'untiring devotion to making others laugh is a comic image for a love that is absolutely
self-giving' is exaggerated; but it is not without foundation.
Falstaff's play-acting, his jokes at his own expense, his teasing,
his apparently large-hearted irony, his parody of all-worshipped
conventions and institutions radiate delight if not happiness,
mainly in Part I, and might even have justified Auden's claims
but for the fact that Falstaff is not only uncharitable himself, but
the cause that uncharity is in other men. Our charity to Falstaff
cannot outweigh our uncharity to his victims. Sir Toby can be
defended, and attacked, in a similar way, but there is nothing in
Toby so wonderfully attractive as the following, and others like
it:

[1] Bishop Butler, op. cit., see page 60.

PRINCE HENRY: Thou say'st true, hostess; and he slanders thee
  most grossly.
HOSTESS: So he doth you, my lord; and said this other day you
  ought him a thousand pound.
PRINCE HENRY: Sirrah, do I owe you a thousand pound?
FALSTAFF: A thousand pound, Hal? A million, thy love is
  worth a million, thou owest me thy love.

(Henry IV, Part I: III, iii. 130–6)

If by saying that Falstaff is a symbol of charity, Mr. Auden
meant that on these occasions we cannot help loving him and
feeling that the wit and the tenderness outweigh all his vices, we
might be disposed to agree – even though we know that the
tenderness is spurious, that Falstaff is play-acting as always, that
no deeds of his will rescue his words from sentimentality, dupli-
city and hypocrisy. Such is the charm that Shakespeare gives to
Falstaff. Hal, Falstaff's fellow egoist, is not deceived, and his
cold response is the fitting counterpart of Falstaff's calculating
exploitation of friendship. Far from being a comic image for self-
giving love, Falstaff's wit is a comic defence against contempt
and retribution. 'All things foul would wear the brows of grace',
and Falstaff's cynicism and cold opportunism masquerade as
frolic and charity. Sir Toby is prepossessing too, but less likely to
impose on perceptive audiences than Falstaff. He is much more
laughed at than laughed with, and his 'fun' at Malvolio's
expense, popular as it is, comes near to spoiling the happiness of
Twelfth Night.

*   *   *

Whether or not Shakespeare hoped at one time to create
happiness out of such as Falstaff, he clearly sought very different
means when he came to write *Twelfth Night*; and when he wrote
The Tempest he reaffirmed his judgement that genuine charity is
the essential ingredient in a recipe for happiness.

It is interesting to notice that Viola and Sir Toby, Falstaff's
successor, have an important feature in common. Both are creatures of impulse. Neither Toby nor Viola is aware of the working
of conscience. Toby, like Falstaff, is a grasping infant. What is

Viola? Viola, on impulse, does what conscience, that is love and reason, would require – the reason that sees far enough to recognise that in the long run one's own good and the good of others 'do perfectly coincide'. Viola does not *observe* this: it is in her being. She is altruistic 'upon instinct'. Either her conscience is perfectly developed from the start, or she has that fully trained conscience that has learned to do by habit what at first requires discipline and choice. Watching the play, we do not consider the question, we *feel* her perfection. And Toby and Malvolio as creatures of defective conscience and examples of the wrong sort of self-love stand in contrast to her, as do Orsino and Olivia whose self-love is a kind of dreaming vanity.

As Toby and Falstaff are images of primitive egoism, so Viola is an image of primitive altruism. She does not live wholly or short-sightedly in the present; love of her brother prevents that, but she cuts herself off from her past by the very disguise that links her with her supposedly dead brother, and she jeopardises the future:

> What else may hap to time I will commit.

Like Sebastian she commits herself quickly and decisively, and once committed remains firm. Any knot too hard to untie she leaves patiently to time; Sebastian, we feel, would cut it, though he too accepts a doubtful situation adventurously. Both are spontaneous lovers, and both are courageous in taking risks, for love and for other purposes. This helps to give them their vividness, it helps to confirm their genuineness and their constancy and while it arouses suspense also gives rise to confidence. We feel that they are natural restorers of order, as true lovers and firm friends are by nature. After *Twelfth Night*, young lovers do not again play so prominent a part in bringing about happy endings. They are of very great importance in the last plays, but the final happiness depends less upon youthful impulse, more upon older characters and upon will and discipline and patience and conscious thought. And Providence.

Twelfth Night is not a play of total reconciliation, and it is too much a play of mocks and 'wounding flouts' to end in perfect happiness; but it is much happier than most comedies because of the natures of Viola and Sebastian, and because in the final happiness of these two some others share perhaps more than they 'deserve'. Orsino and Olivia are saved from their foolish and dangerous preoccupation with themselves by the exchange of a false love for a true. Orsino's 'fancy', like that of the young lovers in *A Midsummer-Night's Dream*, is bred in the eyes, 'with gazing fed'. 'That miracle and queen of gems', Olivia's beauty, attracts his soul. But this is not the worst. He woos by messenger and positively luxuriates in his miseries:

> Away before me to sweet beds of flowers;
> Love thoughts lie rich when canopied with bowers.

He is hardly less narcissistic than Falstaff. Subsequently we observe in every turn of phrase his trust in and growing affection for the 'boy' who is his messenger, so that his discovery that the 'boy' is a woman coincides with the recognition of his *true* love. The change in Orsino appears sudden, but his blindness to true love has been painful to the audience; so all that is necessary for us is that his eyes be opened. And the same is true of Olivia, who at first fancies herself as the world's truest mourner and thinks she can prolong her sorrows and ceremonies for seven years. She is shaken out of this folly by the reality of Viola's love, but only to be the victim of another error, until the coming of Sebastian makes sense of her world and her passion. The untying of the impossible knot is such a relief to us that our pleasure in the denouement depends greatly on it, but it is our strong feeling for the people in the play, and especially for Viola, that makes our desire for the resolution so urgent, and makes the dismissal of Toby and Malvolio not unacceptable as the triumph of good sense over selfish folly.

The first to expose the vanities of Olivia and the pretensions of Malvolio is not Viola but Feste, the jester. It is he also who recommends 'a doublet of changeable taffeta' to Orsino to match his wayward fancies. Though there are touches of the childlike pathos of the 'ordinary' fool in Feste, he is a skilful entertainer and a wit, intelligent enough to be a shrewd commentator on those who pass for wise people. He is frequently a very positive image of good sense, and shows it in action when he first draws Olivia out of her melancholy. There is kindness and insight as well as comedy in the act:

CLOWN: Good madonna, why mourn'st thou?
OLIVIA: Good fool, for my brother's death.
CLOWN: I think his soul is in hell, madonna.
OLIVIA: I know his soul is in heaven, fool.
CLOWN: The more fool, madonna, to mourn for your brother's soul being in heaven. Take away the fool, gentlemen.

(I. v. 61–7)

Though he plays the third 'ass' in Olivia's buttery, his 'wisdom' places him with Viola and Sebastian rather than with those who are 'folly-fal'n'. He is an exploiter of fantasy, not a victim of it, and is a master of his proper role. In this respect he is superior even to Viola, who, though she plays her part well as Cesario, quite loses control of the situation. His function in the play is nearer to Sebastian's – for he is a touchstone – though his understanding, his sympathy, his wit and his brightness, however exploited for professional purposes, are qualities like Viola's and are very important as means to the final impression of happiness.

Like *The Tempest*, *Twelfth Night* is a dream play set in a faraway land where people are cast up from a shipwreck and where people in a state of error and distress are guided to wisdom and happiness. As in *The Tempest*, love and reason are the agents of happiness. In *Twelfth Night* there is no single, overriding authority like Prospero, but there are reflections upon rule and misrule, both in the world and in the mind. The 'world' is that of two households, but the 'mind' reaches beyond what is to what ought to be, beyond fanciful love to selfless devotion, beyond vanity and folly to good sense and good feeling, beyond love triangles and a comedy of errors to a pattern of marriages and friendships, beyond disorder to harmony. If the play is less happy than some of Shakespeare's other plays it is because the sublime image of Viola's love is somewhat obscured by the uncharity of the laughter at the discomfited and rejected Malvolio, and also by the painful and apparently unredemptive self-discovery of Sir Toby and Sir Andrew. The moral is not stated, but the conditions of happiness have been set forth and the underlying imperatives need not be spelt out. This dream, like *The Tempest*, and like the good conscience, sets forth the conditions of happiness and of unhappiness. One way or the other, or both ways, the dream will be realised. The choice is with the audience; but the dream points in a particular direction.

The clown ends by recalling the play's images of disorder in his song, and some of the pains and penalties that go with them. This emphasises the vision of order by drawing attention to the diversity of elements that have been wrought into the unity of the play and have delighted us, both by the range of human experience they cover and by the complexity of the interrelated plots. Like Prospero's epilogue, Feste's song helps to make the transition from the dream world of the play to the everyday world outside the theatre. At the same time it moves us away from the idea of an end to the idea of a process.

> When that I was and a little tiny boy,
>   With hey, ho, the wind and the rain,
> A foolish thing was but a toy,
>   For the rain it raineth every day.
>
> But when I came to man's estate,
>   With hey, ho, the wind and the rain,
> 'Gainst knaves and thieves men shut their gate,
>   For the rain it raineth every day.
>
> But when I came, alas! to wive,
>   With hey, ho, the wind and the rain,
> By swaggering could I never thrive,
>   For the rain it raineth every day.
>
> But when I came unto my beds,
>   With hey, ho, the wind and the rain,
> With toss-pots still had drunken heads,
>   For the rain it raineth every day.
>
> A great while ago the world begun,
>   With hey, ho, the wind and the rain,
> But that's all one, our play is done,
>   And we'll strive to please you every day.

Feste's examples of the process of learning by error and discomfort are mundane and all the more effective in returning us to common life. They are images of discovery and growth and the passage of time. With sad comedy they reflect on the inefficiency of learning by experience – a tragic theme in *King Lear*. The elements in the play that would have prevented the happy ending are precisely the ones Feste uses to remind us of everyday life, 'for the rain it raineth every day'; but in the artistic order of the play and in the harmony of its close, we have dreamed of a beauty that includes and transcends the rain.

The world of Shakespeare's plays is a world of change. In comedy and romance and history there is always a movement towards a new order, not merely to an old order revived. In happy plays the new order is a vision of love, and its symbol is marriage. But it is dynamic, not static. Marriage itself is not an end, but as much a symbol of growth and change and new life as of completion or fulfilment. Act V of *Twelfth Night* is a dream of happiness; Feste's song contrasts with it. There is a continuity between dream and action: between hope and fulfilment, aspiration and achievement, plan and execution; or between despair and ruin, illusion and error, scheming and perpetration. It must have been a long time before man observed the continuity of seed and plant; learning to select the seed and modify the plant perhaps took longer still. Not all seeds grow into plants, and not all dreams issue into action. Man does not yet know how to select his seed-dreams wisely or how to cultivate them, but select he must. Shakespeare's plays contribute to the understanding that precedes wise and effective choice, and the full appreciation of them involves making the choice.

CHAPTER TEN

With Undiscording Voice

FALSTAFF and Viola have this in common: they are both
deviants. Falstaff is the great immoralist; Viola is a woman
in man's clothing. A deviant may be a destroyer or a growing
point. Paradoxically, if he is a growing point he must necessarily
be a destroyer: 'the old order changeth, yielding place to new'.
Growth means development of new systems, either from old
systems or out of chaos. Destruction may imply either the passing away of an old system in favour of a new, or a reduction to
chaos. The former is an essential part of the creative process.
Within the Christian scheme, the Devil attempts the second,
but achieves the first. In so far as Falstaff challenges inhuman
moralities, he is a growing point of charity; in so far as he acts
inhumanely and makes inhumanity attractive he is an agent of
chaos – as he is in the treatment of his own body. The disintegrated body will fertilise the soil and push up daisies, but
that is in spite of Falstaff not because of him; for 'God fulfils
himself in many ways'. A deviant like Macbeth will establish an
order inferior to the old, but Macbeth's tyranny is chaos
wearing the brows of order. Shakespeare presents its nature as
disintegrative.

Viola, as a deviant, has a wholly creative purpose. 'To stand
inquiring right, is not to stray;'[1] and Viola uses her disguise to
give herself a breathing space and a means of independent
livelihood in a strange land, while she awaits news of her
brother. There is something deeper than this, however. The
woman in disguise plays too great a part in Shakespeare's plays
to be explained so lightly. The assumption that, since boys
played the women's parts, it was more convenient to have them
dressed as boys than as women, does not hold, since it is easier
for a boy to play a woman when he is dressed as a woman than
when he is dressed as a boy, and Shakespeare has to take great

[1] John Donne: *Satyre III*, line 78.

198

pains to help the boy to be a woman when he is dressed as a boy. What has to be kept in mind too, is the Biblical prohibition against the wearing of men's clothes by women, and the general view that such behaviour is highly indecorous:

> JULIA: . . . how will the world repute me
> For undertaking so unstaid a journey?
> I fear me it will make me scandaliz'd.
> > (*Two Gentlemen of Verona:* II. vii. 59–61)

At the same time, the good sense of it is understood, and good sense, a strong awareness of reality and necessity, is strikingly characteristic of Shakespeare's heroines of comedy: it is of great importance in achieving the happy endings. If love demands that an irregular journey into the wildernesses and unknown places be undertaken without male protection then, like Shaw's St. Joan in prison, the lady might well be commanded by her patron saint to contravene the Biblical prohibition:

> LUCETTA: But in what habit will you go along?
> JULIA: Not like a woman, for I would prevent
> The loose encounters of lascivious men;
> > (*Two Gentlemen of Verona:* II. vii. 39–41)

Love and good sense alike prompt these young ladies to deviate.

Their deviation is their way to a happy ending. If the happy ending is a vision of order, it implies stability, but as we have seen in the case of *The Tempest* and *Twelfth Night*, not stasis. Marriage is Shakespeare's symbol for the stable and happy order, but marriage is a beginning, not an end. Marriage is preserved – and in *Twelfth Night* and other plays achieved – by constancy; but in every case, since a complication unfavourable to happiness has to be resolved, the happy ending cannot be achieved unless there is an important change. In the case of *The Tempest* and *Twelfth Night, people* have to change; in the case of *The Merchant of Venice*, for example, the *situation* has to be changed. Perfect happiness would require a change in Shylock, and the opportunity to change is offered him, but he rejects it and can only be restrained. In none of Shakespeare's plays is redemption complete or happiness for ever secure. But there is

another sense in which the order achieved is not a closed or final
order: the notion or the idea or the 'dream' of a happy marriage
is not of an unchanging state but a state of change according to
constant laws or principles of continuity. The tension between
stability and change is thus present in every Shakespeare play.
It is implicit in every happy 'ending', and the happiness often
results from some kind of revolution in the established order in
which an individual deviant plays a special part. Every one of
Shakespeare's disguised ladies is this kind of revolutionary.

Of all the deviants who are growing points of happiness,
Portia is perhaps the most remarkable. The imagery of order
and proper spheres is strong in *The Merchant of Venice*, and
Portia herself commits her gentle spirit to Bassanio's,

> to be directed
> as from her lord, her governor, her king.
>
> (III. ii. 164–5)

It is true wifely obedience she vows, in the currently accepted
order of marriage. Of the young ladies in Shakespeare who
defy convention by wearing male dress, Portia is one of the two
who are married, and it is as a married woman that in other
respects too she steps out of her proper sphere. Hardly has the
vow of obedience, couched in these unequivocal if not extreme
terms, passed her lips when she takes complete command,
makes the vital decisions, and talks as if she is still lord of the
wealth she has just bestowed, with the gift of herself, upon
Bassanio. Antonio is in distress and the bond for a pound of his
flesh against the three thousand ducats he owes to Shylock is
forfeit:

PORTIA: What no more?
  Pay him six thousand and deface the bond:
  . . .
  First go with me to church, and call me wife,
  And then away to Venice to your friend:
  For never shall you lie by Portia's side
  With an unquiet soul. You shall have gold
  To pay the petty debt twenty times over.

> (III. ii. 297–306)

What is more, from this time forth Portia remains in command, enters the courts where no woman could plead as a lawyer and disguised as a man fulfils, not a servant's function like Julia or Viola, but the function of a master of affairs. As far out of her proper sphere as Prospero is out of his dukedom, she, like Prospero, orders the lives of all the rest and brings them to a happiness they could not otherwise have achieved. This includes even Shylock, whom she saves from committing murder, as Prospero saves the villains of *The Tempest*. By defying what she herself acknowledges to be the proper order of things, she establishes the new harmony. She is the deviant who is the agent of beneficent change and the growing point of happiness. When the stability of her order is threatened, she breaks its rules to establish a new order. Her new order is superior to the first in that it brings together as one in Belmont all the individuals and groups that were formerly separated, Shylock alone remaining apart and casting a sombre shade over the happiness of the close. It is, however, the lesser law that Portia has broken: the greater law of self-giving love that is the foundation of any happy human order whatsoever she has observed. The continuity with the order of Belmont established by her father is unbroken. Sending Bassanio from her side to Venice is an act both of love and of sacrifice such as the leaden casket enjoins. It shows

> a noble and a true conceit
> of god-like amity;   (III. iv. 2–3)

and that which makes for the new and happier order is the best that grew in the old.

The Merchant of Venice is a love-story. In it hate is contained by love, money and gain are sanctified by love, power and command and intelligence in Portia, as in Prospero, are manifestations of love, and in Antonio love is expressed as charity, forbearance and forgiveness as well as friendship and self sacrifice. Love makes the difference between Portia's scheming and Shylock's, between his litigation and hers, between his exercise of power and hers. To speak in these terms is to show how the meaning of the word 'love' in this play is extending towards the meanings it has when we use it to embrace Prospero's will and actions, as well as his personal feelings, in *The Tempest*. Traditionally, love binds heaven and earth; and both plays present the correspondences between human love and the universal order.

Shakespeare's most perfect *realisation* of self-giving love in an individual character is in Viola; but as a total symbolic image of love *The Merchant of Venice* is more nearly perfect than *Twelfth Night*. Lorenzo's symbolism of the spheres, quoted in our first chapter, is in the final scene of the play and is readily associated with the symbolic by-play of the marriage rings. At the same time as being a description and a reminder of the universe and of our part in it, it is an expression of Lorenzo's romantic mood:

> How sweet the moonlight sleeps upon this bank!
> Here will we sit and let the sounds of music
> Creep in our ears – soft stillness and the night
> Become the touches of sweet harmony:
> Sit Jessica, – look how the floor of heaven
> Is thick inlaid with patens of bright gold,
> There's not the smallest orb which thou behold'st
> But in his motion like an angel sings,
> Still quiring to the young-ey'd cherubins;
> Such harmony is in immortal souls,
> But whilst this muddy vesture of decay
> Doth grossly close it in, we cannot hear it:
>
> (V. i. 54–65)

The last two lines are consistent with the sadness and the sense of the world's darkness that recur throughout this final scene. However, the play does not confirm the contemptuous rejection of the body implied in these Platonic lines. In the rest of the scene there is an attempt to reconcile heaven and earth in human love, where soul and body harmonise. Perfect harmony of these apparent opposites is not achieved in this play, but there is a reaching towards it.

A Romantic idealist such as Lorenzo appears to be in this scene is apt to disparage the body and earthly matters even while, as here, his sensuous delight in beauty gives the lie to his conscious thought. Bassanio, too, is a romantic, and his lady 'of wondrous virtues' lives in a palace, remote and famed through all the world.

> And many Jasons come in quest of her.   (I. ii. 172)

However, the first words of this lady of dreams are in prose, and she herself in very decidedly in the flesh:

> By my troth, Nerissa, my little body is aweary
> of this great world.

Portia is also seen to be intelligent, rational, something of a moral philosopher, and one who will excel in practical affairs where an understanding of human nature is requisite. At the same time, she is no less romantic than Bassanio and she dreams herself a maiden in distress whom he will rescue like

> young Alcides, when he did redeem
> The virgin tribute, paid by howling Troy
> To the sea-monster: (III. ii. 55–7)

When he chooses aright, the ecstasy of her passion of love cannot be contained:

> PORTIA (*Aside*): How all other passions fleet to air:
> As doubtful thoughts, and rash embrac'd despair,
> And shudd'ring fear, and green-eyed jealousy.
> O love be moderate, allay thy extasy,
> In measure rain thy joy, scant this excess!
> I feel too much thy blessing, make it less
> For fear I surfeit.   (III. ii. 108–14)

This passion is not of 'air'; yet, apart from 'rain' and 'surfeit', there are no words of direct physical reference except those relating to the very passions that have now fled into the air. The soul being 'higher' than the body, and Portia being noble, this is to be expected. When she speaks to Bassanio, it is to give herself totally and wholeheartedly to him. Again, however, there is no direct reference to the body, only the word 'myself' twice. Superficially this is true to life, but more deeply it is false to marriage. Cultivated ladies and gentlemen may become affianced without any acknowledgement of the physical bond between them other than the formal kiss and the conventional symbolism of the finger and the ring – whose sexual connotations may be ignored; but the special feature of marriage among love relationships is its own kind of giving and receiving in the flesh. In this scene love's mysteries are displayed in the soul of Portia, but 'pure lovers soules' must

> descend
> T'affections, and to faculties,
> Which sense may reach and apprehend,
> Else a great Prince in prison lies.[1]

Gratiano and Nerissa also plight their troth; and they are different. Their inferior rank and comparative lack of refinement are manifested by a punning and jocular reference to the sex act. And thus, on the one hand, sexual inhibition, in the contemporary shape of Platonic-Christian ideas of the hierarchy of being, is exploited to give superior grace to Portia and Bassanio; on the other, attention is drawn to the incompleteness of the image of love given in their betrothal. Nerissa's jest is a reminder that marriage is of the body as well as of the 'spirit' (III. ii. 163); but a joke is a belittling or a disguise or an apology or a defence. Bawdy language is a kind of prudery, impossible except where there is shame or fear. So the effect of Nerissa's salacity is to preclude the perfect union of mind and body in wedded love. We might not expect to find that perfection expressed in Elizabethan literature, the body being assumed to be lower in the scale of being than the soul or mind; but we do find it in Shakespeare, beautifully realised in the love-language of Perdita in *The Winter's Tale*. The first episode of the scene of the shearer's feast (*The Winter's Tale:* IV. iv. 1–180) presents the beauty and worth of sensual love as *integral* to Perdita's intelligence and judgement, to her sincerity and innocence, to her clear and comprehensive soul, and her sensibility. It is not a case of the body being uplifted by the soul or being turned to 'the soul's essence'.[2] The body is living body, both 'unpolluted' and untransformed. The whole episode contributes to this

---

[1] John Donne: 'The Extasie', 65–8.
[2] See Milton: *Comus*, 416–2.

impression, but the following lines are at the heart of it. Perdita longs for spring flowers to grace her lover, Florizel:

> and my sweet friend,
> To strew him o'er and o'er!
> FLORIZEL: What, like a corpse?
> PERDITA: No, like a bank, for love to lie and play on:
> Not like a corpse; or if – not to be buried,
> But quick and in mine arms.
>
>   (IV. iv. 128–32)

There is no such perfection of art and of psychological insight in *The Merchant of Venice*, but there is a striving for it. Portia's frequent reference to the body and the bed in the teasing love-play of the ring drama does preserve some balance, even though it is in jest and dwells on false love, not true. The tendency of Gratiano's coarser way of speaking is to isolate flesh from soul, and thus reduce it to that 'muddy vesture of decay' which grossly closes us in and deafens us to the non-material harmonies of love. Portia rebukes him (V. i. 266); but, as Portia's own wit has demonstrated, not every sex joke is merely coarse, and it would be very imperceptive and insensitive to dismiss the last words of the play as *mere* bawdry. On the contrary, Gratiano's bravado there conceals a shy affirmation of constancy behind a display of sensual anticipation and jealousy:

> Well, while I live, I'll fear no other thing
> So sore, as keeping safe Nerissa's ring.
>
>   (V. i. 306–7)

A ring is finite and complete, but also endless. It suggests both limitation and limitlessness. In this final scene, even while rings are the subject of the quarrel, they represent the sacred bond of marriage. Correspondingly Lorenzo's heavenly spheres are mighty rings, keeping the stars in their courses. Portia, when she plights her troth gives a magical property to her ring as she places it on Bassanio's finger:

> Which when you part from, lose, or give away,
> Let it presage the ruin of your love,
>
>   . . (III. ii. 172–3)

This is the fairy-story motif: it is also the preparation for the fun of the last act – comic and serious, like Gratiano's jest. The wedding ring stands for the fulfilment of romantic passion and dream, the expression of delicate feeling, of constancy, of devotion and of utter self-giving in a life-long bond; but Portia's images of its meaning are concrete and material: it is, she reminds Gratiano,

> A thing stuck on with oaths upon your finger,
> And riveted with faith unto your flesh.

Consistent with this is the reminder in Gratiano's witty couplet that, besides its emotional and spiritual meaning and its imagery of the heavenly and eternal order, the ring is of the body and in the body, the meeting place of woman and man in the flesh. Gratiano is a shallow but good-natured hedonist, light of tongue and 'full of mocks' like Berowne; he is coarse-grained and imperceptive, the earthy opposite of the romantic Lorenzo. Consequently the flesh is muddied by his joke. Nevertheless, through him as well as through Portia, Shakespeare remarks the *possibility* of a fuller realisation of the oneness of flesh and spirit.

A harmony, if not a perfect harmony, is achieved in the play. Lorenzo's discord is almost resolved; the image of perfect love is taking shape. Had Portia dismissed the teasing and the jesting with a frank and serious giving of body and soul, like Perdita's, she would have held the balance between Gratiano and Lorenzo, reconciling the apparent contraries in the perfection of art, which is the image of both human and universal integration.

The theme reappears in the love-story of Ferdinand and Miranda, which recalls the story of Bassanio and Portia. 'At the first sight', Miranda and Ferdinand 'chang'd eyes'. Similarly, Bassanio, from Portia's eyes, received 'fair speechless messages of love'. So Fancy, the infant love, is born.

> Tell me where is Fancy bred,
> Or in the heart or in the head?
> . . .

206

It is engend'red in the eyes,
With gazing fed, and Fancy dies
In the cradle where it lies:
(*The Merchant of Venice:* III. ii. 63–9)

Fancy dies, unless it grows into true love. Then the Midsummer
Night's rage for possession will be subdued, and the lover will
'give and hazard all he hath': Ferdinand will put off his rank
and carry logs; Bassanio will choose the leaden casket. It may
be noted that while both these instances are symbolic, that of
the log-bearing is the stronger dramatic realisation of giving
through humility and service. The lover's giving is at times a
refraining: Bassanio and Portia part on their wedding day, each
giving up the other in a love that includes Antonio; Ferdinand
does not need Prospero's warning against incontinence, for his
union with Miranda must be unspoiled by greedy haste. For all
the lovers, the bodily fulfilment must be perfect, and their
restraints but sharpen

> The edge of that day's celebration
> When I shall think, or Phoebus' steeds are founder'd,
> Or Night kept chain'd below.
> (*The Tempest:* IV. i. 29–31)

The giving is also a receiving, and the rewards are in the 'bed-
right' and 'Earth's increase' as well as in the blessing of the
gods (IV. i. 96–115).

The union of soul and body, of heaven and earth, is symbolised in the masque by the figures of Juno, 'queen o'th'sky',
and Ceres, goddess of earth, linked by the rainbow, which in
another mythology is the sign of the Convenant between God
and man. Since Juno is queen over Ceres, and since Venus and
her 'blind boy' are excluded, it may seem, looking back from
the twentieth century, that the harmony of soul and body is
imperfectly symbolised. This Venus, however, is goddess
neither of beauty nor of fertility, but is 'Mars's hot minion',
representing the flesh out of place and proportion, and thus
injurious to the perfect union represented by marriage. Thus
Venus and her Cupid are inimical both to Juno and to Ceres, to
heaven and to earth, to soul and body. As for the idea of the

superiority of soul over body, of heaven over earth, that does not preclude the possibility of harmony, though it does preclude the exact balance that is realised in Perdita.

Selecting the theme of sexual love from among those we might have chosen, we have been observing the process of integration, and also the state of integration, that characterises equally a work of art, a human being, a society or a universe. We have taken Lorenzo's images of heaven and earth, both to denote and to symbolise contraries or seeming contraries that need to be harmonised in human thought and action both in art and life: but there are other contraries, discords more difficult to resolve. Lorenzo takes no note of hell. The opposition between Venus and Ceres referred to above raises the problem, but Shakespeare tackles it directly through his villains in *The Tempest* and *The Merchant of Venice*.

Portia's new order, like Prospero's, is not perfect or perfectly happy; for not all the contrasting or discordant elements have been integrated into it. The imagery of the marriage story in *The Merchant of Venice* does point to a reconciliation of Lorenzo's heaven and earth, but a perfectly happy ending would require the reconciliation of heaven and hell, which means the transformation of hell into heaven. Shylock's malice, however, is not transformed to love; so the good deeds of Portia and Antonio, brightly as they shine, are candle flames against the surrounding darkness of a 'naughty world' (V. i. 90–1). In the last act joy is tempered with sadness. A dark shadow crosses the moon, music oppresses Jessica's spirits with a sadness that recalls Antonio's at the opening of the play. Antonio grieves at the distress of Bassanio in the ring-quarrel. The beauty of the moonlight suggests stories of true lovers betrayed or crossed, and of Medea's witchcraft; and the sweet romantic light becomes as 'the daylight sick'. The play ends in joyous anticipation, but it is tempered with a melancholy beauty, and there is the sombre memory of the unreconciled Shylock.

The world of Shakespeare's plays is in constant revolution. An order of things is disrupted but a new order supervenes. The agents of disruption are of two kinds: there is the creative deviant, like Portia, and there is the destructive deviant, like Shylock – the saint and the criminal, the one who is too good for the old order and the one who is not good enough for it. In a play with a happy ending each becomes an image of the integration of disorder into order. In the case of the creative deviant there is full reconciliation of the apparently discordant elements; for the defiance of the old order is directed towards the creation of the new and better order. The destructive deviant, however, whose actions tend only to disruption can do no more than mobilise the forces of order against himself. He succeeds only in providing the conditions for the creation of a new order. He himself is rejected, but he has been the occasion of the revolution and he also is an image of disorder serving the ends of order. If endings are to be happy *without* the transformation of the destroyer, he must be rejected, but his efforts to destroy must have been turned to creative advantage. Reference has already been made to the myth of Satan, which illustrates this point:

> the will
> And high permission of all-ruling Heaven
> Left him at large to his own dark designs,
> That with reiterated crimes he might
> Heap on himself damnation, while he sought
> Evil to others, and enrag'd might see
> How all his malice serv'd but to bring forth
> Infinite goodness, grace and mercy shewn
> On Man by him seduc'd, but on himself
> Treble confusion, wrath, and vengeance pour'd.[1]

Shylock's malice brings forth goodness, grace and mercy, from which, unlike Satan, he benefits. However, he is not able fully to accept the gifts that are offered him, and so, like Satan, he heaps on himself damnation. In Portia's happy order, where all are givers, all must be receivers. Shylock, by his grasping, is a heavy loser. Yet he does not lose so heavily as he would have lost if those who defeat him had been as grasping, as malicious, as legalistic as he. His hate has occasioned the creation of a love whose blessing extends even to himself.

[1] *Paradise Lost:* I. 211–20.

Love between the sexes culminating in marriage is Shakespeare's symbol of happiness, but in *The Tempest* happiness comes, not because Ferdinand and Miranda love each other, but because Prospero loves in a different and a larger sense, and because his love is indistinguishable from his wisdom, from reason and duty and action, and because he is endowed with great power, which enables him to influence the lives of others. His role is a development of Portia's. She too has power and intelligence and benevolence. Because of her love for Bassanio, she undertakes a duty and a mission to save his friend, and she brings blessing to Venice. Because of his love for his daughter, Prospero devises and executes his project, which saves more than one and is designed to save all. Starting from the particular love, each proceeds towards the universal.

Each has villainy to deal with, and the method of each is similar. It may seem to some that Portia and Prospero are cruel, for each deals severely with those whose greed and hate and malice would destroy the best and spoil the happiness of all. But the aim of each is forgiveness. Portia's famous plea for mercy falls on Shylock's deaf ears. If he could have listened and responded, mutual blessing would have followed, forgiveness and reconciliation would have been possible, and the final happiness might have been unalloyed.

It must not be implied that mercy is represented in Portia alone; on the contrary, the Duke of Venice pardons Shylock his life, and Antonio pleads for further remission of sentence. It is interesting that the remission of Shylock's penalties should have been so frequently overlooked. His life is forfeit; the Duke pardons him. Life being granted, his wealth is forfeit; half to Antonio, half to the state. The Duke requires the half, but is disposed to commute the confiscation to a fine. Antonio requests that Shylock be allowed to retain half his goods while the other half be held in trust by Antonio to be rendered to Jessica with interest on Shylock's death. This is mercy and not rigour, but the words Shylock speaks *before* the remission of the fine, being in his powerful vein, are engraved on many minds:

Nay, take my life and all, pardon not that,
You take my house, when you do take the prop
That doth sustain my house: you take my life
When you do take the means whereby I live.

(IV. i. 370–3)

In fact they take neither: half his great wealth is no pittance.
What Shylock is deprived of is vengeance, on Antonio and on
Jessica; but this is a blessing not an injury. He has been saved
by Portia, as Caliban is saved by Prospero, from committing
murder. That he has been and is to be saved is further symbolised by his having to become a Christian. The fact that we
do not now see this as a means to salvation but as perhaps the
worst indignity of all should not blind us to its probable meaning for Shakespeare's audience: it is on Antonio's part an act of
severity, but also of benevolence, since as a Jew Shylock would be
damned.[1]

'Mercy' and 'forgiveness' are not strictly synonymous. The
Duke is merciful; Antonio is forgiving. Antonio has been
injured by Shylock, and might have been expected to take
vengeance, as the common-minded Gratiano would in his
position. Furthermore, Antonio's stipulation that Shylock
become a Christian must not be taken as a mere punishment,
but also as the indication of true forgiveness, a desire to receive
Shylock into the same communion. Mercy may be shown by
one who has not himself been injured: forgiveness is a creative
response by one who has been injured. What is created by it is
a new relationship which at the very least is a tolerance, at the
best may be a love or a friendship all the richer for the increase
of wisdom or the changed quality of feeling arising from the
recognition and understanding of the injurious act by which
relationship was formerly impaired. Prospero's forgiveness
of Alonso is of this latter kind: it is warm and ungrudging
and will grace the marriage of their children. His forgiveness of his brother is not the same; it mars the spirit of the
close:

[1] See *Shakespeare Quarterly*, I (London 1948), 'The Governing Idea' by
Nevill Coghill.

> For you, most wicked sir, whom to call brother
> Would even infect my mouth, I do forgive
> Thy rankest fault, – all of them; and require
> My dukedom of thee, which perforce, I know,
> Thou must restore. (V. i. 130–4)

Prospero shows mercy to his brother, but his forgiveness is no more than tolerance or forbearance. The explanation is perhaps that, since Antonio shows no sign of repentance and is thus perpetuating the injury done to Prospero, tolerance is the best that can be hoped for. Moreover, simply to 'let him get away with it' is not to forgive a man or even to be charitable, and may injure him by confirming him in his fault.

The great problem for Prospero and for Antonio, the Merchant, is that forgiveness is mutual. To take effect it must be accepted: a new relationship cannot be built by one alone. Shylock's 'I am content' (IV. i. 389) sounds like a grudging submission, a fatalistic endurance. He goes away sick and defeated without a word to Antonio: even mutual tolerance is impossible in this case. Thus, however forgiving Antonio may be in spirit or in act, whatever mercy and charity may be shown, forgiveness in the richer sense is rejected and reconciliation is impossible. Evil is foiled and restrained for a time but not transformed to good. Yet forgiveness, in such a case, is the only way to perfect happiness, and perhaps that is what makes the episode of the rings so important in the final act. The joy of that episode is not in the teasing and the parting, but in the reconciliation and the coming together. Antonio, supporting Bassanio's plea for pardon, takes the fault upon himself and dwells not upon the past but on the future relationship of Bassanio and Portia:

> I dare be bound again,
> My soul upon the forfeit, that your lord
> Will never more break faith advisedly.
>
> (V. i. 251–3)

The episode is play, and superficially Antonio's words mean simply, 'he won't do it again'; but the forgiveness and reconciliation impossible in the case of Shylock are presented instead

212

in this comic and sad and joyous symbolism. Here again is the dream, the aspiration, the vision of that perfectly harmonious and happy order, which is the end and aim of morals.

In date of composition, *The Merchant of Venice* falls somewhere between *Richard II* and its sequel *Henry IV*; and it may quite possibly be the only play that separates those two. Since it is a play about forgiveness, this is a most striking fact; for there is no play of Shakespeare's other than *Macbeth* that dwells more sternly and more sombrely on Nemesis than *Richard II*. In the contrast between Richard himself and Henry Bolingbroke, in their persons and in their achievement, there is the very 'form and pressure' of psychological determinism. The inexorable law of causation in the moral sphere, by which follies and vices pursue their inevitable consequences to destructive ends is not only seen in Richard's career but is frequently referred to in so many words:

> But by bad causes may be understood
> That their events can never fall out good.

York warns Richard,

> Take Herford's rights away, and take from time
> His charters, and his customary rights;
> Let not tomorrow then ensue today:
> Be not thyself. For how art thou a king
> But by fair sequence and succession?
> (Richard II: II. i. 195–9)

To use Macbeth's words:

> this even-handed Justice
> Commends th' ingredience of our poison'd chalice
> To our own lips.

Given the initial evil or weakness or folly, it is necessary that the subsequent offences come; but the sequel, *Henry IV*, cries 'woe to that man by whom the offence cometh'; for the deed that punishes Richard is itself a sin and brings its own punishment:

CARLISLE: My Lord of Herford here, whom you call king,
Is a foul traitor to proud Herford's king,

And if you crown him, let me prophesy –
The blood of English shall manure the ground,
And future ages groan for this foul act,

> (IV. i. 134–8)

Carlisle's words are confirmed over and over again both by events and by solemn reference throughout the tetralogy, *Richard II–Henry V*. That this is the law of error as well as of sin, we have seen in *King Lear*.

By this law, Shylock is doomed. He had prepared death for Antonio. The appropriate consequence is that death should be prepared for him, and if Gratiano had his way that is just what would happen:

PORTIA: What mercy can you render him Antonio?
GRATIANO: A halter gratis, nothing else for Godsake!

Gratiano's is the common reaction. Who has not exulted with him vengefully when the Jew is foiled?

GRATIANO: A second Daniel, a Daniel, Jew! –
Now infidel I have you on the hip.   (IV. i. 329–30)

It is the common reaction – and hence the doom on the world; for

> in the course of justice, none of us
> Should see salvation.

Gratiano's call for justice is similar to Shylock's – a call for vengeance. By such means, malice is perpetuated and all its evil consequences multiplied. But Shylock is not given a halter, in spite of Gratiano; for Antonio is wise. Unless the vicious circle of evil deed and evil response can be broken:

> It will come,
> Humanity must perforce prey on itself,
> Like monsters of the deep.
> > (*King Lear:* IV. ii. 48–50)

The means to break that vicious circle and to replace it by a new causal sequence of kindness, love and joy is forgiveness, or, failing that, mercy. To use mercy is thus both virtuous and wise. Shakespeare's plays, as we have noticed in studying *Macbeth*, raise the question whether what is good and right is not also what is good sense and in our interests, whether moral and prudential considerations are not in truth identical.

The vices of Richard II are injurious to his people, but the doom that falls upon England and France in Plantagenet times arises, not from those vices themselves but from the response to those vices by rebellion and usurpation which stimulate further rebellion and usurpation, with progressive increase in malice and murder until sheer weariness and lack of contenders for the throne makes possible a reconciliation between York and Lancaster. Forgiveness is the means whereby this causal chain could have been broken. Mercy shown by Bolingbroke and forgiveness exchanged between him and Richard, while involving supportive restraints like those applied to Shylock, Alonso and Caliban, would have saved generations from misery and transformed both Henry and Richard. The story of Portia and Antonio is thus a sharp comment on the story of the Plantagenet kings, which it interrupts.

Part of the effect of *The Merchant of Venice*, as of other happy Shakespeare plays, is to show how attractive true virtue is, and also how advantageous. Portia's famous speech on mercy is not only highly moral; it is also intelligent. Moreover its poetry presents mercy as gracious and lovely, majestic and powerful, so that we long for it. The play as a whole has a similar effect, but with the addition that malice and hatred are included and made hideous. Love and its attendant virtues of generosity, mercy, charity, forgiveness are made desirable; its opposites are repellent. The contrasts are more broad and clear in *The Merchant of Venice* than in some other plays, *Henry IV* and *Henry V* for example, but even though Shakespeare simplifies, he does not over-simplify. The real opposite of love, for example, is not Shylock's hate, but something else, which masquerades as love. Much of Shylock's hate-language, like Richard III's, sounds like a cry for love or a complaint at being unloved. Shylock's grasping, his possessive 'love' of Jessica, his 'love' of wealth and power, his personal and racial vanity – these self-loves are the real enemies of true love. These father the hate and the cruelty. The love that attracts us, here called 'true', we have formerly described as 'altruistic'. Shylock's 'loves' are egoistic. In other plays, altruistic love has more dangerous opposites than Shylock's varieties of egoism, for his are easily seen in their true colours. Falstaff's spurious good fellowship and Henry V's calculated 'lenity' are more specious.

In contrast to Shylock's grasping, Portia's love and Antonio's are expressed in giving and forgiving; Bassanio as a lover must 'give and hazard all he hath'. Bassanio must risk his all on the choice of a casket to win a rich reward. Shylock, too, gambles for a high stake. Some differences are obvious. Bassanio hopes to receive; but, if he wins, he wins the opportunity to give again and again. Shylock hopes to get, but not to bestow anything but pain and death. However, the similarity is that both take risks in hope to gain. Though the words have different meanings in the two cases, there is self-interest in both. Bassanio and Portia give and hope to receive. Do they give *in* hope to receive? Bassanio may appear a fortune-hunter. Portia's 'weariness' without a husband is unmistakably expressed. If they give in hope to receive, is it just to speak of their love as altruistic?

In this study of Shakespeare we have considered moral development as the progress from infantile egoism to mature altruism. We have observed that egoism in Shakespeare's plays produces tragedy and misery, and that altruism is the way to happiness. We all want happiness. Can we then choose to behave altruistically, so as to gain happiness? Is altruism itself a form of self-interest? The answer appears to be 'yes', and we have already drawn attention to the difference between long-term and short-term self-interest, between narrower and larger loves, between pleasing oneself without regard to others and pleasing oneself by and through giving pleasure to others. Prospero spends all his time preparing happiness for others as far as he is able, but Prospero's chief pleasure is in his daughter, and his whole project is for her:

> I have done nothing but in care of thee,
> Of thee, my dear one; thee, my daughter,

The satisfaction that he gains is in his love and inseparable from it, but it appears also to be part of his conscious aim, premeditated and calculated. Bassanio and Portia too anticipate the greatest joy in their reciprocal giving and receiving. Egoism and altruism seem to be different kinds of self-interest – very different kinds, but from the same root.

Yet one of the characters we have considered keeps the question open. Viola seems human and living and natural, a marvellous imitation of a real person. Viola not only gives her love without hope of return, but acts with the utmost firmness and intelligence in such a way as to sacrifice that very response to her love she so poignantly desires. No doubt it is possible to devise explanations of this in terms of self-interest, but not on the evidence of the play, only by attributing to Viola a motive which is not evident in her actions themselves. From her words and actions relating to Orsino and Olivia in the play Shakespeare has simply omitted any hint of self-interest. We might say, well, it could easily be done: Shakespeare is, after all, a creator before he is an imitator; and here he is intent upon other things. To emphasise the devotion and the sacrifice by leaving out the self-interest would be just what we might expect. But what is remarkable about Viola is that Shakespeare was able to do this without turning her into a statue instead of a breathing human being. Whether this is indeed a test of truth is hard to say, but the character of Viola leaves one wondering whether perfect altruism can exist either by nature in some people or by training and habit, as Wordsworth thought. Wordsworth held that the best portion of a good man's life is in

> His little, nameless, unremembered acts
> Of kindness and of love[1]

and that a person may be strongly influenced to such acts by intercourse with beauty – not detached approval, but the kind of involvement with the object that we may call love. Love alone is the motive given by Shakespeare for Viola's unselfregarding action. Love is of course a wanting as well as a giving, but what Viola wants,

> Whoe'er I woo, myself would be his wife.

is precisely what she gives away.

[1] Wordsworth: 'Tintern Abbey', 34.

The question is open. Bernard Shaw held that drama is a test of truth, and that if a playwright manipulates his characters to suit a personal prejudice or to plead a false cause instead of letting them live and act as such people in such circumstances really would live and act, he will produce bad drama. That is, his play, being untrue, will also be unbeautiful: its inner shape will be destroyed. Keats read a similar message in the Grecian Urn: 'Beauty is truth, truth beauty.' When we say Viola seems real, we mean that her language and behaviour chime in with our experience, and part of the experience we draw upon to co-operate with Shakespeare in recreating the character is the memory of acts of unpremeditated, unreflecting kindness, love or sacrifice. The astonishing reality of Viola may indeed confirm that there exists in human beings an instinctive or at least impulsive altruism which, although it might *after the fact* be explained in terms of personal interest or private pleasure, does not appear *in the act* to be motivated by these. What so convincing a character certainly does confirm is that we have memories of something like it. Perhaps, however, we are remembering our dreams – dreams of how we should like people to act towards us. If we could prove that altruism such as Viola's did not exist, we should wish that it did.

In that case the question is whether our dream can be realised, whether Viola in respect of her disinterested love is an image of human potential rather than an imitation of observable human nature. What Shakespeare does not leave an open question is that the happiness of Man is in proportion to his altruism. When Shakespeare wants to imitate human happiness or visualise a possible happiness, he creates altruistic people and gives them power; or, vice versa, when he creates altruistic people who are more powerful than the egoists, his plays come to happy endings. The egoists in his plays sooner or later destroy happiness or reduce it. Since happiness includes freedom and since freedom implies the power to choose a course that would destroy happiness, and since some of his characters choose or are disposed to choose in that way, Shakespeare's endings are not perfectly happy, but they point to a possible happiness. That altruism, the precondition of happiness, can be cultivated,

King Lear, if it is as true as it is beautiful, demonstrates. The three parts of *Henry VI* and *Richard III* show altruism retarded or atrophied by the deprivation of affection. What can be retarded can alternatively be fostered. Both propositions, that altruism is a precondition of human happiness, and that altruism can be cultivated, are implicit in the studies of repentance and education, service and freedom, power and forgiveness in *The Tempest*. In history we have unforgettable examples of altruism, including men and women who have, in action, loved their enemies. Many of these have claimed to be inspired by a book, though motivated in another way. Reading Shakespeare may not make anyone altruistic, but Shakespeare's dreams of altruistic love may predispose a reader towards it by the realisation, first of the possibility of it, second of its beauty, and third of its value. It is both a means and an end of growth; it is a limitless giving, which implies a limitless receiving; it is thus the condition and the precondition of harmonious relationships, of maximal freedom, not for one or for 'the greatest number' but for all; and so of universal happiness. That men do not choose universal happiness, but strive for personal satisfactions at one another's expense and thus prevent not only universal happiness but also the private happiness they grasp after, accounts for the sadness of Prospero and the dark shadows at the end of *The Merchant of Venice*, as well as the horrors of *Richard III* and *Macbeth*, the rejection of Falstaff, the downfall of Richard II, the miseries of the Wars of the Roses, and the majestic and tragic irony of the life of King Lear, who realises the error of his choice, and strives to make the right choice, but too late.

* * *

We have noted two kinds of altruism, the one conscious, the other unconscious. The first is duty and may simulate the second by the formation of habit; the second we have sometimes equated with love, but love such as Prospero's and Portia's includes both. We have thought of egoism as conflicting with altruism, and opposed to it. Yet, in the loves of Portia and Viola, we have seen passion and desire, both of which in common usage and in Shakespeare are named 'love', and both of which are ego-centric emotions. In Viola especially, we have seen love compounded of intense desire and unwavering altruism. The same we have observed in different forms in Perdita, in Ferdinand and Miranda, and in Prospero. The noblest, wisest, most attractive, most beneficent kind of love that Shakespeare represents or creates is thus in itself, in its own nature, a resolution of discord.

Similarly in action. Love, in the plays, is the reconciler of discordant elements, the maker of harmony. Love is analogous, on the one hand, to gravitational forces in the physical world and on the other to the shaping power of the creative imagination. All three are compounded of tensions; in addition, the last exploits the tensions in the material upon which it works. It is as if they are different modes or manifestations of a universal underlying principle or idea of order. Prospero is an embodiment of that idea or principle; *The Tempest* and Shakespeare's whole dramatic work are explorations of it. At the same time, Shakespeare presents love as the breaker of bounds: Romeo overleaps the traditional as well as the physical barriers between his family and Juliet's and challenges the morality of the feud. We have seen how Julia and Portia defy custom and convention. Grains of dust on a vibrating sheet respond to notes of music, and with each note in the scale form a different pattern. As the note changes so the pattern dissolves and before a new one forms there is a period of feverish activity and apparent disorder. The movement, however, is towards a new order. So people and societies vibrate in response to ideas. Societies dissolve, but society is vital to man; so new societies form. And always in the mind of man is some idea of what society ought to be. Whether or not, in his last four complete plays, Shakespeare was expressing his own faith in the possibility of universal harmony, he was certainly expressing man's desire for it, and giving shape to the dream out of which new societies and new moralities arise.

That love, and not fear or mere obedience, is 'the bond of rule'[1] we have seen demonstrated in *The Tempest* which is a

[1] Tennyson: 'Le Morte D'Arthur'.

dramatic exposition of the central moral imperative, 'love one another'. In prudential terms, Shakespearean comedy and tragedy together confirm W. H. Auden's dictum: 'We must love one another or die'.[1] But Shakespeare does not end his life's statement with a threat: he ends it with patience and hope. An old magician is setting out on a journey. Granted it is a return journey, but man never treads the same path twice. Prospero's tone is that of one setting out into the unknown, not with eager anticipation, not in the full pride of energy and courage, but diffident and stripped of all his former power. Prospero thinks on death, but his last six lines are in the language that Christians use when they look through death, with a moderate hope, a deep humility, and a claim upon forgiving love:

> And my ending in despair,
> Unless I be reliev'd by prayer,
> Which pierces so, that it assaults
> Mercy itself, and frees all faults.
> As you from crimes would pardon'd be
> Let your indulgence set me free.

Shakespeare's last word is a moral injunction, the meaning of which he has explored for many years both through characters who affirm and characters who deny it. Even if the metaphysical context of the words be ignored, a reader who can translate the specialised language into his own idiom will recognise on the one hand Shakespeare's sense of causal necessity and of the darkness of man's heart, and on the other hand his affirmation of the saving bonds of love. The moral implications are not merely for the adherents of a particular religious group, or for those who have beliefs about personal immortality.

When Edmund of Gloucester at the point of death says: 'The wheel is come full circle' he is reflecting fatalistically on the bitter consequences of an evil deed:

> EDGAR: My name is Edgar, and thy father's son.
> The Gods are just, and of our pleasant vices
> Make instruments to plague us;
> The dark and vicious place where thee he got

[1] 'September 1, 1939'.

Cost him his eyes.
EDMUND: Th' hast spoken right, 'tis true.
The wheel is come full circle; I am here.

(King Lear: V. iii. 169–74)

Shakespeare is underlining once again the 'moral' of *Richard III* and *Macbeth*.[1] However, we shall not do violence to Shakespeare's meaning if we extend the application of the image. In Edmund the Shakespearean wheel is coming full circle from *Richard III*. In the last four complete plays, a theme of which is reconciliation and the recovery of that which was lost, it is coming full circle from *The Comedy of Errors*. We have already dwelt upon the meaning and effect of the imagery of rings and spheres in *The Merchant of Venice* and of the word 'rounded' in Prospero's speech on dreams. The connotations of these images are, paradoxically, both endlessness and completion, both finish and infinity. The ring symbolises these qualities in human love; the wheel is a symbol equally appropriate for a life-cycle or for the shape and movement of a work of art. The wheel of life was a sufficiently well-known image in Shakespeare's time, with its seven spokes corresponding to the seven ages of man.[2] Edmund sees the wheel of life bringing in its revenges:[3] but in Shakespeare's final plays we see the cycle of cause and effect bringing in its rewards, love being the cause, and the effect harmony and blessing. 'The Gods' in these plays make of man's virtues instruments to save him.

There is a close correspondence between art and morals; each expresses a longing for the resolution of discord, and each is an attempt to create a more perfect order. This is not to say that the ultimate aim of either is a merely unchanging state. Perfection need not be conceived as fixity: it may be a process of

---

[1] That the wheel referred to is not Fortune's wheel is made evident by Edgar's insistence upon the justice of this causal relation between deed and consequence established by 'The Gods', and by the fact that Edmund agrees with him. Fortune's wheel symbolises the mere alternation of prosperity and adversity, not causal necessity.

[2] See *Shakespeare & the Emblem Writers*, Green, London 1870, p. 406.

[3] Cf. *Twelfth Night:* V. i. 362–3.

ever-increasing integration, not finite but infinite. Every Shakespeare play is about change, and each of his 'endings' is both a reminder of a process taking place in the imagined world of the play, and a returning of the audience to the changing world of everyday life. Yet each play is an image of perfection in the sense of completeness. A work of art is a beautifully finished thing that is never complete in itself, since it implies its audience. Furthermore, being never twice in the same context, it is never twice the same. We have already noted that it is the inferior work of art that does not change with the times; the great one has continuing relevance and does not 'date'. We have also noted the similarity between art and morals in this respect (Chapter Five). Both art and morals are attempts to reconcile the changing and the unchanging; but, if there is anything unchanging, it is not the phenomena, the items, the objects; it is either the principles of their existence, the principles according to which they change, or the pattern within which they exist and in which those principles obtain and the processes of change work. Whether or not the universe actually is patterned and ordered and has its 'laws', that is how man perceives and 'understands' it. Facts become knowledge 'only when we trace the links between them – when we find the underlying principles which hold the facts together and which turn them into an orderly pattern'.[1] Whether perceiving, understanding or imagining, man is either discovering or creating new groupings, bringing things into relation. Even as an analytical scientist or a 'trained' observer, he is impelled to create a pattern of classification according to principles discovered or divined or imagined in the act of analysis or observation. A playwright making plays will discover principles of drama, principles of art and principles of human behaviour, and his discoveries will be inseparable from the act of composition. Principles of moral and social behaviour have been discovered or created in the process of building social orders and of observing or conceiving a universal order. The more immediate aim in each case is a new stage of completion; the process is one of growth, which is never a mere adding process. Man delights to see the wheel come full

[1] Dr. J. Bronowski: *Insight*, a B.B.C. television pamphlet (1961).

circle: in his science, his law, his politics, his religion, his philosophy, his psychology, he shows his longing for new order; but
nowhere more than in art and morals.

Order is both necessary and satisfying. Yet there are some
kinds of order that are injurious and stultifying. The case for
Falstaff is that he strikes for the individual soul against restric-
tive conventions and rigid moralities; the case against him, as is
shown not only in his own story but also in the story of Caliban,
is that licence and self-will exert a tyranny of their own no less
injurious and stultifying. It is deviant love, like Portia's, not
'will peculiar and self-admission'[1] that strikes effectively for the
individual soul as well as for the living and changing society.
The badness of bad morals and bad art lies in unresolved disharmonies like that represented in the opposition between
Malvolio and Sir Toby. Officiousness and licentiousness make
men ugly and sick; responsibility and independence make them
strong and handsome; service and delight make life beautiful.
The last four harmonise; the first two cannot. Portia creates a
circle of joy and fellowship: Falstaff is rejected, and Malvolio
isolated. Harmonious order in life or in art is delightful to share
in and to contemplate. When the order of our own being chimes
with the order we contemplate, we describe what we contemplate as beautiful. The proper aim of morals is to achieve such a
chime between the individual psyche and the social or universal
order. Morals is thus, like art, the pursuit of beauty – beauty in
the patterns of human relationships. Morals is the aesthetics of
living.

Art is a process of selection, and selection implies rejection;
but the beauty of a work of art is in what it accepts, in the
variety of elements it embraces and in the strength and subtlety
of its inter-relationships. The same is true of morals; and, just as
there are failures in art, so there are ugly moralities where the
emphasis is laid on rejection, negation, restriction and condemnation. We have reflected upon such a morality in our
study of Richard III. In life, Shylock is condemned and rejected.
In the story, Portia fails to include him in her happy order. But
in the artistic order of the play he is as much a thing of beauty

[1] *Troilus & Cressida:* II. iii. 161.

as Portia, and his presence casts the shadow without which the close would lack its very special beauty. Much the same is true of more unquestionable villains in Shakespearean drama, and of evils and sufferings and horrors of many kinds. Art makes a thing of beauty out of the moral ugliness of Richard III, the suffering of Lear, the damnation of Macbeth. A whole play by Shakespeare, tragedy no less than comedy, is a harmonious order in which disintegration, disharmony, misrule, deviation, perversion, murder, rapine, jealousy and waste are contained, and actually contribute to the artistic harmony. What we call the beauty of the play is the integration of the parts, and we delight in the

> Inscrutable workmanship that reconciles
> Discordant elements, makes them dwell together
> In one society.[1]

Wordsworth, in these lines, is not writing about art however, but about life, more especially about growth. Shakespeare's stories of Lear and Caliban, his images of the pursuing love of God, from the pilgrimage of Julia to the divine interventions of the last plays, his preoccupation with forgiveness and redemption and the images of blessedness with which his last plays end leave the strongest impression that moral development, like artistic creation, must proceed by the acceptance and consequent transformation of elements that, when they are rejected and denied, show as evil and ugliness. Whether intentionally or not, Shakespeare commented with profound simplicity on his own studies of forgiveness, and laid bare the correlation between art and morals, when he made Prospero say,

> this thing of darkness I
> Acknowledge mine.

and soon after gave Caliban the words,

> Ay that I will; and I'll be wise hereafter,
> And seek for grace.
>
> (V. i. 295)

[1] Wordsworth: *The Prelude* (1850) I. 342-4.

FULL CIRCLE

Hitherto, man's threescore years and ten have not been time enough in which to grow out of his moral infancy, and most of a man's short life has been spent in dying. Fear and self-assertion, infantile and complementary attitudes, make us retreat into 'vain citadels'[1] designed for self-protection but promoting self-destruction, armaments and rejection of the enemy being only the most obvious example among many, most of which are even more deeply entrenched in our daily lives. But man is a maker. In the last hundred years he has lifted himself off the surface of the earth and is reaching out to the stars. And in the same period he has begun to develop new ways of exploring the universe within himself. By new methods he seeks the principles of inner harmony and studies the processes of maturation. Modern psychology is a mere starting-point, but from it may come discoveries and transformations that may yet enable man to achieve that 'perfect Diapason' of personal and social and universal harmony to which Shakespeare's visions of love and wisdom point. In dreams and stories man walked on the moon; observation and imagination taught him the conditions upon which his dream could be realised; he has now walked there in the flesh. There is a nobler dream, and Shakespeare's imagination may help us to grasp some of the conditions for its fulfilment.

[1] Wilfred Owen: 'Strange Meeting'.

Index

INDEX

INDEX

INDEX

C. *Some Key Words*

Note: In this section, references are often given for words related to the head-word

INDEX